LEADING

AT THE EDGE

LEADING

AT THE EDGE

Leadership Lessons *from the* Extraordinary Saga *of* Shackleton's Antarctic Expedition

Dennis N. T. Perkins
with Margaret P. Holtman,
Paul R. Kessler, and Catherine McCarthy

American Management Association

New York • Atlanta • Boston • Chicago • Kansas City • San Francisco • Washington, D.C.
Brussels • Mexico City • Tokyo • Toronto

Special discounts on bulk quantities of AMACOM books are available to corporations, professional associations, and other organizations. For details, contact Special Sales Department, AMACOM, a division of American Management Association, 1601 Broadway, New York, NY 10019.
Tel.: 212-903-8316.   Fax: 212-903-8083.
Web site: www.amanet.org

This publication is designed to provide accurate and authoritative information in regard to the subject matter covered. It is sold with the understanding that the publisher is not engaged in rendering legal, accounting, or other professional service. If legal advice or other expert assistance is required, the services of a competent professional person should be sought.

Acknowledgments for permission to use previously published materials can be found on page 268.

Library of Congress Cataloging-in-Publication Data

Perkins, Dennis N. T., 1942–
    Leading at the edge: leadership lessons from the extraordinary saga of Shackleton's Antarctic expedition / Dennis N.T. Perkins.
       p.   cm.
    Includes bibliographical references (p.).
    ISBN 0-8144-0543-6
    1. Shackleton, Ernest Henry, Sir, 1874–1922. 2. Leadership. 3. Strategic planning. 4. Survival skills. 5. Explorers—Antartica. I. Title.
HD57.7.P46   2000
658.4'092—dc21

99-057868

Printing number

20 19   ·

To the memory of
Private First Class Louis Anthony Leatherbury,
United States Marine Corps,
and all who have gone to *The Edge*
in the service of others

Contents

Acknowledgments

The experience of writing this book seemed, at times, to be something like mounting a polar expedition. There was, of course, less physical hardship, and little risk of life. But the process did involve venturing into the unknown and dealing with some fairly formidable obstacles. I was fortunate to have with me in this adventure a number of colleagues who made it possible to face these challenges with a spirit of creativity and camaraderie.

I deeply appreciate the enormous contributions made by each member of the "Book Team": Peggy Holtman, Paul Kessler, and Catherine McCarthy. Although I had been using the *Leading at the Edge* approach for a number of years, the challenge of translating these concepts into a readable book was not a straightforward matter. The Book Team met regularly from the proposal stage forward, debating every major decision involved in structuring the book. Peggy and Paul drove long distances to my office in Connecticut, while Catherine participated by phone from Chicago. These meetings were often extended affairs, and I sometimes worried that Catherine would carry a permanent imprint of a telephone earpiece.

Each member of the Book Team wrote initial drafts of chapters, critiqued my work, and searched for business examples that would illustrate key lessons of the book. Peggy Holtman was tireless—a "whirling dervish"—in searching for "factoids," and ensuring that the key concepts of the book were bridged to practical organizational applications. Paul Kessler researched and wrote the Malden Mills case, emanated optimism, and demonstrated an awesome knack for catching errors that no one else could find. Catherine McCarthy wrote the Business Communications Systems (AT&T/Lucent Technologies) case, exhibited an impressive "can do" spirit and—at the same time—played an important role in challenging the team's assumptions and keeping us focused.

In addition to these contributions, each member of the Book Team also showed a willingness to practice the leadership strategies highlighted in the book. One of my great satisfactions in this effort is the belief that we, as a team, did our best to practice the principles we espoused.

Words can never fully express my appreciation for the contribution of Anna Gianitsos, my office manager and assistant. The name Gianitsos means "loyal warrior," and Anna embodied the spirit of her family name. Through month after month of the most demanding work, Anna demonstrated an extraordinary level of dedication and breadth of skills. She was conscientious in proof reading and fact checking. She made substantive suggestions about the content of the book. When I was stuck on a small detail, Anna pointed at the "count down" chart that she had made showing the number of days until the manuscript was due—and I got the message. Through late nights, weekends, and stress-filled days, Anna retained her determination, resilience and her winning smile. She and her family can be justly proud of her critical role in making the book a reality. Anna—*S'efharisto apo ta vathi tis cardias mou.*

Steve Elliott not only helped with editorial decisions, he also served as navigator (my own "Frank Worsley") in steering through the uncharted and often turbulent waters of the publishing world. Ellen James provided valuable editorial assistance, and wrote the Weyerhaeuser case study. Nick Appelby expertly created the graphics, including the map of the *Endurance* expedition. Marya Holcombe's counsel was critical in the beginning stages of the writing process as she helped me break the ice off the runners of my writing sledge. And Becky Hoffman, of Knowledge = Power, deserves special recognition for her resourcefulness in finding business illustrations of the ten strategies.

I am grateful to Bob Headland of the Scott Polar Research Institute for his timely fact checking, and for helping me avoid any errors that would qualify as major "howlers." I should emphasize that I am responsible for any remaining discrepancies, and that any conclusions—particularly those concerning Robert Falcon Scott—are my own.

The contributions to the book made by David Nadler and my colleagues at the Delta Consulting Group were invaluable. David has been a friend for more years than I care to remember, and has taught me much about the art of helping organizations achieve their full potential. My friends at Delta have shared their time and expertise generously, and I thank them for their valuable assistance.

I appreciate the steadfast encouragement of Jeff Heilpern, who has been tremendous source of support, and who helped me maintain a healthy perspective on the process of writing and on the process of living. Virginia Herndon showed an unwavering belief in the book and its message, Martha Miller beamed support from far corners of the globe, and Dave Ellis was an important source of inspiration.

Donna Gianini deserves special mention for her early work in developing the *Leading at the Edge* approach, and for her continuing innovation in applying the concept. Donna first coined the phrase, "Onward through the hummocks"—a rallying cry that helped us move through many daunting ice fields. I appreciate the ongoing encouragement of Diane Russ, my long-haul partner in exploring the frontier.

I would like to acknowledge the editors at AMACOM, who helped bring the book from proposal to print. Adrienne Hickey saw the potential of the concept, acquired the book, and provided suggestions about its structure. Christina McLaughlin managed the complex production and editorial processes with laughter and competence, and Karen Brogno's thorough copyediting of the manuscript is greatly appreciated.

A number of other individuals were important in the writing of this book, and each made a unique contribution. I thank and acknowledge Deborah Ancona, Francesca Campolattero, Nancy Cardwell, Fred Courtright, Jack Creighton, Anthony D'Albero, Mark Edinberg, Aaron Feuerstein, Jo-Ann Fleishman, Peg Gilliland, Lois Grady, Andrew Greatrex, Gordon Hellman, Diana Ho, Joan Imhof, Randy MacDonald, Leslie Margolin, Naoko Matsunaga, Chuck Miceli, Phil Mirvis, David Montross, Steve Moran, Renee Murphy, Robert Ostroff, Prakash Patel, Jonathan Patrick, Bill Reinsmith, Gail Robinson, Gayle Rohrbasser, Darien Roseen, Pat Russo, Barry Schlosser, Harold Shapiro, Tom Sheehan, Jane Sheppard, Paul Siegel, Scott Sklar, Lon Smith, Ken Stellar, Jim Tullos, and Grant Withers.

I am grateful to Dr. Elias Marsh, who first gave me a copy of Lansing's *Endurance*, and who exemplified the spirit of exploration. And I thank Bill Gleeson, whose courage and presence under fire helped ensure that I would be around to write this book.

Finally, I thank the members of my family who have supported me through the years, and who have taught me a great deal about leadership and overcoming obstacles. My daughter, Holly, showed me that it is possible to ride a bucking horse with a smile on your face. My son, Jonathan, showed me that it is possible to negotiate tough white water in a kayak with no spray skirt—and still have a good time. My brother, Bob, kept the supply chain intact throughout the expedition. I thank the "Magic Girls," Meghan and Melisa, for their smiles and courage in the face of adversity; and I appreciate Joe Hernandez' help in carrying the load. Most of all, I express my deepest gratitude to Bernadette Bialczak Perkins who supported my quest, and whose love and compassion helped me make it home from *The Edge*.

Preface

On August 3, 1913, a Canadian expedition led by Vilhjalmur Stefansson set out to explore the frozen Arctic, between the northernmost shores of Canada and the North Pole. On December 5, 1914, the British Imperial Trans-Antarctic Expedition, led by Sir Ernest Shackleton, sailed from the island of South Georgia in the Southern Ocean. Its goal was the first overland crossing of Antarctica.

Both ships, the *Karluk* in the north and the *Endurance* in the south, soon found themselves beset in solid pack ice. Trapped by the ice, each crew was soon engaged in a fight for survival. But the outcomes of these two adventures—and the ways in which the two leaders dealt with the obstacles they faced—were as far apart as the poles each leader set out to explore.

In the north, the crew of the *Karluk* found themselves transformed in the months that followed into a band of self-interested, disparate individuals. Lying, cheating, and stealing became common behaviors. The disintegration of the team had tragic consequences for its eleven members who died in the Arctic wasteland.

In the frozen south, the story of the *Endurance* could not have been more different. Shackleton's expedition faced the same problems of ice, cold, and shortages of food and supplies. The response of his crew to these hellish conditions, however, was in almost every respect the obverse of those of the *Karluk*'s crew. Teamwork, self-sacrifice, and astonishing good cheer replaced lying, cheating, and rapacious self-interest. It was as if the *Endurance* existed not just in a different polar region, but in a different, contrary, parallel universe.

What Can Today's Leaders Learn from Explorers at the World's Edge?

There were many variables at play in the *Endurance* and *Karluk* adventures. I believe, however, that these two cases reflect something far different from a simple twist of fate. Having studied numerous situations in which teams faced the edge of life and death—the physical limits of human endurance—I have found that there are systematic differences between those that succeed and those that fail.

Over the past fifteen years, I have examined numerous stories of other groups that have been at the edge of survival, including accounts of shipwrecks, airplane crashes, mountain-climbing expeditions, and polar exploration. From this research, ten leadership principles have emerged as the critical factors that distinguish groups that triumph from those that fail. These core leadership strategies form the backbone of this book.

My goal is to show how these ten principles, employed by Shackleton and others who have succeeded in the face of extreme adversity, can help leaders reach the limits of individual and organizational performance. *Leading at the Edge* will demonstrate how these leadership lessons can be applied to organizations confronting such contemporary challenges as competition, economic uncertainty, and the need for constant innovation, growth, and change.

Each chapter in Part One of the book illustrates how one of the ten strategies has been used under life-and-death conditions. It also includes specific tactics for implementing these strategies and uses brief case examples to show how these concepts can be applied to any organizational challenge. Finally, each chapter poses a set of questions for reflection in the form of a personal Expedition Log.

Part Two of the book includes four extended case studies. These cases show how leaders have applied the ten strategies in situations ranging from short-term crises to cultural transformation. The cases, drawn from different industries, illustrate the power of effective leadership under conditions of ambiguity, uncertainty, and change. They also demonstrate how leaders can create teams that work together and succeed in the face of enormous odds.

In Part Three, I share my perspective on the fundamental issue of success and failure and on learning the art of "leading at *The Edge*." Finally, Part Four includes a number of resources, including tools for individual assessment and for further reading about leadership and adventure.

Origins of the Leading at *The Edge* Concept

A major part of my life has been spent trying to understand what it really means to be a leader—particularly under conditions of adversity, ambiguity, and change. My passion to understand the art of leadership began at the United States Naval Academy. As a midshipman at Annapolis, I looked at the discipline of leadership as the foundation of a military career.

My quest to understand leadership began in earnest after graduation, when I was commissioned as a second lieutenant in the Marine Corps. As a platoon commander, I found myself in the sand dunes of Camp Lejeune, North Carolina, faced with the challenge of leading some thirty-five young Marines.

As a platoon leader I tried to apply what I had learned at Annapolis, and I watched other leaders to see what worked and what did not. I was naively amazed to find that—although we had all gone through the same training—the actual practice of leadership varied tremendously. Mostly I saw good leadership; sometimes I saw exceptional leadership.

The differences between good and exceptional had effects on the attitudes and behavior of the troops, but the consequences in peacetime were not profound. Mistakes were simply mistakes, and no one died. The troops might grumble, but it was the Marine Corps and everyone followed orders.

My leadership "postgraduate education" continued off the coast of Vietnam with the 3rd Battalion, 5th Marines. As part of the Special Landing Force, we sailed along the coast, launching amphibious operations to relieve units that got into trouble near the demilitarized zone. Later, I went "in country" and experienced the war in many roles. As a civil affairs officer, I saw it from the perspective of the Vietnamese. I helped build wells, distribute CARE packages, and bring medical and dental care to the local villagers. Later, as the commanding officer of a rifle company, I saw Vietnam through a different set of lenses.

In Vietnam, the stakes were higher and blind obedience was not something to be taken for granted. Under combat conditions—in an unpopular war filled with Kafkaesque absurdity and contradiction—asking a group of people to move into harm's way required more than just giving orders. It was here that I really began to understand the nature of exceptional leadership.

I saw that some leaders were able to inspire exhausted, wet, tired, and discouraged Marines under the most grueling conditions. They were able to exercise leadership in a way that called on deep reserves of endurance and comradeship. They did things that motivated scared, anxious troops to "saddle up" and move into the dark—to venture beyond the relative safety of the concertina-wire perimeter into the face of death. It was more than the discipline of the Marine Corps. It was something else.

After Vietnam, my passion to understand leadership continued in graduate school—first, at the Harvard Business School, then later as a doctoral student in psychology at the University of Michigan, where I discovered that what I had done in Vietnam was called experiential learning. My ideas about leadership really began to converge, however, when I joined the faculty of the Yale School of Management. There, as a professor, I was confronted with two central questions:

> ➢ What can I tell students about the qualities and behaviors that distinguish truly exceptional leaders and teams?
> ➢ How can I help students display these qualities and practice these behaviors when they leave the classroom and move into positions of leadership?

As I began to reflect on the academic research that I had studied—"the literature," as we affectionately called it—I still felt that something was missing. It was not that the theories were wrong. It was just that academic theories about leadership seemed far removed from the challenges I had faced as a leader, particularly those I experienced in Vietnam. Furthermore, I found it difficult to present these leadership concepts in a way that I thought students would remember after graduation.

In my teaching and consulting outside the university, I was faced with an even more difficult challenge. Working with a diverse array of organizations, I found that leaders were often stretched to the limits and pressured to achieve the impossible in short order. They were totally unconcerned about getting a passing grade on a management-theory exam. They searched for solutions that answered their problems. They required help in identifying the critical steps that they could take to lead their organizations. They demanded ideas in a form that they could remember.

So, a series of life experiences, plus the immediate challenge of teaching and consulting about leadership, led me to blaze a new path. I thought about the power of the leadership lessons learned in Vietnam, and I decided to take a different route: to look for leadership insights in stories of groups that have been to the outer limits of human endurance—the place I call *The Edge*.

This path has led me to believe that the essence of leadership can be found in this ultimate crucible of human endeavor. I am convinced that by understanding the things that work when survival is at stake—when financial incentives or promotions become irrelevant, and when fear and self-interest surface—we can understand how to lead under other conditions. By studying *The Edge*, we can learn the things needed to lead organizations to their full potential, and we can remember these principles when we ourselves are stretched, stressed, and challenged.

In this book, then, *The Edge* is a concept with two dimensions. The first edge is the *Survival Edge*: the limits of human endurance. The second edge is the *Performance Edge*: the limits of individual and organizational potential. Throughout the book, I take lessons from the first and apply them to the second.

Contemporary organizational challenges are not, of course, exactly the same as the life-and-death situations I experienced and studied. I have, however, often observed people reacting to everyday events as if they were life-and-death matters. I have seen people more upset about missing deadlines or giving presentations than Marines under automatic-weapons and mortar fire. In one notable episode, I watched a distraught executive charge down a runway, briefcase in hand, attempting to catch a departing plane. He was apparently prepared to risk his life rather than miss an important meeting.

The challenges that you face as a leader may not involve physical survival, but you will need to deal with the human reactions that are common to any stressful situation. By understanding the leadership practices that work in extreme situations—conditions in which normal or even above-average performance means failure and even death—you will increase your ability to lead and flourish in the face of adversity.

Overview of the Ten Strategies

In my search to find compelling examples of what can be accomplished when people work together to overcome adversity, the saga of Shackleton's Trans-Antarctic expedition stood out. While there are many other accounts of triumph at *The Edge*, the story of the *Endurance* was unique. Better than any other, the Shackleton saga encapsulated the strategies

I had found to be absolutely essential for success. Consequently, I will use Shackleton's story as the primary vehicle for exploring leadership at *The Edge* and for illustrating key ideas about extraordinary leadership and teamwork.

What are these critical factors that determine success at *The Edge*? What are the core elements that made the outcome of the *Endurance* expedition so different from that of the *Karluk*? There were, of course, a number of forces that affected the ending of these two stories: weather, ice conditions, and even luck. Shackleton's luck, however, was not limited to good fortune. He had a boatload of bad luck as well, and it started at the outset of the adventure.

I am convinced that the safe return of Shackleton's expedition can be attributed to much more than luck. I believe that the leadership strategies that enabled Shackleton's crew to beat the odds can be found in a set of principles common to many other stories of survival. The underlying ingredients of triumph are expressed in these ten strategies:

1. *Never lose sight of the ultimate goal, and focus energy on short-term objectives.*
2. *Set a personal example with visible, memorable symbols and behaviors.*
3. *Instill optimism and self-confidence, but stay grounded in reality.*
4. *Take care of yourself: Maintain your stamina and let go of guilt.*
5. *Reinforce the team message constantly: "We are one—we live or die together."*
6. *Minimize status differences and insist on courtesy and mutual respect.*
7. *Master conflict—deal with anger in small doses, engage dissidents, and avoid needless power struggles.*
8. *Find something to celebrate and something to laugh about.*
9. *Be willing to take the Big Risk.*
10. *Never give up—there's always another move.*

The ten strategies are closely interwoven. A single leadership action might include several strategies, in much the same way that an athlete might employ several techniques such as balance, focus, and dynamic relaxation to hit a ball or score a goal. A chapter will be devoted to each of the ten strategies, but it is important to remember the interconnectedness that exists among them all.

The chapters that follow show how each strategy is critical to the success of groups and organizations at *The Edge*. Most important, they outline ways in which these strategies can work for you as a leader. First, however, let us look more carefully at Shackleton's extraordinary adventure.

Expedition Log

1. Before we begin our explorations at *The Edge*, you may want to reflect on a situation in which you were stretched to your own limits of performance or endurance. The situation can be one that involved leading others, or it can relate to a personal obstacle or goal.

   ➢ What were the qualities that enabled you to succeed or persevere—your behaviors, values, or personal characteristics?
   ➢ If the situation involved others, what was the nature of the teamwork or support that you were able to inspire? How did you work with others to achieve your goal?

2. If you have difficulty thinking of a personal experience, you may want to reflect on a leader who has taken a team or organization to *The Edge*—to the highest possible limits of performance.

   ➢ What were the qualities that made this individual so exceptional—behaviors, values, or personal characteristics?
   ➢ What was the nature of the teamwork that this leader was able to inspire? How did the group work together to achieve its goals?

The Shackleton Saga

The saga of Shackleton's Imperial Trans-Antarctic expedition has been told many times. I first encountered the story some fifteen years ago when a friend—knowing my interest in survival accounts—gave me a copy of Alfred Lansing's *Endurance*. I was so captivated by the story that I simply could not put it down. I knew that the account, while an engaging tale of adventure, was something more. It was a powerful metaphor that I could use to help leaders who were taking their organizations to *The Edge*.

A number of other excellent books on Shackleton are listed in Part Four, including Caroline Alexander's recent volume with superb photographs. My goal in writing *Leading at the Edge* is not to duplicate these historical accounts, but rather to examine the story in a different way using the lenses of leadership and teamwork.

Later chapters will highlight important aspects of the story, each one illustrating how Shackleton and others used the ten *Leading at the Edge* strategies. These illustrations will have more impact, however, if they are understood in the context of the overall story. This chapter, therefore, provides an overall chronology of key events, many of which will be explored in more detail in subsequent chapters.

Setting the Stage

The Shackleton expedition's extraordinary tale is one of the most exciting adventure stories of polar exploration. It is a story about a leader and a group of explorers who endured conditions of hardship and deprivation more extreme than most of us can even imagine.

To help frame the story, consider this question: Have you ever been cold? I mean really, really cold? Try to recall the coldest, most miserable time in your entire life. It might have been on a camping trip when you got caught in a hard rain and had to spend the night in a wet sleeping bag. It might have been while waiting for a tow truck in the winter with a dead battery.

Now, hold that feeling and imagine that someone said to you: "You're going to live this way for the next 634 days. You'll be out of touch with the rest of the world; your family will have no idea whether you are dead or alive; and you will be hungry to the point of starvation."

If you can conjure up that feeling of coldness and desolation, it will give you some sense of the conditions faced by Ernest Shackleton and the members of his Trans-Antarctic expedition.

The adventure began with an advertisement, perhaps apocryphal, that appeared in the London papers:

> Men wanted for Hazardous Journey. Small wages, bitter cold, long months of complete darkness, constant danger, safe return doubtful. Honour and recognition in case of success.[1]

Who in the world would volunteer for this journey? Some of you reading this book may feel that this is your job description and that you have already volunteered. Amazingly, thousands of would-be explorers came forward, each wanting to join Shackleton's expedition.

But what was it they were signing up for? Shackleton's mission was the first overland crossing of the Antarctic Continent. He had a clear vision and a plan for how to achieve it. Shackleton intended to sail from London to Buenos Aires and then to the island of South Georgia. From South Georgia, the expedition would enter the Weddell Sea, cross Antarctica, and exit on the other side, where a ship would be waiting. Having calculated the times and distances, Shackleton believed the transcontinental journey could be completed in 120 days.[2] One way of understanding what he was trying to accomplish is to imagine walking from Idaho to Texas, except the geography is dramatically different.

The terrain of Antarctica is depicted well in a passage from Stephen Pyne's *The Ice*:

> Ice informs the geophysics and geography of Antarctica. . . . Out of simple icy crystals is constructed a vast hierarchy of ice masses, ice terranes, and ice structures. These higher-order ice forms collectively compose the entire continent: the ice bergs: tabular bergs, glacier bergs, ice islands, bergy

bits, growlers, brash ice, white ice, blue ice, green ice, dirty ice; the sea ices: pack ices, ice floes, ice rinds, ice hummocks . . . ; the coastal ices, fast ice, shore ices, glacial-ice tongues, ice piedmonts; the mountain ices: glacial ice, valley glaciers, cirque glaciers . . . ; the ground ices: ice wedges, ice veins, permafrost; the polar plateau ices: ices sheets, ice caps, ice domes . . . ; the atmospheric ices: ice grains, ice crystals, ice dust, pencil ice, plate ice, bullet ice.[3]

This description makes it clear: The surface of Antarctica is nothing but ice. The continent's perimeter begins with an ice shelf, in places as tall as a ten-story building. Once past the shelf, there are other obstacles. There are ice hummocks—jagged ridges thrust upward like so many small mountains. Crevasses that can swallow a dog-sled team abound. And, then, there is the climate. The coldest temperature on earth has been recorded in Antarctica: minus 128.6 degrees Fahrenheit.

The Leaders and the Crew

Crossing Antarctica was a formidable undertaking. What kind of a person would attempt a feat such as this? Ernest Shackleton believed he was the person to do it.

Shackleton was an explorer who had already gained fame in Britain in 1909, when he came within ninety-seven nautical miles of the South Pole before he was forced to turn back because of physical exhaustion and a shortage of food. On that expedition, in a characteristic gesture, he gave one of his last biscuits to a comrade, Frank Wild.

The South Pole was reached in 1911 by Norwegian Roald Amundsen and then early in 1912 by the ill-fated expedition of Robert Falcon Scott. No one, however, had traversed the continent by 1914, and this frontier of exploration remained. Shackleton yearned for a challenge, and this was one of the few remaining arenas in which to test his skills.

Much has been written about Shackleton, but I believe the essence of his character can be found in the values transmitted by his family. The Shackleton family's Latin motto, *Fortitudine Vincimus* (By endurance we conquer) was his rallying cry, and the expedition put his motto to the test.

Because he was the leader of the expedition, and because of his forceful personality, much emphasis has been placed on Shackleton. As in any complex enterprise, however, leadership was exercised by many individuals. In fact, a key theme of this book is the importance of mobilizing leadership from multiple sources.

One of the most important sources of leadership came in the form of Frank Wild, Shackleton's old companion. Wild's low-key style balanced Shackleton's bold temperament, and they were so close they would finish each other's sentences. This partnership, born of deep respect and shared hardship, would serve them well when both would be stretched to their limits to maintain the integrity of the expedition.

Wild and Shackleton selected twenty-five other explorers for the expedition. Complex and diverse, the group was composed of men with a range of temperaments, personalities, and technical skills, including medicine, navigation, carpentry, and photography. The team was also diverse in social class, ranging from university professors to fishermen, and in age. The oldest, McNeish, the carpenter, was fifty-seven.

Officially numbering twenty-seven, the full complement of the ship proved to be twenty-eight with Blackborow, the stowaway. When Shackleton discovered that there was a stowaway aboard, he was furious and declared, "If we run out of food, and anyone has to be eaten, you will be first."[4] Despite this inauspicious start, Blackborow eventually became fully integrated as a member of the expedition.

Shackleton was also faced with the task of finding a seaworthy vessel to carry them south. He chose a barkentine-rigged ship, which he named *Endurance,* after his family motto. Built by a famous Norwegian shipbuilding yard, the vessel was powered by both steam and sail.

Endurance was specifically designed for polar travel, constructed of carefully selected wood to withstand the pounding of the ice. Unlike modern icebreakers, however, *Endurance* was not designed to ride over the ice but was constructed with a V-shaped keel.

The Adventure Begins

While Shackleton stayed behind to raise money, *Endurance* sailed at the end of August 1914 under the command of Frank Worsley. Shackleton joined the expedition in Buenos Aires, and they all set out for Grytviken, a whaling station at rugged South Georgia (Figure SS-1, map position 1 at the end of this chapter).

At the whaling station, Shackleton received disturbing reports that the ice had moved much farther north than usual. With these warnings, and knowing that wintering aboard was a distinct possibility, they sailed on December 5, 1914, with extra clothing and a great deal of apprehension.

Shackleton portrayed the scene:

> The ship was very steady in the quarterly sea, but certainly did not look as neat and trim as she had done when leaving the shores of England four months earlier. We had filled up with coal at Grytviken, and this extra fuel was stored on deck, where it impeded movement considerably. . . . We had also taken aboard a ton of whale-meat for the dogs. The big chunks of meat were hung up in the rigging, out of reach but not out of sight of the dogs, and as the *Endurance* rolled and pitched, they watched with wolfish eyes for a windfall.[5]

As the ice thickened, the going became more and more difficult. As Worsley enthusiastically rammed the ship through the floes, Shackleton became increasingly worried by the lack of progress. They wormed their way through the "gigantic and interminable jigsaw puzzle devised by nature."[6]

Trapped in the Ice

On January 19, 1915—forty-five days after their departure from South Georgia—disaster struck. The ice of the Weddell Sea closed around *Endurance* like a vise. The expedition was stuck, sixty miles from the Antarctic Continent (Figure SS-1, map position 2).

Working with picks, saws, and other hand tools, the expedition made two attempts to break free. The first time, with all sails set and engines on full ahead, the crew tried for hours and never moved a foot. In a second attempt, working from 8 A.M. to midnight, they advanced 150 yards. But they were still hopelessly stuck. The "elastic" sea ice prevented a solid blow from ramming a passage, and *Endurance* was trapped.[7]

On February 24, sea watches were canceled, and the crew resigned themselves to wintering on board. The men moved to a warmer between-decks storage area that they called "the Ritz." Their only entertainment was a hand-cranked phonograph and Leonard Hussey, the geologist, who played his banjo and a homemade violin. As the days wore on, *Endurance* became caked with snow and ice. It would be difficult to imagine a colder, bleaker scene. In these extreme conditions, members of the expedition became closer than ever.

How did this happen? I believe the answer lies in Shackleton's understanding of the absolute importance of managing the dynamics of his crew. He had learned from accounts of previous expeditions of the severe morale problems that could arise, and he made a number of conscious decisions to ensure the cohesion of the team. Foremost, as *Endurance* sat securely on the ice, Shackleton kept the crew fairly busy until the end of July 1915. At that point, deep in the Antarctic winter, high winds caused the ice pressure to increase. The ship heeled, the bilge pumps began to fail, water poured into the ship, and the stern was thrown upward twenty feet. As the ice moved relentlessly against the hull, both the timbers of *Endurance* and the crew's sense of security began to crack.

Worsley, the captain, recalled:

> Two massive floes, miles of ice, jammed her sides and held her fast, while the third floe tore across her stern, ripping off the rudder as though it had been made of matchwood. She quivered and groaned as rudder and stern-post were torn off, and part of her keel was driven upwards by the ice. To me, the sound was so terribly human that I felt like groaning in sympathy, and Shackleton felt the same way. It gave me the horrible feeling that the ship was gasping for breath. Never before had I witnessed such a scene, and I sincerely hope I never may again.[8]

Endurance Goes Down

Day 327 of the expedition—October 27, 1915—marked the end of *Endurance*. The masts toppled and the sides were stove in, as shards of ice ripped the strong timbers to shreds. Frank Wild made a last tour of the dying vessel and found two crewmembers in the forecastle, fast asleep after their exhausting labor at the bilge pumps. He said, "She's going boys, I think it's time to get off."[9]

Imagine yourself in Shackleton's position. Your ship is crushed, and you are 346 miles from the nearest food depot on Paulet Island (Figure SS-1, map position 3). You have lifeboats and sleds, but they weigh almost a thousand pounds. Now what?

Shackleton proposed to head toward open water by undertaking a march across hundreds of miles of solid pack ice. Men in harness began pulling the lifeboats on sledges. The task was grueling, and after two days of hauling, the team had covered less than two miles.

Ocean Camp

Realizing that it was futile to go on, the men found a large floe more than half a mile in diameter, made camp, and came to a decision. They agreed to stay on the floe until the drift of the ice carried them closer to Paulet Island. They sat at Ocean Camp from October 30, 1915, until the end of December. So far, Shackleton's leadership had kept the team intact. Now, however, it was more than a year from the time they had set sail from South Georgia. Morale was understandably low, and Shackleton knew that something had to be done to combat the growing sense of futility. On day 384, although they were still a long way from the sea (Figure SS-1, map position 4), they once more attempted to drag the boats across the ice to open water.

The Mutiny

This second sledge march was no more successful than the first, and it set the stage for what has come to be called the "one-man mutiny." McNeish, the carpenter, refused to go on. He argued that the articles he had signed specified serving "on board" and, since *Endurance* had sunk, they were no longer binding. Despite a special clause in the articles that bound him "to perform any duty on board, in the boats, or on the shore," McNeish stood his ground.[10] He defied orders to march, so Shackleton was summoned, defused the mutiny, and enabled the expedition to move forward.

Patience Camp

Exhausted and discouraged because the ice was still impassable, the expedition crewmembers again made camp and waited. The men knew they had to get off the ice, but they had no sense of controlling their fate. Reginald James, the physicist, summed it up this way: "A bug on a single molecule of oxygen in a gale of wind would have about the same chance of predicting where he was likely to finish up."[11]

They continued to deal with the anxiety of waiting, hoping to drift to open water. As their food supply dwindled, they stayed alive on a diet of seal steaks, stewed penguin, and their favorite: penguin liver. There were some moments of excitement, including a near-fatal encounter between Thomas Orde-Lees, the storekeeper and former Royal Marine, and a sea leopard.

By the beginning of April, the floe had shrunk from a half mile to 200 yards wide. With the floe literally cracking out from under them, the men wanted to launch the boats. But they knew that abandoning the floe prematurely might mean disaster: The unstable ice could close, crushing the boats and their only hope of survival.

Escape from the Ice

Finally, on April 9 (Day 491), the pack opened and the boats were launched (Figure SS-1, map position 5). The men tumbled into the three lifeboats, put out every available oar, and pulled with all their strength for open water. The temperature was so cold that when the waves broke over the boats, the water froze to the rowers' clothes in an instant. The men bailed furiously, but the water rose quickly to their ankles and then to their knees. Blackborow, who was wearing leather boots, soon lost all feeling in his feet.

They were all emaciated, suffering from diarrhea, and desperately craving fresh drinking water. The first night they camped on a flat, heavy floe and fell asleep. Late that evening, "some intangible feeling of uneasiness" moved Shackleton to leave his tent. He stood in the quiet camp, watching the stars and the snow flurries. Suddenly, the floe split under his feet, and from the darkness he could hear muffled, gasping sounds. Shackleton ran to a collapsed tent and threw it out of the way, exposing a member of the crew who was struggling in his sleeping bag in the frigid water below. With a tremendous heave, Shackleton pulled him onto the ice, just as the two halves of the broken floe came back together with a crash.

As the winds and currents changed, the group was forced to change its destination four times during the five-and-a-half-day voyage. Finally, they found respite on a rocky, barren speck of land known as Elephant Island. The beach was only 100 feet wide and 50 feet deep, but for the first time in 497 days they were on solid ground.

Elated, but on the verge of collapse, the men ate their first hot meal in almost six days. Given their enfeebled condition, even the most basic tasks were painful. They built shelters out of lifeboats, sails, and clothing. Unfortunately, the shelters were constructed on snow that had been mixed with hundreds of years of penguin guano. Body warmth and the heat from a blubber stove melted the guano, and the crew soon found themselves wallowing in a foul-smelling yellow mud of penguin guano. So they had made it to safety—sort of—but what now? There was only a small food supply on the island—a few penguins, some seagulls, shellfish, and some elephant seals. Still, the chance of rescue was slight and another decision loomed: whether to stay and wait for rescue, or to sail for help. If you sail, where do you go?

The Scotia Sea

There were no good options, and the danger of running out of food also weighed heavily on Shackleton. He confided in Worsley: "We shall have to make the boat journey, however risky it is. I'm not going to let the men starve."

Shackleton decided that part of the crew would sail for help. Because the region's gale-force winds blew from west to east, he elected to make the 800-mile run to South Georgia, sailing through the most treacherous stretch of water on the planet, with winds of hurricane intensity and enormous waves.

Shackleton chose the *James Caird,* the one lifeboat that was the most seaworthy, and attempted to create a vessel that would survive the voyage. Although McNeish was a troublemaker on occasion, he was also a skilled and creative carpenter. His ingenious solution for decking and outfitting the lifeboat for this risky journey proved invaluable. Shackleton selected five members of the expedition to sail with him. After a farewell breakfast, all hands mustered to launch the *James Caird* on Day 506 (Figure SS-1, map position 6).

The next sixteen days were even more harrowing than the journey to Elephant Island. The boat was constantly pounded by immense waves known as Cape Horn Rollers. Each watch, one of the men was forced to risk his life to chip away ice that was constantly forming on the deck and lines.

On May 10, 1916, the exhausted sailors sighted South Georgia. As they made their landing, the rudder fell off the *James Caird,* but by late afternoon Shackleton and his companions were standing on the island they had left 522 days earlier (Figure SS-1, map position 7).

Across the Glaciers

A safe landing was the good news. The bad news was that they were on the wrong side of South Georgia, an island abounding with uncharted and treacherous glaciers. Shackleton and the two best able to travel proceeded overland to reach the whaling station of Grytviken at

Stromness Bay. It took the men three days and nights—each filled with danger and enormous physical challenge—to reach the station.

The men left behind on the far side of South Georgia were soon rescued. Shackleton and five others were finally safe. Back at Elephant Island, however, conditions were desperate. Frank Wild, whom Shackleton had left in charge, worked desperately to keep up the crew's spirits. After four months of waiting, however, the men were wondering if they would ever be found.

The Rescue

Shackleton struggled to get help for the rest of his crew, making three attempts in three different ships. Finally, at the end of August—128 days after the launching of the *James Caird*—he succeeded on the fourth attempt. The timing was providential: The pack ice opened for only a few hours, just enough time to get a boat ashore and to complete the rescue.

Captain Worsley's final journal entry reads:

> Rescued! August 30, 1916
> All well! At last! All ahead full.
>   Worsley[12]

With that entry, the saga of Ernest Shackleton and the men of the Trans-Antarctic expedition ended, 634 days after their departure from South Georgia.

Every time I relive this story, I want to give these explorers a round of applause. I want to applaud them, not just because they made it to safety, but because of the extraordinary leadership and teamwork they exhibited. Not only did they survive, they all survived with a unique level of caring and camaraderie.

Sir Edmund Hillary, the first person to climb Everest and to cross Antarctica successfully, later wrote, "When disaster strikes and all hope is gone, get down on your knees and pray for Shackleton."[13]

But why pray for Shackleton's leadership in desperate times? What was it, exactly, that made him such a great leader? What was it that enabled Shackleton and his team to overcome such seemingly insurmountable obstacles? The chapters that follow provide answers to these questions.

Figure SS-1. Map of the *Endurance* expedition.

PART ONE

Ten Strategies for Leading at *The Edge*

1

Vision and Quick Victories

Strategy 1

Never lose sight of the ultimate goal, and focus energy on short-term objectives.

> . . . I feel sure that it is the right thing to attempt a march. . . . It will be much better for the men in general to feel that even though progress is slow, they are on their way to land, than it will be simply to sit down and wait for the tardy northwesterly drift to take us out of this cruel waste of ice.[1]
>
> Ernest Shackleton

Leaders who take their organizations to *The Edge* must channel energy toward two equally important goals. First, they must continually be aware of their ultimate destination—their longer-term, strategic objective.

This ultimate goal, however, may be distant and uncertain. So while pursuing this long-term target, leaders also must be vigilant in focusing the scarce resources of the organization on the critical short-term tasks that create momentum and ensure survival. Ernest Shackleton demonstrated an almost uncanny mastery of these two essential, but very different, leadership skills.

Be Willing to Find a "New Mark"

It is hard to imagine a bleaker scene than the one surrounding the demise of *Endurance*. Shackleton and his crew had suffered as the ship was slowly, inexorably crushed by millions of tons of ice. For days, they watched the death agony of the ship, waiting helplessly as their floating home disintegrated plank by plank.

Even with the uncertainty of the shifting ice, wind, and ocean, life aboard ship had followed a relatively predictable routine. The crew had warm food and the comforting security of a familiar environment. Now, marooned on the ice and snow, their familiar, stable world had been turned upside down.

With the end of *Endurance*, Shackleton saw his dream of crossing the Antarctic Continent die as well. And he faced more than failure: Shackleton was not expected by the world to reappear until February 1916, and his chances of rescue were nonexistent.

In this wrenching moment of personal challenge, however, Shackleton was able to shift quickly his long-term goal from the crossing of the continent to bringing every man back alive. Refocusing his efforts, he wrote, "A man must shape himself to a new mark, directly the old one goes to ground."[2] With no prospect of rescue, facing an unknown future with little chance of survival, he turned to his crew and simply said: "So now we'll go home."[3]

How was Shackleton able to exercise this kind of tenacity in the face of such overwhelming adversity? He certainly had his private doubts, writing in his diary, "I pray God I can manage to get the whole party to civilization."[4] Acutely aware of his responsibilities as the leader, Shackleton let go of his original plan, shifted his focus, and devoted himself completely to this new mission. By the intensity of his conviction and the force of his will, he instilled in others the deep belief that they would achieve their new goal: returning safely, without loss of life.

Lessons for Leaders

Efforts to explore the unknown are inherently filled with unexpected events. Changing environmental conditions and shifting opportunities are part of any truly innovative, challenging adventure. This means that, as a leader, you need to be willing to shift both long- and short-term goals without clinging to the past. Additionally, you must be able to commit to these new goals with as much passion and energy as you did to the original mark.

CEO Andy Grove's decision to alter Intel's direction provides a clear example of how this tactic can be applied in a business setting. Intel, a company now synonymous with microprocessors, was once primarily a maker of memory chips. In the mid-1980s, Japanese chip-makers moved to win away Intel's chip business by undercutting its prices by 10 percent. The Japanese were successful, and Intel lost $173 million in 1986.

After considering many options, Grove determined to take Intel out of the memory-chip business and make a full-fledged commitment to microprocessor manufacturing. In coming to this decision, Grove asked his colleague and former Intel CEO Gordon Moore a hypothetical question. "If we got kicked out and the board brought in a new CEO, what do you think he would do?"[5]

Moore told Grove that this new CEO would take the company out of the memory-chip business. Grove decided that rather than wait for his successor to change things, he would do it himself. Thereafter, resources were redirected into developing Intel microprocessors, a business sector then secondary to chips. This new direction provided the foundation for Intel's future success.

Do Something!

When *Endurance* went down, the crew's anxiety might have been overwhelming. Instead, their energy was focused and channeled. Although many of their activities did not produce positive results, Shackleton was tireless in finding ways to capture the free-floating anxiety that permeated their situation. Shackleton looked for every opportunity to do something concrete, to take decisive action.

The initial attempt to drag *Endurance*'s heavily laden lifeboats was a complete failure. Their goal was to head northwest for Paulet Island, hoping to reach the emergency food stores that Shackleton knew had been left some twelve years before. This trek of some 312 miles was an unbelievably ambitious undertaking. Even Shackleton had expressed doubts that it could be accomplished at the projected rate of five miles a day—the best they could hope for, dragging sleds and lifeboats across the jagged ice. The boats were essential, since their plan was to reach open water and then to sail to safety.

In spite of the dangers, Shackleton understood the need to try. The task was nearly impossible, but this immediate activity shifted attention from the loss they had just suffered to the clearly defined task ahead. After recovering supplies from the ship and packing the sleds, the journey began. Shackleton and three others forged ahead, searching for a passable route.

Their route was obstructed by a series of pressure ridges, each of which required heavy chopping with shovels and mountaineering pickaxes. The advance party was forced to perform the mind-numbing work of clearing a level trail, and the rest of the expedition followed, man-hauling the sleds in relays. After three hours on the trail, the expedition had gone only a mile from the ship in a straight line.

Ironically, the rising temperatures of the next day made things even worse. The expedition was now plowing through snow stew, bulldozing their way inch by inch, foot by foot. The men sweated profusely, swore at the snow, and made little progress. At the end of the day, they had bulled their way just one more mile. Realizing that it was impossible to go on, Shackleton faced reality and called a halt to the march.

Not surprisingly, this change of plans created no small measure of disappointment. After all, this was to be a march to the open ocean, and eventual rescue. Once more, Shackleton defused a potentially destructive mood, turning the crew's attention toward salvaging any remaining food, clothing, and other supplies from the wreckage of *Endurance*. Wild and six others returned to retrieve gear and—most important—the third lifeboat. Then, all hands focused on the new task of establishing Ocean Camp.

Shackleton's first decision after *Endurance* went down was in some ways a glaring mistake. They had no chance of covering the vast distance to Paulet Island, and precious energy was wasted on an unreachable goal. Or was it?

Shackleton had discovered the absolute importance of sustaining psychological momentum on an earlier adventure, the British Antarctic expedition of 1907–1909. Marooned in McMurdo Sound, he sensed growing frustration and anxiety among the expedition members. To create an outlet, he proposed climbing Mount Erebus. The ascent was marked by days of suffering, sickness, and fatigue, but it concluded with a major achievement: the first ascent of an Antarctic peak.[6]

The "sledge march," like the ascent of Mount Erebus, served its purpose. The march kept the crew from dwelling on its misfortune and redirected their energy toward concrete action. Perhaps most important, the effort forced the members of the expedition to work together toward a common goal.

Lessons for Leaders

Leading at *The Edge* means seizing every opportunity for decisive action, and refusing to be discouraged when some efforts prove unsuccessful. The very act of doing something concrete creates a sense of momentum, and a series of small victories will lay the foundation for eventual success.

James Burke, CEO of Tylenol-maker Johnson & Johnson, faced a difficult decision in September 1982, after an unknown person laced Extra-Strength Tylenol capsules with cyanide—causing seven deaths. His handling of the Tylenol danger is a powerful illustration of the value of decisive action in a crisis situation. He had to choose between waiting for conclusive evidence of a nationwide threat or incurring the cost of recalling all the capsules.

The public had come to equate Johnson & Johnson's products with health and safety; now people were panicking. The company's response would be critical to restoring trust in Tylenol, the company's top-selling product, and the rest of the firm's product line.

The way in which Burke and J&J responded is now regarded as the gold standard of crisis management. Burke's and the firm's actions were guided by the company credo: "The first responsibility is to the customer." Burke quickly formed a strategy team to deal with the crisis, posted a $100,000 reward for finding the killer, ran full-page newspaper and television ads offering consumers an exchange of capsules for tablets, set up a toll-free hotline to field questions, and established public programs to reach doctors and other significant constituencies.

The company redesigned its packaging and eventually retrieved some 31 million capsules from stores and homes around the country. Three months after the crisis, thanks to the company's quick action, tablet sales had returned to 80 percent of the pre-crisis level. The Tylenol capsules were eventually replaced with more tamper-resistant caplets. Decisive action saved the company's market and—more important—its reputation.[7]

Although the problems facing Continental Airlines in 1994 did not involve loss of life, the company and its leaders were faced with a similarly daunting situation. Greg Brenneman, president and COO, described the state of the organization:

> Managers were paralyzed by anxiety. The company had gone through ten presidents in ten years, so standard operating procedure was to do nothing while awaiting new management. The product, in a word, was terrible; the company's results showed it . . . And the company hadn't posted a profit outside of bankruptcy since 1978.[8]

On the verge of an unprecedented third declaration of bankruptcy, and with employee morale in shambles, Brenneman and CEO Gordon Bethune devised a strategy for Continental that they called the "Go Forward Plan"—then they went forward. Brenneman remembers:

> If you sit around devising elegant and complex strategies and then try to execute them through a series of flawless decisions, you're doomed. We saved Continental because we acted, and we never looked back.[9]

Bob, a senior manager in a large federal agency based in Washington, D.C., exemplifies this spirit of moving forward. Bob was given the task of revitalizing two regional offices, one located in New York, the other in Boston. Although he was in constant contact with the two offices by phone, he was often required to be physically present to troubleshoot. He did this by using the New York–Boston airline shuttle.

During one particularly hectic week, Bob ran to the airport and boarded the shuttle for Boston. As the plane was taxiing down the runway he realized, panic stricken, that he was not absolutely sure he had boarded the right plane. He could be going to the wrong city. Then, he took a breath and said to himself, "Don't worry, Bob, it's not such a big deal. You have so much to do that either city will work!" He kept his nerve, kept his momentum after the plane did land in Boston, and the revitalization effort succeeded.

There is a caveat here. A few years ago, I worked with a leading technology organization to try to discover why it expended so much time and resources and accomplished so little in the marketplace. What we found was a culture that valued activity over results.

A cultural icon within the company was the belief that it was important to be seen working late and on weekends. As I interviewed a number of senior executives, it became clear that many of them were more concerned about the appearance of working hard than they were about the work's outcome. This focus on activity over results diverted energy from more important tasks and was a significant barrier to the company's economic success.

Look Beyond Your Own Needs for Action

Shackleton's focused vision and decisive team actions contrast dramatically with those of Vilhjalmur Stefansson on the *Karluk*. The tragedy of the *Karluk* expedition resulted, in part, from a leader who failed to understand the distinction between individual actions and team motivation. Conceived by Stefansson, the Canadian Arctic Expedition of 1913 was intended to explore the possibility that there might be an undiscovered continent somewhere beneath the polar ice.

The expedition was, from the beginning, a flawed effort. Stefansson was an anthropologist and a self-promoter, not a seaman. Short of time, he chose the only available vessel, a twenty-four-year-old wooden barkentine known as the *Karluk*. It was a sailing vessel with an auxiliary engine designed for fishing. The ship was capable of limited speed, only five to seven knots. *Karluk*'s main assets were her cheap price and her availability.

The captain, Robert Bartlett, was a better choice. He, too, was selected at the last minute, but at least he was a distinguished mariner. A native of Newfoundland, he had sailed with Admiral Robert Peary in his historic Arctic exploration in 1909. Captain Bartlett was disappointed in the ship and knew that it would never survive a winter trapped in the ice.

Confusion reigned from the start. Having left preparations to others, Stefansson reached Victoria, British Columbia, just three days before the *Karluk* was to sail. He arrived to find the boat a shambles and the crew anxious about their safety. Already, Stefansson had made incredible public statements that *Karluk* would press northward as far as possible and would probably be crushed and sink. Understandably, the crew was nervous about its uncertain fate.

The *Karluk* sailed from Vancouver Island on June 17, 1913. After fog, engine failure, and five broken hawsers, she finally reached Nome on July 8. On July 26, she sailed from Point Clarence, only to encounter an early blizzard and unusually heavy field ice.

The *Karluk* was not designed for these ice conditions, and Bartlett advised turning back while there was still time. Stefansson refused, and they plowed ahead. On August 13, the ice pack closed around the *Karluk*. No one was particularly concerned, since they expected the sea conditions to change. In fact, they "cavorted about on the ice for hours," enjoying the scenery.

After sitting for five weeks waiting for the ice to open, Stefansson became impatient. He was a leader who thrived on activity, and the delay hardly suited him. He concluded that "the *Karluk* was not to move under her own power again, and that we were in for a voyage such as that of the *Jeanette* or the *Fram*, drifting for years, if we had the luck to remain unbroken. . . ."[10]

Having reached that conclusion, and dreading the prospect of inaction, Stefansson set out on a personal expedition. On September 19, he abruptly announced that he was going to hunt for caribou. Caribou were apparently extinct in the region, so this appeared to many as simply an excuse to leave the ill-fated ship. Stefansson loaded two sledges with food and ammunition and, after posing for photographs, set out with four others for Point Barrow. He left a letter with Bartlett promising to be back to the ship in ten days "if no accident happens."

In September 1913, with the expedition trapped and separated from its leader, the *Karluk* drifted into the realm of "ultimate inaccessibility," into the frozen Arctic Sea. When the *Karluk* was carried out to sea, Stefansson made an effort to follow, but by then it was too late. Apparently reconciled to the loss of the ship, Stefansson went on with his plans for mapping and geographic discovery. He was not seen again until 1918, when he suddenly reappeared after five years of exploration.

Stefansson later rationalized his decision to abandon the expedition, and he minimized the plight of the crew. He was, as he later reported, convinced that the destruction of the *Karluk* would take place slowly and that the crew would be able to salvage their critical supplies and reach safety. He was partly right. They were able to retrieve most of the stores and equipment. What he did not foresee, or apparently care about, is that many would not reach safety and would die in the ice.

Stefansson left behind a leadership vacuum that was never filled, but one thing is clear: If the energy of the crew had been focused and directed, the story of the *Karluk* expedition might have had a very different and much happier ending.

Lessons for Leaders

Vilhjalmur Stefansson did a good job of focusing anxiety—but only his own. Stefansson's caribou hunt is a glaring example of a leader who focused on his own needs for action while neglecting the rest of the organization. This sort of self-involved activity is not, of course, unique to polar explorers.

I observed one senior executive at a leading aerospace firm whose behavior under stress paralleled that of the *Karluk* leader. Whenever this executive was faced with a financial downturn, he closed his door, sat behind his computer, and stared at spreadsheets for hours. By endlessly running the numbers, he focused his own anxiety. This self-absorption left the rest of the management team adrift, wondering who was steering the company.

Leaders at *The Edge* need to maintain a balance between their own needs and the needs of the team, and they must concentrate on engaging the whole organization. By doing so, they will channel their own anxiety and simultaneously ensure that the expedition maintains momentum and focus.

Overcome Uncertainty with Structure

There are times at *The Edge* when it is simply not possible to take proactive, decisive action. But there are other ways of focusing team energy, even when direct forward movement is blocked. Shackleton's ability to create structure and order was effective even when there was little to do but wait. These routines provided a sense of stability, and they helped quell the ever-present anxiety about the future.

To understand just how important these structures were to the stranded crew, picture the inherent chaos of their environment. Adrift on the ice, they were a sorry collection of castaways. Their equipment was primitive at best, with reindeer-skin sleeping bags and rudimentary tents. Their new home was a seesaw of shifting, grinding ice that moved without warning.

In the middle of the first night, a crack opened in the middle of their encampment. The men were awakened by Shackleton blowing the alarm whistle. Tents and stores were moved to the larger section of the floe, but the incident made it clear that their temporary refuge was not a safe home.

While the environment had changed for the worse, the crew's routines had not. From the outset, Shackleton had understood the importance of these essential systems; the necessity of organization had been underscored by the state of his crew after the voyage from London to South Georgia.

Shackleton had stayed behind in England to deal with the perpetual problem of raising money for the expedition. There were harbor and coal bills to contend with and wages to be paid to the crew's families while they were away.[11] This left Frank Worsley, the captain, to take *Endurance* on the first leg of the journey, from London to Buenos Aires, Argentina.

Worsley would later show himself a brilliant navigator, but his initial command was a disaster. He was a leader who shared Shackleton's ebullience, but lacked an understanding of the importance of order and organization. Early on, the captain's erratic nature gave Shackleton reason for concern, and he expressed his doubts in a letter to Ernest Perris of the *Daily Chronicle*. Shackleton wrote that Worsley "was not the type to hold men well together," and that he was eager to have "the whole show under my own eyes."[12]

The effects of this inconsistent, haphazard leadership were apparent when Shackleton arrived in Buenos Aires. He found the crew surly, fragmented, and often drunk.[13] With Shackleton's arrival, everyone breathed a sigh of relief. His very presence restored a sense of order and security. As Orde-Lees put it, it was "splendid having Sir Ernest on board. Everything works like clockwork & one knows just where one is."[14]

Unlike Worsley, Shackleton demonstrated fiery enthusiasm that was complemented by an ability to make order out of chaos. From the start, he established routines that continued after their original purpose had evaporated. Sea watches were kept even after *Endurance* was locked in the ice, and the daily chores of living together proceeded effortlessly. Ice was hauled on board for water, seals were hunted, and the radio watch was maintained.[15]

This tactic of "business as usual" went a long way toward offsetting the bitter disappointment and frustration that everyone felt. Scientists did their work, even if the work was restricted to identifying stones from penguin stomachs. Frank Hurley, the photographer, recorded the changing panorama of ice and sky, and a routine was established for training the dogs.

Shackleton had learned from a previous journey the critical importance of managing the dogs, and he still held out hope that the transcontinental journey could be achieved. So each dog-team leader was assigned the task of producing an effective "work group" through regular practice and exercise.[16]

The stabilizing role of structure became even more important after *Endurance* had been crushed and the expedition was cast out on the ice. Given the strain he was under, Shackleton demonstrated astonishing attention to detail. He realized, for example, that they might be forced to abandon their makeshift quarters in a hurry. He wrote up a detailed plan of just how that would be accomplished and pinned a copy of it to each tent. After reviewing the plan with the crewmembers, he warned them that an evacuation drill could be called at any minute—a sort of "pop quiz" to test their ability to respond.[17]

These stabilizing structures, then, provided a foundation of organized activity that had vital, positive effects on the morale of the team. In his diary, Worsley summed up the sense of security and confidence that this contributed to the expedition:

> I don't think we have a genuine pessimist amongst us. Certainly a good deal of our cheerfulness is due to the order & routine which Sir E. establishes. . . . The regular daily task & matter-of-fact groove into which everything settles inspires confidence in itself, & the Leader's state of mind is naturally reflected in the whole party.[18]

Lessons for Leaders

When leaders move into unexplored terrain, ambiguity and uncertainty are inevitable. Establishing critical organizational structures—a "matter-of-fact groove"—can give people the sense of order they need to be productive. Lawrence Bossidy's leadership of AlliedSignal illustrates the power of this approach.

Lack of confidence throughout the organization was the glaring concern for Bossidy when he took over the reins as CEO. "People were downtrodden, disillusioned, and disappointed. So the essential thing was to try to lift all boats, to communicate things that we could specifically do."[19]

Bossidy's solution was to design a rigorous structure for the company's key processes. He reorganized human resources, detailing systems for selection, reward, development, and motivation. He established structures for strategic planning, including a process for identifying the obstacles that blocked AlliedSignal's success and for deciding how these barriers would be overcome. He revamped the operating plan and developed contingencies—"pre-considered options"—that could be implemented in response to changing external events. He also put in controls to ensure that the company would maintain a focus on its customers.

Bossidy's campaign of systematization extended to manufacturing. He made sure, for example, that the six sigma quality process—defined as 3.4 defects per million parts—was deeply embedded in the organization. He also instituted an employee-education program called "forever learning" in which every employee—including the operators on the floor—received forty hours of training a year.

The investment in these core processes halted AlliedSignal's drift, and it has paid off in financial performance. These efforts also changed the personality of the organization. As COO Fred Poses stated: "[Larry] can be relentless, but he also gives us a burning desire to win."[20]

Create Engaging Distractions

At times during the twenty-three-month ordeal, the Shackleton expedition members, as a practical matter, had very little to do. Naturally, attention often turned to thoughts of home and, of course, food. Shackleton was always on the alert to find distractions that also made real contributions to the expedition. In one notable instance, a crewmember was so discouraged that he literally wanted to lie down and die. Shackleton fixed the problem: The despondent man was given the job of cook, and he became so preoccupied with his new role that he snapped out of his depression. Shackleton later recalled:

> The task of keeping the galley fire alight was both difficult and strenuous, and it took his thoughts away from the chances of immediate dissolution. In fact, I found him a little gravely concerned over the drying of a naturally not over-clean pair of socks which were hung up in close proximity to our evening milk. Occupation had brought his thoughts back to the ordinary cares of life.[21]

The transformation was remarkable. When challenged with a demanding task, a crewmember waiting to die became a valuable contributor.

Lessons for Leaders

Winning leaders cultivate the ability to monitor the condition of each person on the team and to sense when individuals are becoming overwhelmed. They need to direct negative energy toward activities that divert people's attention from their problems and harness this energy for positive results.

I recently came upon a contemporary example of an "engaging distraction." I was discussing human behavior under stress with a friend who is an airline pilot. He had just returned from an intensive training course on dealing with emergency water landings, and he shared an interesting observation.

The lifeboat section of the course dealt with procedures for instructing surviving passengers on a process for setting up a shelter over their rafts. The cover provided, he admitted, very limited protection from the elements, and the assembly task was complicated. The central purpose of the task, however, had little to do with physical protection. Instead, it was designed to give people a concrete activity that would occupy their minds while waiting for rescue.

There is nothing quite like responsibility—especially a role in which others depend on you—to focus your attention. As a leader at *The Edge*, you must continually scan for people who exhibit nervousness and anxiety. When you find them, figure out a way to capture that free-floating energy. Assign them a special project. Give them added responsibility. As a martial arts instructor of mine used to say, "Anxiety is energy without a goal."

Expedition Log

Defining a Long-Term Vision

Before you can communicate a long-term vision to others, you need to be clear in your own mind about your goals. This clarity needs to exist on two levels: a personal vision for you as a leader, and second, a vision for the organization.

1. What is your personal leadership vision? What are the qualities and behaviors that will be required to lead your organization to *The Edge*?
2. What is *The Edge* Goal for your organization—the ultimate destination for the expedition you have undertaken? Is there a "new mark" that you should consider?

Focusing Energy on Short-Term Goals

1. What are the key opportunities for action? What concrete things can you do to create a sense of momentum and forward movement?

2. What are the structures and routines that you use to create a sense of stability? What other things might you do?
3. Can you think of any "engaging distractions" that would contribute to the morale of your organization?
4. What are your short-term milestones? How are you measuring success on the journey your expedition has undertaken?

2

Symbolism and Personal Example

Strategy 2
Set a personal example with visible, memorable symbols and behaviors.

Speaking with utmost conviction, Shackleton pointed out that no article was of any value when weighed against their ultimate survival, and he exhorted them to be ruthless in ridding themselves of every unnecessary ounce, regardless of its value. After he had spoken, he reached under his parka and took out a gold cigarette case and several gold sovereigns and threw them into the snow at his feet.[1]

Alfred Lansing

Chapter 1 stressed the vital importance of keeping energy flowing toward short- and long-term goals. This chapter highlights a set of specific leadership tactics for mobilizing that energy through personal example and with clear, concrete images and symbols.

Particularly under conditions of stress and discouragement, visible leadership can mean the difference between success and failure. Shackleton understood this well. He knew just how important it was for the crew to *see* him as the leader—and to outline the work to be accomplished with unmistakable clarity. We do not all have to be Ernest Shackleton, but leaders need to be aware that their personal presence is a unique source of energy and power. They need to draw on this power to lead their organizations to *The Edge.*

Give the Right Speech

When the situation is dire, the power of the right words is striking. It is impossible to exaggerate the devastation the men felt when *Endurance* was crushed by the ice. As Captain Frank Worsley wrote:

> Actuated by an invisible force countless miles away, the rigging tautened and sang like harp strings, then snapped under the strain as the ship was twisted and wrung by the giant hands of ice that grasped her. . . . To talk was impossible. Each man knew that it was the end of the ship. We had lost our home in that universe of ice. We had been cast out into a white wilderness that might well prove to be our tomb.[2]

The loss of the actual ship, dramatic though it was, was made more poignant by the men's sure knowledge of its consequences. They had only a four-week supply of food; their linen tents were so flimsy that they provided minimal protection; the lack of tent floors meant that the crew were sleeping in pools of water as the heat from their bodies melted the ice. Even though *Endurance* would not sink immediately, everyone knew that, as Frank Worsley wrote, "Many of our stores were irretrievable. . . . A shortage of food was not a pleasant prospect."[3]

The explorers were standing on an ice floe, in the middle of the Weddell Sea, listening to the beams of their ship snapping in two, knowing they could never get to their stores, and wondering what would happen next. Despite Worsley's quaint Victorian understatement, their anxiety must have been palpable. At this point, Shackleton made a speech. Frank Wild remembered:

> Shackleton made a characteristic speech to hearten our party, the sort of speech that only he could make. Simply and in brief sentences he told the men not to be alarmed at the loss of the vessel, and assured them that by hard effort, clean work, and loyal cooperation, they could make their

way to land. This speech had an immediate effect: our spirits rose, and we were inclined to take a more cheerful view of a situation that had nothing in it to warrant the alteration.[4]

The crew knew that nothing had physically changed. But Shackleton used precisely the right words and tone. He chose words that gave members of the expedition a sense of control over their fate. Shackleton later recalled:

> After the tents had been pitched I mustered all hands . . . and stated that I propose to try to march with equipment in the direction of Paulet. . . . I thanked the men for the steadiness and good morale they have shown in these trying circumstances, and told them I had no doubt that, provided they continue to work their utmost and to trust me, we will all reach safety in the end.[5]

It is axiomatic that people who do not believe they can influence their destiny become anxious and fearful. Shackleton's words gave them the belief that they could influence their own survival and that of the expedition.

In addition, Shackleton chose the right tone—calm, confident, and reassuring. It might have been tempting to dramatize the situation, but Shackleton chose a calm demeanor, probably using his characteristically solid stance with his hands on his hips. His speech was not a pep talk or a locker-room rallying exhortation. That would have been incongruent, given the gravity of the situation. Shackleton's speech provided a balanced, realistic look at the situation and assured the men of his confidence that they would survive through their own efforts.

Lessons for Leaders

I have worked with a number of senior executives who are uncomfortable in large group settings. As a result, they exercise leadership in their most natural style, emphasizing one-on-one or small group interactions.

Establishing strong individual relationships is an important part of leadership. But there are times when the role demands something different, when the energy of the entire group or organization needs to be mobilized. On these occasions, the leader needs to face his or her team and communicate a message to the team as a whole—to make a speech.

I have seen speeches take the form of "get one for the Gipper" motivational addresses. I have also seen speakers deliver extended, dry remarks filled with complex financial projections, or sermons filled with dire predictions about the future—and admonitions to work hard or else.

There are occasions for financial projections and times when a standard set of motivational remarks will suffice. There are other times at *The Edge,* however, when something more is needed. These are the times that call for the "right speech."

The right speech needs to be more than a recital of remarks written by a staff member given the job of coming up with something clever. The right speech needs to be authentic, and it needs to be delivered with sincerity. But it need not be filled with histrionics. It is more important for the message to be delivered from the heart than with flowery language, and there are times when a cheerleading speech is counterproductive.

When the situation is grim—when people are fearful and obstacles loom large—an excessively cheerful and overly emotional message is the wrong speech. What is called for is calm reassurance, straight talk, and unmistakable resolve.

Franco Bernabe, CEO of Eni, Italy's large energy-focused industrial group, faced more challenges than most executives when he took over as CEO in 1992. The circumstances of the government-owned, debt-ridden firm included a senior management team that was arrested and jailed for corruption, the suicide in prison of the former CEO, and a baseless claim from a former employee that Bernabe himself had accepted a huge bribe.

Bernabe's announced goal had been to transform the company from a government-run, politically handcuffed entity into a market-driven business that answered to shareholders. Regardless of the turmoil around him, he kept his focus on this goal, and he relied on speeches to spread his message through the organization.

Bernabe recalled:

> I had to learn as CEO how to communicate. I was used to writing articles and preparing reports, but those are not really very effective communication tools. People can fall asleep after two minutes of reading. And you can talk to five senior managers around a table, but you find a month later that no one in the second or third levels of the organization knows you or your objectives.
>
> I realized the most effective thing to do was give

> speeches to large groups within the organization. I try to
> give one a month. You can reach so many people, so many
> levels of the organization. But a speech can be like an article
> if you're not careful. So the speech has to have emotional
> content. To be effective, you have to tap into people's senti-
> ments, feelings, and emotions.[6]

Bernabe did more than give speeches, but his ability to speak clearly
and sincerely was a powerful leadership tool. Since Bernabe became
CEO, Eni's labor productivity has increased 112 percent, and profits
have risen sharply. In 1995, the company made its first public offering
and by July 1997, 49 percent of the firm was publicly held.

Use Vivid Symbols

Although Shackleton deliberately took a low-key tone in describing
the expedition's situation, he was far more dramatic when he outlined
the work to be done to reach the expedition's goals. Not an alarmist
about things he could do nothing about, he was a genius at drawing
on drama, even theatricality, when he needed to mobilize the expedition to overcome extraordinary obstacles.

Shackleton had demonstrated his ability to use symbolic behavior
earlier—in Buenos Aires—when First Officer Lionel Greenstreet fouled
the propeller while attempting to maneuver *Endurance*. Greenstreet expected to be called on the carpet, perhaps even disciplined. Instead,
Shackleton helped him repair the damage and never again spoke about
the incident. The message he had visibly demonstrated was clear: We
will all make mistakes; fix them and move on. This public act became
a symbolic gesture for the whole expedition.

When *Endurance* was crushed by the ice, Shackleton again acted
symbolically. He was convinced that a successful sledge march to the
ocean could only be accomplished if every nonessential item was discarded. He had to communicate to the crew that anything that would
not contribute to the success of the expedition—no matter what the
emotional attachment or how intrinsically valuable elsewhere—had to
be left behind.

Shackleton realized that some personal items, though they did not
necessarily contribute to physical survival, were essential for psychological well-being. He struggled to find a balance between weight and
speed:

> I rather grudged the two pounds allowance per man, owing
> to my keen anxiety to keep weight at a minimum, but some
> personal belongings could fairly be regarded as indispens-
> able. The journey might be a long one, and there was a
> possibility of a winter in improvised quarters on an inhospi-
> table coast at the other end. A man under such conditions
> needs something to occupy his thoughts, some tangible me-
> mento of his home and people beyond the seas.[7]

So mementos of home were indispensable, while other items that
might have had great value in a different situation were expendable.
After issuing the order that each man could carry only two pounds of
personal gear, Shackleton set the example for traveling light with a
dramatic gesture. He reached inside his parka, took out a handful of
gold sovereigns, and threw them to the ground at his feet. Again, he
reached into his parka and found a gold cigarette case. This too he
threw to the ground.

The message, as Worsley recalled, was clear:

> Shackleton now determined to cut down every ounce of su-
> perfluous weight, in the hope that we could sledge to Gra-
> ham Land, the most northerly part of the Antarctic
> Continent. He himself set the example, throwing away,
> what a spectacular gesture, a gold watch, a gold cigarette
> case, and several golden sovereigns. Naturally, after wit-
> nessing this action, which brought home to me at any rate
> the shifting values in life and the knowledge that there are
> times when gold can be a liability instead of an asset, we all
> discarded everything save the barest necessaries.[8]

In this dramatic gesture, Shackleton personally demonstrated that only
items that had value in terms of survival were important. He provided
a focus for the expedition that was unmistakable and unambiguous:
We must jettison anything that will not directly enable us to accomplish our goal.

Lessons for Leaders

It is one thing to tell people that a task needs to be done, and it is
another to dramatize the challenge with visible, memorable symbols
and behaviors. These symbols can be as dramatic as throwing gold
sovereigns into the snow, or they can be more prosaic. Whatever the
symbol, it needs to be vivid and memorable.

Gordon Bethune, the CEO of Continental Airlines, described an example of one such symbolic act. In the early 1990s, Continental—ranked last in customer service among the ten largest airlines—was stifled with a bureaucratic set of rules that specified everything from the color of pencils to be used on boarding passes to the kind of fold used in a sick-day form. The problem was that these rules had tied the hands of airline employees to the point that they had no real discretion to solve problems—and they were punished for disobeying the rules.

If a plane was canceled, for example, a full-fare passenger might get a hotel room, whereas a next-in-line bargain-fare passenger could get a meal voucher. Naturally, this sort of rigid decision making did little for Continental's public image. It also subjected gate agents to the wrath of irate customers, practically making gate agents eligible for hazardous-duty pay.

The policy manual—the "Thou Shalt Not Book"—was an icon for this rigid system. To symbolize the need for change, Bethune took a group of employees into the parking lot. They threw the manual into a fifty-five-gallon drum, poured gasoline onto it, and set it afire. By burning the manual, they sent a message to the organization: Do not blindly follow the book—use your ingenuity and do what is right for the company and for the customer.[9]

Be Visible: Let People See You Leading

Shackleton understood the importance of demonstrating through action as well as words that he was a leader doing his duty. He was a visible presence throughout the experience, yet one of the most striking examples took place during the open boat voyage from Patience Camp to Elephant Island.

This grueling journey was one of their most physically exhausting, demoralizing experiences. The men were soaked by constant rain, and the cold was so severe that sleep was often impossible. The tiny boats were surrounded by the hisses of killer whales, and the men dealt with the fear that they would capsize when the creatures came up to blow.

The winds and currents were so strong that—after hours under sail—they were sometimes dismayed to discover that, not only had they made no forward progress, they were actually farther from their destination than when they had begun. Exacerbating the situation, they lacked fresh water and their thirst could only be relieved by chewing raw seal meat and swallowing the blood. Finally, to cap it off, many of the men suffered from seasickness as the small boats wallowed in the heavy swells.

Shackleton described the scene:

> The temperature was down to four degrees below zero, and
> a film of ice formed on the surface of the sea. When we were
> not on watch we lay in each other's arms for warmth. Our
> frozen suits thawed where our bodies met, and as the slight-
> est movement exposed these comparatively warm spots to
> the biting air, we clung motionless, whispering each to his
> companion our hopes and thoughts. Occasionally from an
> almost clear sky came snow-showers, falling silently on the
> sea and laying a thin shroud of white over our bodies and
> our boats.[10]

Conditions were so severe that there were times when Shackleton
doubted that all hands would survive the night. If ever there was a
time for visible, inspiring leadership, this was it. Understanding the
importance of his role, Shackleton made a point of standing erect in
the stern of the lifeboat *James Caird*, "conning the course," showing
that he was keeping vigil and inspiring the men.

When Hurley, the photographer, lost his mittens, Orde-Lees observed Shackleton's response:

> At once [he] divested himself of his own, and in spite of the
> fact that he was standing up in the most exposed position
> all the while he insisted upon Hurley's acceptance of the
> mits, and on the latter's protesting Sir Ernest was on the
> point of throwing them overboard rather than wear them
> when one of his subordinates had to go without; as a conse-
> quence Sir Ernest had one finger rather severely frost-
> bitten.[11]

Shackleton's presence as a leader and his example of self-sacrifice were
critical to the crew's success in reaching the safety of Elephant Island.
A more recent example, one from the Vietnam War, confirms the
power of visible leadership. Phil Caputo was a Marine lieutenant in
Vietnam. In his personal memoir, *A Rumor of War*, Caputo describes
the way his platoon sergeant, "Wild Bill" Campbell, dealt with the
panic of an ambush. Caputo and his platoon had come under heavy
automatic-weapons fire. Bullets were smacking into trees, shredding
leaves, and snapping twigs. The Marines panicked, emptying their
magazines and wasting ammunition by firing at targets they could not
see. Caputo recalled:

I wasn't frightened, just confused. Or maybe I was confused because I was frightened. Then I heard Campbell's voice booming above and behind us. "Cease fire, you silly shits! Cease fire!" Several enemy bullets walked up the trail behind him, splattering dust, the last round striking less than an inch from his heel. He kept walking as casually as a coach at the rifle range. "Cease fire, Second [Platoon]. Can't see what the hell you're shooting at. Let's have a little goddamned fire discipline."[12]

Encouraged by the sergeant's calmness while under intense enemy fire, the Marines came to their senses and stopped wasting ammunition. The gunfire halted, and Lieutenant Caputo climbed out of the trench in which he had taken cover. When Caputo complimented the sergeant on his presence of mind, Campbell brushed off his heroism, attributing it to a back injury he'd sustained jumping off the chopper. Most likely, the veteran Marine knew that his platoon was spooked and out of control and needed reassurance. His personal example turned the platoon around in a tough situation.

Lessons for Leaders

Leaders can be quietly competent, but they must be visible. The open boat journey to Elephant Island was physically demanding and one of the most extreme stress points that the expedition had encountered. It was stressful for everyone, but especially for Shackleton, who bore the principal burden of leadership.

In spite of the personal hardship, Shackleton recognized the importance of being in the forefront and was willing to face the freezing ocean spray. "Wild Bill" Campbell also understood the importance of visible leadership and stood conspicuously under fire to stabilize his platoon.

This type of action is all too easy to talk about in the abstract, when one is warm and dry, or in a case study discussion of leadership. It is quite different to be a visible leader when you are exhausted and facing danger—whether the threat comes from weather, sniper fire, or angry customers, analysts, or shareholders.

These difficult situations, however, are those during which it is most important to let people see you "standing in the stern sheets." If you are conscious of this necessity, you can create opportunities for visibility that allow you to use the power of your role as a leader to provide assurance, direction, and inspiration.

At Continental Airlines, CEO Bethune and his COO, George Brenneman, loaded bags and stood alongside their agents at ticket counters. They talked to mechanics, and they talked to pilots. They got out to airports, rode planes, and spoke with employees at every possible opportunity—and their presence made a difference in the company's turnaround. The power of visible leadership is not, however, restricted to turnarounds and crises.

Ray Kroc, the founder of McDonald's, had a penchant for stopping unannounced at the McDonald's restaurants near the company's headquarters in Oakbrook, Illinois. He relayed this story of what happened on one such occasion:

> One sunny July afternoon, I pulled into a McDonald's parking space and noticed that the flowering bushes were littered with shake cups, Happy Meal boxes, napkins, and other trash. Inside, I asked for the manager. Only the assistant manager was there, so I had him call the manager and waited for the anxious man to rush in after a speedy drive from his nearby home. "What can I do for you, sir?" the manager asked me. I led him to the parking lot, pointed at the shrubbery, and said, "Look! We don't want trash around our sites!" In a matter of minutes, I, my driver, and the manager had picked up all the garbage out of the bushes.[13]

By working side by side with this manager, Kroc conveyed that it is more important to fix a problem than to establish blame, and he also set an example that no one is above doing the work that needs to be done. This story has become part of the corporate lore at McDonald's and has helped to establish a culture where attention to detail and collaboration are valued.

The point of these stories is clear: You, as a leader, have a unique role and a special power. Chart your course and—with presence, symbolism, and personal example—use that power to lead your organization to *The Edge*.

Expedition Log

1. As you look at and think about the things your team needs to do to reach *The Edge*, what are the most critical priorities?
2. How can those priorities be dramatized with vivid, memorable

symbols or images? Is there a story or metaphor that portrays the work to be done? What is your equivalent of throwing gold sovereigns into the snow?

3. Have you given "the right speech" to mobilize the power of the team? Do you need to address your team members again, to reenergize the organization?

4. What are you doing to ensure that you are visible as a leader? What is your "visibility plan"? How much time do you spend out of the office or in situations that allow you to project your presence?

3

Optimism and Reality

Strategy 3
Instill optimism and self-confidence, but stay grounded in reality.

> Shackleton had a wonderful and rare understanding of the men's attitudes towards one another and towards the expedition as a whole. He appreciated how deeply one man, or a small group of men, could affect the psychology of the others. Therefore he almost insisted upon cheeriness and optimism; in fact his attitude was, "You've damn well got to be optimistic."[1]
>
> Frank A. Worsley

Keen intellect, business competence, and strong interpersonal skills are essential leadership qualities. But if there is one quality that makes the difference at *The Edge*, it is the ability to remain optimistic in the face of daunting adversity. It is the capacity to look at odds that are impossible, to believe that it is still possible to win, and to convince others that you are right.

Some critics might say that Shackleton's entire plight came about because he was too optimistic and should have never embarked in the first place. After all, the Norwegian whaling skippers had warned him that ice conditions were treacherous, and yet he elected to continue when a more prudent course might have been to turn back.

This is an issue I will pick up in this chapter and later in the book.

Nevertheless, the fact remains that the expedition was able to prevail against enormous obstacles largely because of Shackleton's dogged optimism—and his superb skill in spreading this positive outlook to others.

Cultivate Optimism in Yourself

Before you can instill optimism in others, you first need to find it in yourself. Shackleton's family motto—*Fortitudine Vincimus* (By endurance we conquer)—sums up the explorer's personality. His indomitable spirit, however, was more than a family legacy. It was a quality that he worked to develop.

Shackleton spent his time nourishing the spirit of optimism within himself. It seemed to pervade everything he did, especially his reading. For example, he was fond of quoting Robert Browning's "Prospice":

> I was ever a fighter, so—one fight more,
>> The best and the last! . . .
> For sudden the worst turns the best to the brave
>> The Black minute's at end . . .[2]

Shackleton framed the world in an invariably optimistic way. On his first expedition to the South Pole, when the march was stopped by a blizzard, he spent time reading Darwin's *Origin of Species*. He embraced Darwin's belief that natural selection leads to perfection and felt buoyed in spite of his ill health.[3]

The spirit of the times was unflaggingly optimistic, of course, but Shackleton took it to a new dimension. He was more than just a salesman, although his salesmanship was revealed by his dogged refusal to take no for an answer when he was gathering financing for his expedition. Shackleton believed he would succeed, and his belief spread to others.

Lessons for Leaders

A reasonable question to ask is whether optimism like Shackleton's is something you either have or not. He was, after all, a charismatic leader with special qualities. Shackleton and other great leaders often seem to have been born with a special belief in their own ability. General George Patton, for example, grew up with a belief in the inevitability of his place in history.

Many people may have a difficult time identifying with Shackleton's boundless optimism, and his enthusiastic belief that things would somehow work out in the end. Few of us grew up in families whose mottoes were as inspiring as "By endurance we conquer." I have one client, for example, who—after reading accounts of the *Endurance* expedition—volunteered that his family motto was "We meant well." Not quite so inspiring. Another leader quipped, "It's easy for me to be an optimistic leader anytime except when I'm depressed."

For many leaders, questions remain. Is this capacity for optimism an innate characteristic? Can optimism really be acquired or cultivated? How can I develop a more optimistic personality if I do not already have that predisposition?

Optimism may not be a natural act for everyone, but there is reason to believe that it is an ability that can be learned and greatly improved. The key lies in the inner dialogue that goes on, often unnoticed, almost all the time for all of us.

I will sometimes ask a group the question, "How many of you talk to yourselves?" Usually, about half of the group members raise their hands. The other half say (to themselves), "I don't talk to myself."

The reality is that this "self-talk" is part of human nature, and the first step in cultivating optimism is to pay close attention to what you say to yourself. If you are aware of this inner dialogue, especially during times of adversity or setback, you will be conscious of the messages you are sending yourself about failure or success. The right messages are energizing, and the wrong ones are deflating.

The way to develop a feeling of optimism is to consistently send positive messages that override voices of discouragement and pessimism. Some of the mechanics of sending these positive messages may sound hokey or contrived. I agree: They may seem contrived—but they often work.

One of my clients had the task of leading a team with an extremely difficult assignment. The task was to complete a thorough report in a business field in which no one on the team had prior direct experience. Progress was glacially slow. Operating under a tight deadline, everyone was discouraged, even the leader. The goal seemed unreachable.

Then one day the team leader was looking at a magazine ad with the words "You can do it!" emblazoned in color across the page. He cut out the words and taped them to the mirror in his bathroom. Every morning, the first thing he saw was his face with the caption, "You can do it!" This optimistic image literally changed the way he began the day. Contrived, yes—but effective, because the team completed a well-received report by the deadline.

There are more complex ways of thinking about how to change these self-messages. Psychologist Martin Seligman has pioneered one systematic approach that he calls "learned optimism."[4] Seligman has studied the effects of optimistic self-talk, or "explanatory style," in real-world conditions ranging from selling insurance to surviving plebe (freshman) year at West Point. His conclusions are that optimists do better than pessimists and that their success rate is greater than objective data (such as SAT scores) would predict.

Seligman argues that his "ABCDE" model is more effective than simply sending positive messages. His process, which I have simplified, involves five concepts and related actions:

1. *Adversity.* Identify the adversity you have encountered (e.g., a computer crash in the middle of an important project).
2. *Beliefs.* Note your thoughts and beliefs about the event—that is, your interpretation (e.g., "I'll never get the report done").
3. *Consequences.* Recognize the consequences of your belief (e.g., you feel discouraged).
4. *Dispute.* Dispute the negative belief with a sound argument based on evidence (e.g., "I have overcome other technology disasters through persistence").
5. *Energy.* Generate the energy and feelings needed to overcome the adversity (e.g., "I feel more relaxed and confident that I deal with the problem and finish the report").

The learned optimism approach can be a valuable tool, but the process requires rehearsal. Practice using the method to deal with minor setbacks so that it will become second nature under conditions of more serious adversity. And, whatever approach you use, be aware of your inner dialogue. As Henry Ford once said, "Whether you think you can, or whether you think you can't, you're right."

Spread the Spirit of Optimism

Shackleton did more than cultivate optimism in himself. He was able to communicate his positive outlook in a way that had a profound influence on every member of the expedition, even the cynics. He exercised this remarkable power in a number of ways.

Shackleton's fundamentally ebullient personality was a contagious force that simply infected others. In large measure, he believed so completely in success that it was difficult not to subscribe to his cheerful outlook. Shackleton also established the attitude that "you've damn well got to be optimistic" as a core operating principle of the expedition. It was a discipline to be learned and cultivated.

There were also times in which Shackleton's ability to inspire confidence lay in his ability to put on a good face—the traditional British stiff upper lip and steely self-control. This was illustrated by his behavior at a ship's "party" that was held before the other members of the expedition realized the extent of their predicament.[5]

These festive events, held in the below-deck area known as the Ritz, were in keeping with a tradition of polar exploration. They consisted of skits, songs, and whatever makeshift costumes the crew could devise. While the crew was preparing for the fun of the masquerade party, Shackleton met with Frank Wild and Captain Worsley to deliver his grim assessment of their situation. He had become convinced that the ship was doomed, and he gave Worsley the news with no equivocation.

> The ship can't live in this, Skipper. . . . You had better make up your mind that it is only a matter of time. It may be a few months, and it may be a question of weeks, or even days. . . . But what the ice gets, the ice keeps.[6]

Immediately after this dire prophecy, First Officer Greenstreet knocked on the cabin door and announced that the crew was ready to begin the party. Minutes later, Shackleton was laughing with "the boys" in the Ritz. No one would have ever guessed the thoughts that must have lain heavy on his mind.

There were times, of course, during which even Shackleton's dogged optimism flagged under the enormous stresses of responsibility. This was especially true during the time before their escape from Patience Camp to the relative safety of Elephant Island. It was a difficult time for the leader, with his expedition sitting on a dwindling cake of ice, buffeted by wind and weather and threatened by collision and heavy swells. Shackleton recalled his feelings at the time:

> I confess that I felt the burden of responsibility sit heavily on my shoulders; but, on the other hand, I was stimulated and cheered by the attitude of the men.[7]

Shackleton took heart from the optimistic spirit of the team and, in return, Shackleton's presence and demeanor engendered optimism among his crew. But the Boss did not simply exhort people to be hopeful. He was masterful in the subtle ways in which he created a pervasive spirit of future possibility and positive energy.

He kept the group engaged, for example, with a lively discussion about—remarkably—the prospect of an expedition to Alaska![8] For a group stranded in the middle of a frozen Antarctic sea, the idea of another polar undertaking could have seemed preposterous. But the prospect provided an engaging alternative to dwelling on their predicament or thinking about the potential dangers that lay ahead. Captain Worsley recounted:

> We look up all the maps & books on the subject that we can lay our hands on, & are enthusiastic about our next trip before we can definitely settle how the devil we are going to get out of this one.[9]

Planning an expedition to Alaska was clearly a method for entertaining the expedition during the long empty hours. In this sense, it was an "engaging distraction." But it was more than that. It provided a future focus and a promise that there would be other adventures—with the obvious implication that they would triumph over their present situation. It represents just one way in which the whole culture of the expedition encouraged confidence and hope.

Lessons for Leaders

Leaders who are successful at *The Edge* are able to instill in others the belief that the organization will achieve its goals. But just how does a leader radiate optimism? How does a leader spread "the spirit" when survival is not at stake?

Maytag CEO Lloyd David Ward has one formula. Before being named CEO of Maytag in August 1999, Ward—then head of the company's appliance division—took a bold step that nearly doubled Maytag's profits within three years and helped turn the appliance industry on its ear.[10] In an industry traditionally characterized by relentless competition and persistent price pressure, Ward was able to rally his Maytag colleagues around his outside-the-box belief that consumers would be willing to pay a premium for water- and energy-efficient, feature-laden, high-priced appliances. In 1997, Maytag introduced the Neptune washing machine; positioned as water-saving, environmentally friendly, and gentle on clothes, the appliance sold at the theretofore unthinkable price of $1,000.

How did he do it? Describing Ward as a "master motivator who listens as well as he speaks," *Business Week* observed:

> Ward has convinced Maytag veterans that change was both necessary and possible. Colleagues laud his ability to challenge people's beliefs without criticizing them personally, to seize on nuggets of common ground and exploit them. . . . He greets people with a firm handshake, pulling himself closer to them, putting a palm on the back of their elbow, and quickly asking questions about their own life. . . .

This description of Ward's engaging, personal approach is remarkably similar to accounts of Shackleton's interactions with members of his crew. As one of the nation's few African-American CEOs, Ward says, "My whole life I've been faced with 'no'." In seeking the top job at Maytag and facing tough personal and professional challenges, Ward has been able to overcome the prejudices of society and the challenges of business. Ward relates, "Knock on the door, pull on the handle, and, if you have to, dismantle the hinge."

This tenacious approach worked for Shackleton, and it appears to be working for Ward. But there is another question that surfaces for me as I think about optimism at *The Edge:* Just how candid should leaders be in sharing their uncensored doubts and inner feelings when faced with adversity?

There are those who believe that personal authenticity demands complete openness, and that leaders should reveal the depths of their emotional inner life. They argue that anything other than this level of disclosure is patronizing—and that openness creates space for others to be similarly revealing.

My perspective is different. I believe there are times in which leaders need to maintain their composure, despite the natural inclination to express feelings of discouragement, fear, or even despair. This is not to say that they should shield others from reality or withhold basic information about the situation. Rather, it is to say that there are times at *The Edge* in which the perceived attitude of the leader is a powerful force that can create energy and optimism or fear and pessimism: It becomes a self-fulfilling prophecy.

When fears and doubts are expressed openly, it may be difficult or impossible to rekindle the optimism that is so important for success. Therefore, I believe the role of the leader demands that personal fears are best controlled or dampened until negative information is digested. Then a discussion of concerns can be coupled with potential solutions and a positive message of hope for the future.

Build the Right Team "Optimism Quotient"

After hearing the story of the Trans-Antarctic expedition, some people conclude that the success of the expedition can be traced to the initial selection process and Shackleton's ability to assemble such a capable team. In fact, Shackleton's interviews were often cursory and haphazard. But he did succeed in filling several critical roles with extremely competent individuals and in making the best use of those finally selected.

His knack for putting the right team members in the right job showed itself in technical tasks, but Shackleton was also sensitive to having the right mix of temperaments and outlooks. In particular, he seemed to have a sense of the threshold level of what might be called an "OQ"—the optimism quotient, or ratio of optimistic to more pessimistic team members—needed to take on arduous tasks.

Probably the most important team choice Shackleton made was his second in command, Frank Wild. Shackleton had endured extreme hardship with Wild on their previous expedition to the South Pole and, consequently, had a complete grasp of the man's character. Wild was not only steadfast and loyal. He also shared Shackleton's fundamental belief that obstacles existed to be overcome.

Wild's optimism was important on numerous occasions. After Shackleton's jarring pre-party announcement about the fate of *Endurance*, for instance, Wild saw that Captain Worsley was shaken. Wild immediately rose to reassure the captain with softly spoken but confident words: " . . . We are not going to let the ice get us. Poor little *Endurance* may go, but we won't."[11]

It was the perfect remark, and Worsley was comforted. Worsley later remembered:

> . . . [Wild] had said just [the] right thing. To an old seaman like myself, the very idea of giving up a ship is something like having an arm or leg amputated; but Wild's words made me realize that in spite of the importance which the ship might have in my eyes, there were human lives at stake . . . and that our job was to see that the ice didn't get them— even if it got my ship.[12]

This was not an isolated event. Wild's ability to maintain an optimistic spirit was an anchor that remained solid throughout the ordeal. And it was a quality tested dramatically after Shackleton sailed with the *James Caird* for South Georgia. Shackleton left Wild in full command of the twenty-two men left behind on Elephant Island. Managing the emotions of the "castaways" was an enormous leadership challenge. In fact, it may have been even more difficult than that faced by the Boss in his run to South Georgia.

Shackleton's fate was unknown for 128 days, and Wild had the daily challenge of maintaining hope in the face of the obvious possibility that disaster might have overtaken the rescue party. There were also other potential sources of despair. Orde-Lees, ever the pessimist, predicted that their supply of penguins would disappear, and conditions continued to become more and more desperate. They all suffered, especially Blackborow, the stowaway, whose foot had to be amputated from the ball joint forward.[13] Given all this (along with the extreme dismay when the tobacco supply ran out), an atmosphere of doom easily could have prevailed.

Shackleton's confidence in Wild's ability to hold the party together was well founded. Wild not only maintained the routines that had served the group so well in the past, but he also kept the men infused with the positive attitude that they had exhibited under Shackleton.

In the absence of the Boss, it became clear that Shackleton's optimism had become embedded in the ethos of the team, and it was nourished constantly by Frank Wild. He refused to entertain even the slightest possibility that they would not be rescued. As an unwavering symbol of his conviction, Wild roused the men every day with a cheery shout of "Lash up and stow, boys, the Boss may come today."[14] Even the morose Orde-Lees was forced to admit that Wild's ability to maintain the spirits of those likely to be despondent was "a fine thing."

Shackleton's choice of Wild was central to the crew's successful return, but there were other instances in which optimism seemed to be an explicit selection factor. When choosing a crew for what was to be the most arduous and dangerous part of the journey thus far—the voyage to South Georgia—Shackleton looked for men with a number of qualities. He seemed to have an innate understanding of the importance of having someone he could rely on to keep up the spirits of the team.

Shackleton filled one of the five scarce billets on the *James Caird* with Timothy McCarthy, an "able seaman" whose good-natured personality had endeared him to everyone on the expedition. True, McCarthy could contribute physical strength, but his most important contribution was probably his ability to maintain a positive outlook under the worst sea and weather any of them had ever experienced.

"Macty" maintained his cheery outlook throughout the sixteen-day journey. Worsley recalled one vivid example:

> Macty [McCarthy] is the most irrepressible optimist I've ever met. When I relieve him at the helm, boat iced and seas pouring down your neck, he informs me with a happy grin, "It's a grand day, sir, I was feeling a bit sour just before. . . ."[15]

McCarthy's indomitable good spirits undoubtedly buoyed the morale of the soaked sailors. He was a good choice for such an arduous voyage.

Lessons for Leaders

When selecting people for key roles, it is natural to think about the knowledge, skills, and abilities needed for top performance. Other personal qualities, such as the ability to work with others, and values, such as integrity, are often considered carefully. But it is less obvious that an individual's characteristic tendency toward optimism or pessimism may be an important—in some cases, the most important—factor in a particular role.

This is not to suggest that everyone take a personality test as part of the selection process. But it does argue for looking carefully at the way individuals respond to adversity and for explicitly including those with optimistic attitudes in difficult team assignments.

As a "frequent flyer," one of the most difficult assignments I can imagine is having to contend with exhausted, weary travelers. At Southwest Airlines, building the right optimism quotient starts with the hiring process.[16] According to Herb Kelleher, chairman, president, and CEO of Southwest Airlines, "We want people with positive attitudes, who enjoy helping others."

To foster optimism, training exercises are structured so that everyone must contribute in order to complete the exercise. In discussions following the exercise, the trainer points out how each person contributed and notes differences in personality and temperament. By hiring employees who have positive attitudes and building upon that through training and acknowledgment, Southwest has been successful in fostering both diversity and optimism in its workforce.

Exactly what should the team OQ be? The answer is not a team comprised solely of individuals who view the world through rose-colored glasses. As I will discuss later, there is value in diversity in this dimension. However, the team OQ should be high enough to sustain the belief in success, even when the task seems insurmountable. Every team needs a "McCarthy"!

Know How to Reframe a Tough Situation

Optimism can be sparked by leaders who reframe disastrous events in positive, empowering ways. An example comes from the survival story recounted in the book *Alive*.

On October 12, 1972, a group of Uruguayan rugby players and their families crash-landed high in the Andes Mountains. In their struggle to survive, there were many setbacks and challenges. One of their consolations was the daily radio broadcast on the progress of the rescue effort. After four weeks, however, the search was called off. Three of the group, upon hearing this news, discussed whether to tell the rest of the group. Finally, Gustavo Nicolich, one of the emergent leaders of the group, insisted that they must tell the rest of their predicament:

> He climbed through the hole in the wall of suitcases and rugby shirts, crouched at the mouth of the dim tunnel, and looked at the mournful faces which were turned toward him. "Hey boys," he shouted, "there is some good news! We just heard it on the radio. They've called off the search." Inside the crowded cabin, there was silence. As the hopelessness of their predicament enveloped them, they wept. "Why the hell is that good news?" Paez shouted angrily at Nicolich. "Because it means," he said, "that we're going to get out of here on our own."[17]

The optimism and confidence exhibited by Gustavo Nicolich enabled the group to get through what was undoubtedly one of the most depressing and potentially debilitating events that had occurred since the crash. By reframing the situation in an empowering way, he was able to rally the group. Then, they, as a whole, began to take responsibility for their own rescue.

Lessons for Leaders

I had read that the Chinese character for crisis, Weigee, incorporates two figures: The upper character represents "danger," the lower one "opportunity" (see Figure 3-1). I first doubted this was true, so I asked a Chinese student at Yale what the real story was. He hesitated, drew the figure, and looked at me with a smile. It was true, he confirmed, although he hadn't really seen it until I asked him the question.[18]

Effective leaders, like Nicolich, are able to look at adversity and see the opportunity, even if others see only the danger. This perspective may be resisted. A standing joke in one organization I worked with is that people were tired of "major opportunities" and would be satisfied just to have a few "minor problems." Nevertheless, a leader who is able to reframe events in a positive light, and stick by that point of view, can turn the tide.

The success of the Dodge Ram illustrates how a seemingly intractable problem can, indeed, become an opportunity. In the 1980s, sales of the pickup were abysmal—at times below 6 percent of the full-size truck market. Since pickup trucks generate high profits, Chrysler President Bob Lutz saw not only a problem but also a missed opportunity in the market.[19]

The conventional wisdom, however, was that brand loyalty dominated buying decisions. The urban cowboy bought a Ford or a GM product, and a copycat vehicle—no matter how well engineered—was not going to succeed. Faced with this reality, Lutz and Chrysler's chief designer decided to do something dramatically different.

Searching through a book called *Pickup Trucks*, Chrysler designers looked at sketches and photos from the 1930s, 1940s, and 1950s. Although each of the old trucks was distinctive, the design that stood out was the Dodge Power Wagon. With squared-off fenders and bug-eye headlamps, it was unique. And it became the inspiration for a series of designs that eventually culminated in the new Ram.

Some people hated the new design, but some loved it. It was different. By 1993, the first of the "new Rams" went into production, and in three years, Dodge had captured 20 percent of the full-size pickup market. In addition, some 85 percent of sales were the most profitable, top-of-the-line models. Lutz and the Chrysler team had turned a daunting problem into a major opportunity.

It is important to note that the concept of reframing is not simply saying blithely that things will be all right. There are three steps to the process. The first step is to take a difficult situation and envision all the possible outcomes, both positive and negative. The second step is to focus on a positive way of thinking that is consistent with the reality of the situation. This positive view may not, in a statistical sense, be the most likely outcome. But it must be a conceivable scenario. Finally,

Figure 3-1. Chinese character for crisis.

this positive outlook must be maintained in spite of resistance and cynicism.

Stay Grounded in Reality

Shackleton's insistence that "you've damn well got to be optimistic" was one of his most admirable qualities as a leader. But the relentless optimism that Shackleton exuded also had its costs. There were times when this singular focus seemed to blind him to reality, and it created dissension among the crew.

One such occasion was Shackleton's conflict with his crew over stockpiling food. First Officer Greenstreet was convinced that the expedition needed to be prepared for an extended time on the ice. Shackleton thought that a month's supply was sufficient and was content when a hunting party returned with four seals. When Orde-Lees skied into camp and announced that he had killed three more, Shackleton refused to allow additional slain seals to be brought into camp. Greenstreet wrote:

> . . . [T]he present shortage of food is due simply and solely from the Boss refusing to get seals when they were to be had. . . . His sublime optimism . . . being to my mind absolute foolishness.[20]

Shackleton was recklessly optimistic, and he was also angered by Greenstreet's argument, interpreting the first officer's behavior as an act of disloyalty. Had this become a habit—had Shackleton continued to reject people's alternate views of reality—he might have lost the confidence of the expedition.

Lessons for Leaders

A *Fortune* article entitled "CEOs in Denial" sounds an ominous note:

> There's something in the nature of CEOs—pride, vanity, a primal need for control, an obsession with success, good old-fashioned idealism—that makes many smart, well-regarded chief executives into idiots when the world turns against them. They rationalize. They justify. They circle their wagons, build their bunkers, mollify their troops. They

claim themselves "victims" of their "situations." In these trying times for executives, denial is more popular than ever.[21]

Optimism is an important leadership quality, but denial is deadly. Leaders at *The Edge* need to engage in "Janusian thinking."[22] Janus, the Roman god of gates, was able to look in two directions at the same time. Effective leadership in demanding situations means being able to see the optimistic view and, at the same time, deal with stark reality.

This duality is often difficult to achieve. Under stressful conditions, no one wants to hear bad news. As movie mogul Samuel Goldwyn Jr. once commented, "I don't want any yes-men around me. I want them to tell me the truth, even if it costs them their jobs." Leaders often send similar messages.

Refusal to hear contrary points of view can have disastrous consequences. The story of Robert Haas and the Levi Strauss company controlled by his family provides a compelling example.[23] Following an organizational restructuring in 1996, Haas became accountable only to three people, his uncle and two cousins. Haas invested time and energy in creating a socially conscious, values-driven organization. The goals were admirable. The business results were not. While programs designed to create an enlightened workplace flourished, product innovation lagged, costs soared, internal battles raged, customer service dropped, and competitors encroached. In three years, Levi Strauss's market value shrank by some $6 billion.

How could this happen to a great American brand such as Levi's? It appears that Haas simply had the power to ignore reality. A *Fortune* article argues that "Levi Strauss is a failed utopian management experiment. It's a story of what can happen when well-intentioned but misguided managers run a private company answering to no one."[24] Free from accountability, Haas lost touch with the business focus needed to achieve commercial success.

The lesson is clear. Resist the temptation to exclude contrary ideas; stay in touch with reality. Find people who will tell you the truth, and reward them for doing so.

Expedition Log

1. How do you typically react when faced with adversity or potential setback? What do you say to yourself—what goes on in your inner dialogue?

2. Are there changes that you can make to this "self-talk" that will create a more optimistic view and enable you to bounce back more quickly?
3. Think about a current business challenge you are facing. What are you doing to instill optimism in your team or organization? Does your language communicate confidence and hope? Have you been able to reframe this situation in a convincing way?
4. Think about your most difficult individual or team assignments. Is the optimism quotient high enough to ensure success?
5. What are your mechanisms for staying in touch with reality and getting the full picture? Are people comfortable in giving you bad news? How do you know?

4

Stamina

Strategy 4
Take care of yourself: Maintain your stamina and let go of guilt.

> I had not slept for eighty hours . . . I had been steering for nine
> hours while leading the other boats and found it almost impossi-
> ble to keep awake. Greenstreet—a fine seaman—continually urged
> me to hand over the tiller and have a nap. I had, however, become
> so obsessed with steering for the island . . . that I kept on when I
> should have handed it over to him. The consequence was that at
> intervals I fell asleep for a few seconds and the Docker . . . sheered
> off course. Everyone through fatigue and loss of sleep had slightly
> lost his judgment.[1]
>
> Frank A. Worsley

Those who choose to lead at *The Edge* are often individuals gifted
with high energy and drive. At the same time, pursuing lofty goals
places heavy demands on physical and psychological reserves. These
demands are most obvious under extreme survival conditions, but
they are endemic to any tough organizational challenge. There is an
inherent tension between taking care of one's self—of preserving one's
own well-being—and accomplishing the mission at any cost.

Some choose to ignore the dilemma. I recently heard a senior executive remark, "A leader needs to be there 100 percent or not at all—

even if it means sacrificing your health; that's what it means to be a leader." I disagree.

The tension is real, of course, and it needs to be acknowledged. Strategy 2, for example, highlights the importance of personal example, and there are times in which setting an example may mean making personal sacrifices. When Shackleton gave Hurley his "mits" on the journey to Elephant Island, he wound up with a frostbitten finger. Sacrifices can take a physical or psychological toll, and there is a trade-off to be recognized.

There may be times when you choose deliberately to make this sacrifice—but be careful. As the leader, you are the foundation of your expedition. If you fail to maintain your own stamina, then you will be unable to summon the energy needed to reach *The Edge*. Furthermore, taking care of yourself is essential because others in your team will take their cues from your behavior. If you want others to have the reserves of energy they will need to do their jobs, you will need to reinforce that message by personal example.

This chapter explores the critical importance of taking care of yourself and your team so that you will have the stamina needed to reach your goal. It addresses the burden of responsibility often experienced by leaders at *The Edge,* and suggests ways of dealing with feelings of guilt that can accompany mistakes and errors of judgment.

Look Out for Yourself as Well as Your Crew

Polar exploration calls for individuals who can withstand almost continuous physical and emotional challenges: extreme temperatures, lack of sunlight, possible starvation, painful snow blindness, social isolation, and physical hardships, including frostbite. Shackleton was a man who yearned to explore the outer reaches of the earth, where he pushed himself to the physical and psychological edge.

Surprisingly, Shackleton was not blessed with good health. A boy who always dreamed of being a sailor, he was able to convince his parents to let him join the merchant marines at the age of sixteen. While on his first voyage, he became ill with what Shackleton called the "Mauritius fever." His biographer Roland Huntford suspects that this illness, which has no mention in medical diagnostic history, was in fact some kind of malaria or maybe even rheumatic fever that caused irreparable damage to the young explorer's heart.

Perhaps because of his own insight into his health liabilities, Shackleton deliberately avoided the physical examination before joining the *Discovery* expedition when he, Robert Scott, and Edward Wilson attempted to reach the South Pole in 1902. It was a grueling journey, and after ninety-four days in the bitter cold of the Antarctic, the twenty-eight-year-old Shackleton was close to death. Delirious, having difficulty breathing, and unable to walk, he was lucky to make it back to the *Discovery* in time to receive shelter, food, and medical attention from the ship's physician. Shackleton was diagnosed with a severe case of scurvy and what might have been pneumonia.[2]

Shackleton was devastated by Scott's decision to send him home early from the expedition to recuperate. This event seemed to reinforce the need for Shackleton to keep himself at arm's length from the medical profession, and he developed a pattern of avoiding the physical evaluations necessary for joining future expedition crews. Huntford observes:

> Exactly what ailed Shackleton, however, remained an enigma . . . but Shackleton shied away from doctors. Perhaps he was afraid of what he might find. If for no other reason, in the Edwardian cult of manliness, sickness was a stigma. In any case, his health remained part of the secret core of himself he shared with nobody at all.[3]

In spite of these physical limitations, Shackleton never complained either to his men or in his personal diaries about the physical difficulties he experienced while exploring. He seemed to deal with what must have been intense discomfort and, sometimes, excruciating pain by denying its existence and willing himself to continue.

In the light of this, it is somewhat ironic that Shackleton placed tremendous importance on the physical and psychological needs of his men. He constantly monitored the crew's condition. For example, Shackleton was aware of the toll of moving everyone onto the ice floes from the crushed *Endurance*. He watched closely for signs of trouble and wrote, "I took a final survey of the men to note both their mental and physical condition, for our time at Ocean Camp had not been one of unalloyed bliss."[4]

Shackleton was also known to let the men sleep late after a night in which the weather had made it difficult to get any rest. When the sun would shine and the temperature was warm enough to allow them to be outside safely, Shackleton would order the sleeping bags and other gear to be hung out to dry to make things more comfortable. He encouraged everyone to eat until they were full before or after days when they overextended themselves. He noted:

Although I had to keep in my mind the necessity for strict economy with our small store of food, I knew how important it was to keep the men cheerful, and that the depression occasioned by our surroundings and precarious position could be somewhat alleviated by increasing the rations.[5]

His vigilance for the well-being of others was maintained with consistency as the days dragged on. Reflecting on Shackleton's leadership toward the end of the expedition, during the 800-mile sail to South Georgia, Worsley wrote:

Looking back on this great boat journey, it seems certain that some of our men would have succumbed to the protracted strain but for Shackleton. So great was his care for his people that, to rough men, it seemed at times . . . even to the verge of fussiness. If a man shivered more than usual, he would plunge his hand into the heat of the spare clothes bag for the last sodden pair of socks for him.[6]

Shackleton was also consistently willing to put the well-being of others above his own. He would unselfishly volunteer to stand extra watches and to stay at the helm for extended periods—often three times longer than the other men.

His self-control, lack of self-pity, and ability to care for others are admirable qualities. But his disregard for his own health undoubtedly contributed to his early death. On his last expedition, while attempting to circumnavigate Antarctica, he suffered a massive heart attack. He called Macklin, the surgeon, who had joined the expedition to be with the Boss again. But Shackleton refused to be examined and, against medical advice, stayed on the bridge four nights in a row, keeping his vigil during a storm.[7]

Days later, while anchored at the whaling station where *Endurance* had been moored some eight years earlier, he suffered a second heart attack. The indomitable leader, who had cared so much for others, was gone, just over a month shy of his forty-eighth birthday.[8]

Lessons for Leaders

There is considerable evidence showing that effective leaders have high levels of energy, stamina, and the ability to deal with stress. This makes sense, since leadership—especially at *The Edge*—typically means putting in long hours, making decisions under ambiguous conditions, and dealing with adversity. And we sometimes think of exceptional leaders as superhuman beings who have been blessed with perfect health and boundless energy.

The poster boy for this image may be "Neutron" Jurgen Schrempp, the chairman of DaimlerChrysler. As an analyst at J. P. Morgan, Nick Snee, once commented, "He's so full of energy, you feel you should ground yourself before you touch him."[9]

Schrempp may have been the perfect person to revitalize the moribund Daimler culture. He recharges himself at home with a treadmill, stationary bicycle, and stair machine. His hobbies range from mountaineering to safaris, flying in jet fighters, and driving fast Ferraris. Schrempp's worldview is captured by his comment, "Work out for two hours, take a cold shower, and the world changes."

As Shackleton demonstrated, however, the idea that every leader is a picture of health is clearly a misconception. Shackleton was physically flawed, but in spite of his limitations, he was able to summon the courage and the stamina to overcome his physical limitations.

Unfortunately, the care that Shackleton extended to his own crew was never turned inward. Certainly, if any one of his men had exhibited these symptoms, the Boss would have been the first one to ensure that he got adequate treatment. Shackleton's denial of his own health problems, and perhaps his feelings of invincibility, prevented him from doing the things that would have enabled him to extend his days of exploration.

This attitude is not unique to polar explorers. Schrempp may exercise like crazy, but he also has a passion for cigarettes and Cuban cigars. While cigars in moderation may not be a problem, it does not take a health fanatic to wonder if there is not an inconsistency between his workout routine and his cigarette smoking.

This problem extends beyond the behavior of an individual leader. I spoke with a senior executive at Texas Instruments (TI) after the sudden death of the company's leader. He described the shock that hit the organization when Jerry Junkins, the company chairman, chief executive officer, and president, died unexpectedly on a business trip to Germany.

Junkins's obituary described him as a relaxed leader who was not a workaholic and who had no history of heart disease. Yet the TI culture was one that rewarded heroic efforts, long hours, and machismo. The death of their leader prompted many in the organization to reexamine their values and to think carefully about the limits of extended performance pressures. As a result of this shock, an intensive effort was made to examine the expectations placed on leaders and to promote wellness throughout the workplace.

Junkins's death is an extreme case, but I have observed other instances in which leaders pushed too hard and lost their effectiveness. In one case, a newly appointed CEO felt that he needed instantly to "get his arms around" his new role. This meant long hours and relatively little sleep. Unfortunately, this also meant that he was bone-tired in meetings.

The problem came to a head when he started dozing during presentations. Many times presenters had worked for weeks in preparation for the event and were looking forward to their moment in the spotlight. Understandably, the sight of their leader nodding off was a deflating experience. The CEO, fortunately, was able to hear my feedback in a coaching session and changed his behavior. The problem was easily solved. He stopped trying to do more than was humanly possible and became more effective as a result.

The message here is clear. At *The Edge,* leaders need to demonstrate concern for others and monitor the health of those who work for them. They also need to extend this awareness to themselves and to recognize that even the most energetic individual has limits.

There is a nautical expression that applies to this dilemma: "One hand for the sailor and one hand for the ship." In other words, do what you need to do to accomplish your work—but make sure that you keep one hand free to keep yourself from being washed overboard.

Beware of "Summit Fever"

How is it that smart people can completely lose sight of their physical limits? One cause is a psychological phenomenon known in mountaineering as "summit fever." The individual becomes so fixated on reaching the summit that all else fades from consciousness.

The ill-fated 1996 Everest expedition, recounted in Jon Krakauer's *Into Thin Air,* provides one such example. Of the twenty climbers who fought their way to the summit, five were to die. One survived with such severe frostbite that his right forearm, his nose, and most of his left hand had to be amputated.

Although some elements of Krakauer's account have been disputed,[10] one conclusion stands out. While a "rogue storm" was the immediate cause of the disaster, attributing the death of the five climbers to bad weather misses the point. The underlying causes are complex, but it is clear that—in their relentless drive to reach the summit—both the guides and their charges completely lost sight of their physical and psychological limits.

Scott Fischer, who died on the mountain, was a world-class

climber. His strength and stamina were legendary. In 1994, he had climbed the 29,028-foot peak without oxygen. But on the day of the 1996 ascent, Fischer had gone beyond the limits of his strength. As Krakauer wrote:

> "That evening," recalled his tent-mate Charlotte Fox, "I couldn't tell that Scott might have been sick. He was acting like Mr. Gung Ho, getting everyone psyched up like a football coach before the big game." In truth, Fischer was exhausted from the physical and mental strain of the preceding weeks. Although he possessed extraordinary reserves of energy . . . by the time he got to Camp Four they were nearly depleted.[11]

Fischer was strong, but he was not invincible. Although he concealed his inner turmoil, the strain and worry of the ascent, coupled with physical exhaustion, took its toll.

The proclivity to ignore all but the goal is not limited to mountain climbers. Pilots on dive-bombing missions have been known to fly their aircraft into the ground trying to find their target. The label "target fixation" is different, but the phenomenon is the same. It is a human tendency to be so concerned about the goal that all else fades into oblivion. At the *Survival Edge,* this obsession can mean death.

Lessons for Leaders

In work situations, the emotional fever to meet deadlines, complete projects, or accomplish business goals can be dangerously analogous to that experienced by mountain climbers and pilots. Leaders need to be aware of this threat and build in safeguards to ensure that they maintain a sense of perspective and recognize when it is time to make camp, turn around, or pull out of a dive.

Periodic process meetings, for example, can be devoted to reviewing the physical and emotional health of the team. Leaders can help ensure that team members schedule regular downtime—even if only fifteen minutes a day—to regroup, reassess, and relax. Leaders can also sense when target fixation is setting in and intervene with something "completely different."

During the push to design the Nissan Pathfinder, for instance, pressure was extremely high.[12] The deadline was looming, and the design team had yet to submit a promising concept sketch. Jerry Hirshberg, president of Nissan Design International, could have turned up the heat, but he took another path. He chose to close up shop and take everyone—designers to secretaries—to the movies!

The decision not only enhanced the team's health—it had a direct business payoff as well. Shortly afterward, ideas began to flow and the project got back on track. According to Hirshberg, "The cost to Nissan for our truancy was fifty movie tickets, fifty bags of popcorn, and about fifty extra minutes of lunchtime. The payoff was a flood of ideas for an international product representing hundreds of millions of dollars in development investment."

Find Outlets for Your Own Feelings

Shackleton was amazing in his ability to maintain the morale and psychological health of his expedition. What was not obvious to most of the other explorers, however, was that Shackleton was dealing with his own fears at the same time he was managing others' anxieties.

He dealt with these potentially destructive internal forces in a number of ways. For one, he talked to Frank Wild, a partner in whom he had complete trust. He could confide in Wild in a way that he could not with others.

He also shared private feelings with Frank Worsley, the captain. At one point during the open boat journey, exhausted and anxious for the safety of his men, Shackleton became discouraged and worried and was close to depression. In a rare moment, he said to the captain one day: "I will never take another expedition, Skipper."[13]

Shackleton also kept a private journal in which he recorded doubts that he could not share with others. These entries revealed, for example, just how much the loss of the *Endurance* had affected him. After the ship went down, he wrote:

> The end of *Endurance* has come . . . It is hard to write what I feel. To a sailor his ship is more than a floating home, and in the *Endurance* I had centered ambitions, hopes, and desires. Now, straining and groaning, her timbers cracking and her wounds gaping, she is slowly giving up her sentient life at the very outset of her career.[14]

As painful as this experience must have been, the ability to write down his feelings provided some relief from despair.

Finally, he wrote letters home. After his third unsuccessful attempt to rescue the castaways on Elephant Island, Shackleton was so distraught that his misery was palpable. Worsley observed: "So deep were his emotions that, in contradistinction to his behavior after the first two attempts, he did not even speak of the men on the island now."[15] In the depths of his despair, he found an outlet in a letter to his daughter, Cecily:

> I am very anxious about . . . our men for they must have so little to eat now. . . . We are very short of water, and have not been able to wash since we left South America . . . but that is nothing for I had no wash from October last year until 25th May this year. . . .
>
> I will have many stories to tell you . . . when I return, but I cannot write them. I just hate writing letters but I want you to get this to know I am thinking of you my little daughter.[16]

Thus, while he could not share his doubts publicly, he was able to express his feelings in a poignant letter to his daughter.

Lessons for Leaders

Leaders need not be completely stoic, solitary figures. They can, and should, enlist the support and guidance of those around them to assist them in taking the right next steps for the team. Shackleton's approaches to dealing with his inner fears suggest ways in which leaders in other situations can find outlets for their own anxiety:

➤ *Talk to friends.* Find a Wild or a Worsley—someone you can trust who understands the challenges you face and can deal with your candid thoughts.

➤ *Keep a journal.* Shackleton expressed many of his private doubts in his journal. The simple act of recording one's emotions can provide relief.

➤ *Write letters home.* Communicate with others you care about, even if they may not fully understand the conditions you face. Shackleton wrote letters, even though there was no way to send them. Of course, we have access to technology not available in the days of early polar exploration, including e-mail and voice mail. Use whatever works. The point is to find effective outlets to ease the weight of leadership.

➢ *See a counselor or coach.* Periodic meetings with a professional can be invaluable as both a way to express your feelings and a way to get an independent perspective on the challenges you face as a leader.

Some organizations make it easy to get coaching assistance. At Damark International, for example, Mark Johansson has a unique job: He helps executives function in a more cooperative way and guides them through career concerns and people conflicts.[17]

As director of leadership and team development, Johansson essentially works as a relationship coach. Managers can vent their frustrations, brainstorm, and get coached through interpersonal conflicts. One executive says that, by speaking to Johansson, he has been better able to respond to his colleagues: "If not for him, I would have misinterpreted reactions that were neutral or positive as negative."

Managers at Damark who seek out Johansson's counsel have both an outlet for their feelings and a confidential adviser to help them better perform their jobs. Helping others maintain perspective, however, need not depend on a designated coach. It is a role that effective leaders can play as well.

Dave Marsing—vice president of the technology and manufacturing group and general manager of assembly and test manufacturing at Intel—learned the hard way the importance of maintaining perspective under pressure.[18] After suffering a massive heart attack (the result of a hereditary condition aggravated by stress while he was working to turn around one of Intel's microprocessor fabrication plants), Marsing has made it a point to encourage others to keep their work and personal lives in balance.

> I try to be as objective as possible in discussions, and if I'm in a face-to-face meeting with someone who has a short fuse, I'll sit right next to that person to make sure the fuse is never lit. I do that by being calm, even overly calm. When things get heated, I even change my voice. I will consciously take a deeper breath, or two deep breaths, in front of everybody to get them to calm down a little bit and talk about the specifics, about solutions.

Marsing adds, "When I coach the people who report to me, who manage very large sites around the company, I tell them how important it is to spend more time with their families, to spend more time exercising, to get some help to assist them to work through administrative things, rather than putting in extraordinarily long, tense days."

With his heart attack providing the wakeup call, Marsing has created an outlet for his own emotions and found a way to encourage stress-reducing behavior in his colleagues as well.

Let Go of Guilt (But Learn from Mistakes)

Those at the *Survival Edge* are often placed in positions that require split-second decisions that can have disastrous consequences. One such instance occurred when Joe Simpson and his climbing partner, Simon Yates, found themselves on a 21,000-foot peak in the Andes Mountains. Attempting to negotiate an ice wall, Simpson fell to the slope below. He hit the base of the cliff with both knees locked, felt his bones splitting, catapulted backward, and slid screaming down the slope, head first on his back.

Yates somehow checked Simpson's slide and Simpson came to a violent stop. Simpson's right knee, which had literally exploded in the fall, had been shattered beyond repair. He was alive, but just barely.

In the hours following the accident, Yates attempted to lower Simpson down the mountain to safety. Each movement was agonizingly painful. It appeared that they might succeed in their painful progress until Simpson slid unexpectedly into space, spinning helplessly as an avalanche of snow poured over him.

Above, Yates clung to the cliff, as immobilized as Simpson. He had two choices. He could hold on indefinitely, lose consciousness, and be pulled from the mountain. Then he and Simpson would both fall to their deaths. Or he could cut the rope.

Yates cut the rope, but was consumed with guilt:

> It wasn't until I had descended half the rope's length that I glanced down and saw the crevasse. I jammed the belay plate shut, and stopped abruptly. I stared at the endless black depths at the foot of the cliff, and shuddered in horror. Joe had undoubtedly fallen into the crevasse. I was appalled. The idea of falling into that monstrous blackness yawning below me made me grip the rope tightly. I shut my eyes and pressed my forehead against the taut rope. For a long nauseous moment feelings of guilt and horror flooded through me. It was as if I had only just that minute cut that rope. I might as well have put a gun to his head and shot him. . . .

If I hadn't cut the rope I would certainly have died. Yet, having saved myself, I was now going to return home and tell people a story that few would ever believe. No one cuts the rope![19]

Yates finally overcame his remorse and—certain that Simpson had died—returned to their base camp.

Simpson had fallen 100 feet into the crevasse and was badly injured. But he summoned enough strength to make four attempts to escape before giving up hope of climbing out. After lying trapped in the dark for seven hours, Simpson rappelled to the bottom of the crevasse. Then, energized by the light of a sunbeam, his outlook was transformed:

> In seconds, my whole outlook had changed . . . I could do something positive. I could crawl and climb, and keep on doing so until I had escaped from this grave. Before, there had been nothing for me to do except lie on the bridge trying not to feel scared and lonely, and that helplessness had been my worst enemy. Now I had a plan. The change in me was astonishing. I felt invigorated, full of energy and optimism. I could see possible dangers, very real risks that could destroy my hopes, but somehow I knew I could overcome them.[20]

This confidence enabled Simpson to overcome the pain of his broken leg and continue his descent. Using his ice axe to cut his yellow foam sleeping bag, he constructed a crude splint using straps from his crampons and rucksack. Then, bent over and using his short ice axe as a cane, he developed a pattern of movement: "Place the axe, lift the foot forward, brace, hop, place the axe, lift brace-hop, place-lift-brace-hop."

Simpson knew that time was running out. Since Yates would be convinced Simpson had died in the fall, his partner would soon be breaking camp. If Yates left, Simpson was a dead man. Spurred on by that knowledge, he hopped, then crawled and—in the final stages—dragged himself backward down the mountain.

Three days later, Joe Simpson crawled into base camp, just as Yates was preparing to break camp. Simpson was crippled, starving, and frostbitten, but he was alive. If Yates had refused to cut the rope, or lost his will to survive through guilt, both climbers would almost certainly have died on the mountain.

Lessons for Leaders

The very act of exploring at *The Edge* puts leaders in situations that call for tough decisions. Some of those decisions will be the wrong ones, mistakes in judgment, and those mistakes can create feelings of self-recrimination.

While mistakes are to be avoided, if possible, leaders who dwell on them only compound the problem. Feelings of guilt can be distracting, causing a loss of focus and an inability to deal with the next challenge.

Michael Dell, chairman and CEO of Dell Computers, reflects this philosophy in *Direct from Dell,* the story of his journey from a college dorm room to the board room of an $18 billion organization. He devotes a chapter of the book to "learning the hard way" and concludes:

> Someone once said that the difference between Dell and other companies is that while all companies make mistakes, Dell never makes the same mistakes twice. We've always seen mistakes as learning opportunities. The key is to learn well from the mistakes that you make so that you don't repeat them. In our case, learning took the form of some notable public missteps—or, as we sometimes joke, learning opportunities of massive proportions. Fortunately, the lessons we learned helped us identify and implement the practices that gave us a secure foundation for future growth.[21]

Dell's forward-looking philosophy was a core element in the success of the organization and sets the tone for leaders at the Edge. Make decisions, make mistakes, and move your expedition forward.

Expedition Log

1. Step back and take stock of your physical health. Are you taking care of yourself, as well as those who work for you? What more can you be doing to maintain your stamina as a leader?
2. Think about a current challenge, change, or "summit" that you are facing. What, specifically, can you do to keep your perspective and avoid "summit fever"?
3. Assess your emotional well-being and stress-resistance. Whom

do you turn to when you need to vent? Identify a person, process, or activity that will alleviate stress and reenergize you.

4. Reflect on a time when you have made a significant mistake or faced a disappointment. Did you let your feelings of guilt or frustration distract you? If so, what changes did you make to get yourself back on track? Do you need to alter the way you characteristically react to mistakes—especially those "massive learning opportunities"?

5

The Team Message

Strategy 5

Reinforce the team message constantly: "We are one—we live or die together."

Shackleton was always opposed to splitting the party, and he very wisely refused to consider such a move . . . although the temptation to explore . . . was almost overwhelming.[1]

Frank A. Worsley

Teamwork has become something of a modern rallying cry in today's high-performing organizations. Sometimes the word appears so often that it seems to be just another corporate buzzword, and leaders invoke the teamwork mantra whether or not the task calls for collaborative effort. Or, as happens in many academic organizations, teamwork is preached but individual achievement is rewarded.

Why is teamwork so popular? Although the concept of teamwork can be faddish, the reality is that the challenges faced by most organizations can only be overcome through unified effort. It is not surprising that, in *Fortune*'s "All Star" list of the world's most admired companies, teamwork consistently appears as a critical part of the organizational culture. Whether in the wilderness, the classroom, or the corporation, sustained success turns on cohesive effort. This chapter explores tactics for creating a solid team and sending a strong message of unity.

Establish a Shared Identity

There was no question in Ernest Shackleton's mind that survival depended on exceptional teamwork. Under the conditions faced by the Imperial Trans-Antarctic expedition, a fracture in the group would mean energy wasted. This disharmony might well mean the difference between life and death.

Since Shackleton so consistently emphasized teamwork in everything he did, it is curious that he does not mention the subject more explicitly in *South*—his story of the expedition. Perhaps the importance of a solid team was so clear to him that it needed no special notice. He had certainly seen the potential danger of fragmentation on his earlier expedition with Scott, when interpersonal frictions were rampant. Or, perhaps, solid teamwork was simply something whose importance he instinctively understood—and that he had a knack for instilling in others.

The ability of individuals to work with others was clearly on his mind from the beginning. For example, when interviewing Reginald James, who later became the expedition's physicist, he asked whether the prospective scientist could sing. He was not, however, probing for vocal ability. In asking whether James could "shout a bit with the boys,"[2] Shackleton was undoubtedly looking to see if James could live and work with others in close quarters under difficult conditions.

With some notable exceptions, Shackleton seemed to have largely succeeded in selecting a group of people who had the capacity to work together. But he clearly did not select a homogeneous group that could be expected to gel of its own accord. There was a diverse mix of temperaments: some cheerful and gregarious, others introverted and reserved. There were physicians, scientists, seamen, and artists. Shackleton did not simply assume that teamwork would happen.

Almost everything that he did was designed to promote the message of team unity. Before *Endurance* went down, for example, Shackleton brought all hands together in the wardroom after evening meals. These gatherings served to promote spontaneous discussion and to build the social bonds that would become so important later in the journey.

As the days wore on, Shackleton proposed a ceremonial haircutting for all, and he volunteered to be the first shorn. As Worsley described the scene:

> [Rickenson] gloatingly seizes the clippers & plies them till not a vestige of hair longer than a bristle is left, & his victim looks like one of the Roman Emperors. But it is when the

> roles are reversed, that we [are] all clipped . . . & looking
> like a group of convicts. When the commotion was over,
> an official group photograph was taken "to perpetuate this
> evening & to cure us, where necessary, of conceit."[3]

The incident, although comical, was much more than entertainment.
The ceremony and the haircuts themselves were also vivid statements
of the men's common identity.

This shared identity was only to grow as their adventure continued. Later, during sledge marches, the group advanced in relays to
ensure that the party would remain together if cracks appeared in the
ice. On Patience Camp, the tents were kept together. Still later, during
the open boat journey to Elephant Island, the three lifeboats stayed in
constant contact.

As a result of this continuous affirmation of team unity, near the
end of the expedition, when Shackleton was forced to split the party
and sail for South Georgia, the sense of cohesion remained intact.
There was no fear that their comrades would abandon the "castaways"—they were as one.

Contrast this episode at *The Edge* in Antarctica with that of the
Everest expedition described by Jon Krakauer. On May 9, 1996, dozens
of climbers camped side by side, preparing for their assault on the
summit. Judged by the standards of their equipment, the Everest
climbers were much better prepared than any of Shackleton's team.
Instead of reindeer-skin sleeping bags and linen tents, they relied on
ripstop nylon and the finest cold-weather clothing.

Thanks to the backbreaking work of a sherpa, New York socialite
Sandy Pittman was equipped with a thirty-pound satellite telephone
that would enable her to file Internet dispatches from 26,000 feet. They
had everything money could buy, but they lacked the one thing money
could not buy on Everest—teamwork.

Krakauer describes the scene:

> There were more than fifty people camped on the Col that
> night, huddled in shelters pitched side by side, yet an odd
> feeling of isolation hung in the air. The roar of the wind
> made it impossible to communicate from one tent to the
> next. In this godforsaken place, I felt disconnected from the
> climbers around me—emotionally, spiritually, physically—
> to a degree I hadn't experienced on any previous expedi-
> tion. We were a team in name only, I'd sadly come to real-
> ize. Although in a few hours we would leave camp as a

group, we would ascend as individuals linked to one another by neither rope nor any deep sense of loyalty. Each client was in it for himself or herself, pretty much. And I was no different.[4]

At another time, this fragmentation, isolation, and lack of unity might not have been fatal. After adding the elements of an unexpected storm, exhausted guides, and the cognitive deterioration that occurs in the oxygen-depleted "death zone," however, the concoction was deadly.

Climbers came upon others who were lying close to death in the snow and simply moved on without offering food, water, or oxygen. They passed the other climbers without a word, and as one later explained: "We were too tired to help. Above 8,000 meters is not a place where people can afford morality."[5]

Lessons for Leaders

I have seen organizations that operate like the Everest expedition. One global financial institution, for example, was known as "the lumberyard." In an effort to establish a presence in the United States, it hired a number of investment bankers with contracts that took the dimensions of lumber, such as two-by-fours and three-by-tens. In economic terms, this translated into assured compensation contracts of $2 million annually for four years, $3 million annually for ten years, and so forth.

The reward structure created an individualistic culture in which institutional loyalty was almost nonexistent. The problem was that the financial success of the organization depended on making money "between the boxes"—that is, between the institution's different divisions. It required collaboration of investment bankers, commercial and institutional bankers, and others throughout the organization. With no common identity or loyalty, this teamwork often failed to occur.

Success at *The Edge* demands a different outlook, and this sense of identity can be fostered in a number of ways. Values statements, for example, can be used effectively to create a common culture and identity. The effects are not automatic, and there are instances in which corporate values statements are little more than superficial window dressing. They make attractive wall hangings, but little else. In consulting to one organization, for example, I was once asked to create a corporate values statement because the senior management team was too busy to participate in the process. As one remarked, "You're the expert, you take care of it." Faced with this lack of engagement, I declined.

I have seen other organizations, however, in which statements defining organizational values were taken seriously and used with great impact. At Johnson & Johnson, I was asked to help create a survey that would measure the extent to which their Corporate "Credo" was practiced throughout the organization.

I interviewed employees throughout the company and found that they not only knew the Credo, but also used it as a guide for making business decisions. The Credo was cited, for example, as an important source of guidance during the Tylenol crisis. It was a foundational building block for the culture of the firm, and it helped define the shared identity of every member of the organization.

The actions of top leaders can help unify an organization, but the spirit of collaboration can also be initiated in other ways. In 1998, for example, Ann Livermore—then head of software and support at Hewlett Packard—joined with William V. Russell, the company's UNIX computer chief, to explore an Internet strategy for HP.[6]

After analyzing each division's numerous product offerings, Livermore and Russell cooperated to commercialize a host of web technologies. They began packaging the two divisions' computers and software into unified web product solutions for the company's customers. The promising initial results of this combination prompted them to make a radical request: that their two divisions be merged. In addition, each pledged his or her support to whoever would receive the top job at the new entity.

HP's CEO at the time, Lew Platt, merged the two divisions into Enterprise Solutions. Livermore was named to head the new unit; Russell became her second in command. According to Chief Marketing Officer Nicholas J. Earle, "This was a big deal—like bringing two armies together . . . the Net became the great unifier."

Maintain the Bonds of Communication

Establishing a shared identity is an essential first step in creating unity, but more is needed to reinforce the team message. To maintain a sense of connectedness, the bonds of communication need to be nurtured in every way possible.

On January 25, 1990, a Boeing 707 carrying 159 passengers on Avianca Airlines Flight 52 crashed on a wooded hill in Cove Neck, Long Island, after running out of fuel. On impact, the plane sheared into two sections, with the nose of the aircraft resting on the house deck of a terrified elderly couple.

The scene was horrific. Debris and wreckage were scattered everywhere. Oxygen masks hung from the trees, screams filled the air, children were crying, and there was little light to aid the rescuers.

The seventy-three who had died in the crash were mixed with survivors, children were separated from parents, and many of the passengers spoke only Spanish. The potential for confusion was enormous. In spite of the danger that the aircraft would explode, police, firefighters, physicians, paramedics, and local volunteers worked together to pull the passengers from the wreckage. Joan Imhof, a key figure in the rescue effort, vividly described the scene:[7]

> The focus was on saving lives. Ordinary people were doing things they had never done before, working side by side with surgeons in this nightmarish environment, applying tourniquets, and comforting survivors as best they could. Words are just so inadequate to explain the situation. People pushed away all other thoughts and focused on doing what needed to be done.

The rescue effort worked almost seamlessly. For hours, workers pulled people out of the aircraft, separated the dead from the survivors, and tried to reunite terrified children with their parents. The teamwork was extraordinary, but it was also physically demanding and emotionally wrenching. As she worked to save lives, Joan was struck by the way the rescuers were interacting:

> People would pass each other, reach and take a hand for a moment. Or they would look at each other, make a brief comment, and then move on. Sometimes they would embrace or nod, then continue applying bandages or moving bodies to the makeshift morgue. People needed that brief, but meaningful contact to continue working with determination. It rejuvenated us.

Afterward, she met with a surgeon to discuss the events of the night. They stood in the hospital hallway talking about the rescue, how many limbs had been saved, and what the experience was like. At the end of this animated conversation, she realized that they had been talking in the middle of the hallway, oblivious to the traffic that went on around them, never breaking eye contact, and holding hands.

This spontaneous contact, whether it took the form of an embrace, a comment, or simply eye contact, served as the connective tissue that held the team together as its members worked successfully to save lives. It was an extraordinary rescue effort, made possible—in part—by the ability of each individual to maintain contact with the other members of the team.

Members of the Avianca rescue effort could look at each other, talk to each other, and even embrace. But the bonds of communication can be used to bind a team together even when human touch or face-to-face contact is impossible.

American POWs held in the Hanoi Hilton prison in North Vietnam were isolated, placed in solitary confinement, tortured, and subjected to systematic efforts designed to fragment the group. The prisoners maintained their integrity and sense of solidarity, however, using what became a second language known as the "Tap Code."[8] Tapping on the thick walls between prison cells, the POWs communicated with an alphabet matrix consisting of five rows and five columns of letters, as shown in Figure 5-1.

"A"—the first row, first column—was sent with a *tap, tap*. "B"—the first row, second column—was sent with a *tap,* (pause) *tap, tap*. Each letter of the alphabet thus had its own unique code. "K" was omitted and "C" substituted.

Tapping went on throughout the day and night. As one POW described it, "The building sounded like a den of runaway woodpeckers, with everyone tapping." To signal another prisoner, a POW would tap the sequence familiar to every American—"Shave and a haircut"—and wait for the response: "Two bits." The North Vietnamese tried to intercept the messages but, unfamiliar with the tune, they invariably tapped the wrong response and could not figure out what they did wrong.

The prisoners tapped the equivalent of *War and Peace* several times over during their time in captivity. They built up speed, tapping at rates of five or six words per minute. They were also ingenious in finding different ways to use the Tap Code. They swept in code with brooms. They shoveled in code. They flashed pans across holes in code. They coughed, sniffed, spit, and sneezed in code. Since they often had colds, the communication went unnoticed.

The code was used to pass information, of course, but it was much more than that. Prisoners would tap to other prisoners for years, without ever seeing each other's faces. Yet the POWs were so intimately connected they knew each other's moods, simply by sensing the sound of the taps. Anger, sadness, and happiness were all interpretable through prison walls by strangers who had never met.

Their captors tried repeatedly to split the prisoners so that they

Figure 5-1. The Tap Code.

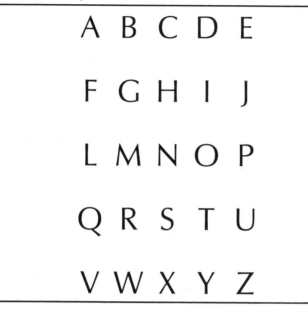

A B C D E

F G H I J

L M N O P

Q R S T U

V W X Y Z

would be unable to gain strength from each other. They never succeeded, though, and the bonds of communication held.

Lessons for Leaders

Few organizational challenges are as emotionally demanding as coordinating an aircraft rescue or maintaining team integrity in a prisoner of war camp. But the need for frequent communication is always important in maintaining a sense of team unity.

Traditionally, we have had the luxury of working in close proximity with other team members. This means having the ability to look others in the eye and communicate face-to-face. Increasingly, however, teams are geographically dispersed entities that rely on other means of communication: electronic mail, letters, phone calls, and videoconferencing.

We are just learning how to use these media effectively. I have frequently heard the lament that electronic media are depersonalizing the workplace, draining organizations of the personal quality that is such an important part of human connection. There is growing evidence, however, that people can work together effectively in ways that were never thought possible before the advent of these new technologies. The effectiveness of the Hanoi Hilton Tap Code in communicating nuances of mood suggests that there is nothing inherent in electronic communication that makes it ineffective for bonding. In fact, the burgeoning of romance on the Internet makes it clear that a form of intimacy can flourish at a distance.

The challenge in all this is to ensure that the efficiency of technology is linked with the personal dimension so important for team cohesion. In addition, since different people are more comfortable with different media, multiple channels are needed. A handshake is, after all, a time-honored way of connecting with other humans.

Lawrence Weinbach of Unisys is one leader who takes communication seriously. When Weinbach took over as president and CEO, the company's poor performance had caused its 33,000 employees to lose confidence in the company and themselves. He was determined to regain their trust and to transform Unisys into an effective service organization.[9]

First, Weinbach went on the road, visiting more than 12,000 employees in three months. His message: Employees could look to him as a cheerleader, but the success of the company was on their shoulders. Second, he elicited ideas from employees on how to deal more effectively with customers. He received 4,500 e-mail suggestions within six weeks. Weinbach answered about 2,000 messages and then sought help to respond to the balance. Third, he launched an "Ask Larry" section on the company intranet to respond to the more generic questions. Fourth, he issued a monthly newsletter to employees so that they could feel a part of what was going on.

In addition, Weinbach encouraged employee participation in two of the company's major efforts: debt reduction and advertising image. He promised additional employee benefits for an improvement in cash collection and a reduction in receivables. And he created a contest among employees to come up with a new company tag line. Nearly 4,500 employees submitted entries; the ten winners each received 100 shares of stock.

Weinbach's communication methods are credited with significantly improving employee morale and productivity while leading to a financial turnaround at Unisys. Weinbach stated: "I use communication as my way of getting people to understand what I call 'the X factor,' the success factor that was going to be built around how well these 33,000 people were motivated to do what I believe they had the ability to do."

Keep Everyone Informed, Involved, and Thinking About Solutions

A unified team is one in which every member understands the task to be done and feels a sense of deep personal responsibility for the success of the group's efforts. For this to happen, each person must have a clear picture of the challenges faced by the team. This implies the open sharing of information, options, and potential consequences of choices. The unity of the Trans-Antarctic expedition reflects, in many ways, Shackleton's ability to create this broad sense of active engagement.

Shackleton was a proactive leader who took on a great deal of personal responsibility. He was intimately involved in almost every aspect of the expedition, including the routine details of food preparation and how they would live together. He thought through how they would deal with emergencies, such as their plans for quickly striking camp. He wrestled with the life-and-death issues of how they would obtain their rescue—deciding, for example, who would make the open boat journey through the Scotia Sea.

It is remarkable, then, that he was able to sustain this level of personal involvement while creating a strong sense of empowerment and encouraging personal initiative in others. A key element to this duality lay in his ability to keep people psychologically engaged and continually thinking about potential solutions to the obstacles they faced. Undoubtedly, he had dual motives: One was to maintain morale, the other to solicit practical ideas that would contribute to their survival.

How was he able to express his own ideas strongly and, at the same time, keep people thinking about solutions? One of his actions was to create the "Directive Committee," an inner circle of key advisers. The Directive Committee—comprised of Frank Wild, Frank Worsley, and Frank Hurley—acted as a sounding board for all major decisions.

"The Quorum," as Hurley described the group, had unanimously agreed to establish Ocean Camp after the failed sledge march. The committee also weighed the difficult alternatives they faced. These choices were grim ones and the outcomes uncertain. As Worsley described it, the Directive Committee debated and prepared:

> . . . for the worst eventuality of having to stop on the Pack for another winter. . . . On the other hand if by the end of January we have, as is probable, drifted near enough to

Graham's Land, or the S. Orkneys, we may make one or the
other by aid of the leads we hope to have come to. . . . The
third alternative is a risky but a necessary dash to the West
at the end of Jan, abandoning boats but sledging the small
punt the Carpenter has made. This we would only do if the
drift became arrested . . . so . . . that we were fairly certain
we would otherwise have spent the winter on the floe running the risk of it opening and crushing the boats some dark
winters midnight.[10]

Although Shackleton had strong ideas about the right course of
action, he listened to the counsel of the Directive Committee, and these
meetings influenced his views. In addition, this advisory group helped
build the strong core of support that Shackleton would need later
when the odds against their survival grew, along with the potential for
mutiny and resignation.

As important as the Directive Committee was, Shackleton's willingness to consult with others was not restricted to this inner circle. As
he made the rounds, Shackleton continually asked "whether there was
anything we might be doing that we aren't doing."[11]

He did not, of course, make decisions by majority vote or act on
all suggestions. Shackleton was approachable, however, and he gave
each person the feeling that he had a role in affecting the course of
events. Especially when plans changed—as often happened—the Boss
encouraged open discussion and comment. As a result, everyone was
made to feel that his opinion counted.[12]

Lessons for Leaders

Information really is power. It can be shared openly or it can be
closely held and doled out reluctantly. But I have never seen a cohesive
team when vital information is hoarded or restricted to a few key decision makers.

This is not to argue that every detail of a developing situation need
be instantly shared without interpretation. There were times when
Shackleton waited until the crew was rested to announce bad news,
and every leader needs to be sensitive to the timing and context in
which information is shared. However, for a group to succeed at the
Edge, all of the essential facts of the situation have to be understood
and integrated into the collective consciousness of the team.

To change the culture at Ford, Jacques Nasser—first as a member of Ford's leadership team and now as CEO—has undertaken an intensive educational program for all 55,000 salaried employees.[13]

This program, which will expand to include the company's hourly workers, is designed to communicate two fundamental concepts: First, employees should think like shareholders, and second, the company as a whole must be able to respond swiftly to—if not anticipate—consumers' needs. Ford's program is taught in-house with its own people leading the effort; those who are taught, in turn, become the teachers to the next level of direct reports. By becoming teachers, employees are helping to reinforce the change process and the company-wide commitment to it.

According to Nasser:

> We realized that the change had to be understood on the individual level. Every manager, every designer, every engineer, every person in the plants had to change his or her way of thinking. And the only way to change at the individual level, I believe, is through teaching. Teaching, we've found, is an amazingly effective way to change an organization. With the teaching programs we've used over the past three years, our people have delivered $2 billion to our bottom line, either as increased revenues or decreased costs. And they've delivered [these results] because their mindsets have changed.

By sharing knowledge about Ford and its marketplace challenges with everyone in the firm, Nasser has put employees in a better position to focus on problems and suggest solutions.

Leverage Everyone's Talents—And Deal with Performance Problems Constructively

Shackleton displayed a unique ability to understand each person's temperament and skills, and then to match those qualities with the needs of the expedition. As a result, all crewmembers contributed as best they could, and Shackleton avoided many performance problems that might have otherwise arisen. There were, nevertheless, times at which he had to bring people back into line. His ability to manage poor performers is somewhat surprising, given his unusual sensitivity to the feelings of others.

This sensitivity is illustrated by one incident that occurred in the perilous journey to South Georgia. The plug tobacco carried by the crew eventually disintegrated through the constant pounding of waves. The leaves washed around in the ballast and mixed with hair from the reindeer-skin sleeping bags, creating an odiferous concoction.

An ingenious seaman collected the leaves, dried them with the Primus stove, and created cigarettes using soggy toilet tissue for rolling paper. When the creator offered this special treat to the Boss, Shackleton would take a few obligatory puffs, then quickly pass it on as soon as the donor's back was turned.[14]

As much as he took great pains to avoid hurting others' feelings, Shackleton was quick to act when corrective measures were needed. The eccentric Orde-Lees, for example, took to riding his bicycle out onto the ice, amusing himself with feats of trick riding. On one ride he became hopelessly lost and had to be rescued by a search party. Thereafter, he was sternly ordered never again to leave the ship by himself.[15]

Orde-Lees's odd disposition and eccentric ways caused repeated conflicts with others, and he could easily have been scapegoated by the rest of the crew. He even managed to antagonize the agreeable Wild—but he never became the outcast he could have been. As a result, he was able to contribute when and where he could. Thus, on the sail to Elephant Island, Orde-Lees took Blackborow's frozen feet and warmed them against his chest.

The principal factor in keeping Orde-Lees within the team was Shackleton's unerring dedication to maintain team unity and his ability to avoid even the appearance of favoritism. He was acutely sensitive to the possibility of splintering and took great pains to ensure that fragmentation was nipped in the bud. Worsley observed:

> When there are twenty-eight men herded together in partially enforced inactivity, with nothing but snow and ice to look upon, life is bound to become irksome. The irritation of trying to drift north and knowing ourselves powerless to combat the inexorable laws of nature . . . was bound to result in a certain fraying of nerves and consequent ebullitions of temper. Little cliques and factions grew up, but Shackleton's tact and diplomacy soon destroyed that spirit. He

would redistribute the occupants of tents . . . and would remind each man that strength lay in unity.[16]

This commitment to avoid bias even extended to his relationship with Worsley and Wild. Shackleton leaned heavily on both of these key figures for counsel, and they were clearly the ranking officers in the expedition's hierarchy. But they were never seen as "cronies"—all were as one under the aegis of the team.

Lessons for Leaders

Probably no leadership task is more difficult than dealing with poor performers while, at the same time, maintaining sensitivity to individual feelings and team unity. Leading at *The Edge* involves dealing with that complicated mix, however, and team cohesiveness is never advanced by overlooking individuals who fail to pull their weight.

When it comes to performance problems, I have seldom, if ever, heard a leader say, "I acted too quickly to deal with the issue." The tendency is to do just the opposite—wait until performance has deteriorated to the point that there is no possibility of recovery or until others have been alienated by being let down by the poor performer. An unwillingness to deal with performance detracts from, rather than supports, team integrity.

As important as it is to deal with poor performers, it is equally important to act in a way that avoids isolating the individual and that gives him or her a chance to recover. Bob, for example, was head of R&D at a leading chemical company. Bob had a star performer on his team—a research chemist responsible for some of the firm's most innovative, creative, and profitable new products. In accordance with organizational goals, he rewarded Charlie (not his real name) with a promotion to senior management.

Not long afterward, however, Charlie's performance began to suffer. Accustomed to hands-on work, Charlie was lost when it came to supervising a research staff, and his administrative abilities were severely lacking. Not only was he not developing new product ideas, he was hindering the ability of his staff to do so.

Bob confronted the problem, but he dealt with it in a constructive way. Rather than reprimand his colleague, Bob recognized that the company and Charlie would be better served if Charlie were freed from daily management responsibilities. Bob created a position that had comparable status to senior manager. As "senior research fellow," Charlie returned to a creative role and his management duties were assigned to an executive who was strong in that capacity.

Bob's creation of an alternate career path for Charlie not only supported organizational goals but created an opportunity for Charlie (and other creative members of the organization) to succeed in a situation that could easily have produced resentment and fragmentation.

The best leaders are sensitive to individual needs and skills, and they find ways of using diverse talents. When corrective action needs to be taken, it is done in a way that avoids isolating or scapegoating people. Successful leaders continually drive home the team message: "We are one: We live or die together."

Expedition Log

Shared Identity

1. What have you done to promote a sense of shared identity for your team?
2. Are your team values explicit and understood by all? Are they used in making decisions?
3. What else can you do to promote identification with the team?

Communication

1. What do you do to stay in touch with the members of your team? Could you be doing more?
2. How would you assess the quality of communication among team members?
3. Are there occasions when the team is able to come together for face-to-face discussion and contact?

Information and Involvement

1. Do all members have a clear picture of the challenges faced by the team as a whole, and a sense of personal responsibility for the team's success?
2. Are there occasions for open discussion of options and decisions—and of potential consequences of different courses of action?

3. Is there anything more you might be doing to keep everyone engaged and thinking about solutions?

Performance

1. How do you assess your ability to deal effectively with individual performance problems? Are there issues you should be dealing with, but are avoiding?
2. Are there factions, or individuals, within your team that are now isolated or scapegoated? If so, what can you do to bring them into the group so they can be fully engaged?

6

Core Team Values

Strategy 6

Minimize status differences and insist on courtesy and mutual respect.

> Shackleton privately forced upon me his one breakfast biscuit, and would have given me another tonight had I allowed him. I do not suppose that anyone else in the world can thoroughly realize how much generosity and sympathy was shown by this: I do, and By God I shall never forget it. Thousands of pounds would not have bought that one biscuit.[1]
>
> Frank Wild

All of the ten strategies for dealing with situations at *The Edge* are tightly interwoven, but the tactics in this chapter are most closely associated with Strategy 5, which emphasizes the importance of reinforcing the team message. In fact, many of the approaches described in this chapter could have been included in the previous one and considered simply as another set of tactics for developing a cohesive team. Strategy 6, however, plays such a vital role in success at *The Edge* that it deserves a chapter of its own.

Minimize Status Differences and Special Privileges

Robert Falcon Scott is one of the most famous explorers of all time. Scott, who reached the South Pole just over a month after Norwegian Roald Amundsen, died with his companions on their return journey. Yet Scott secured his immortality by capturing the imagination of the British public, which saw the expedition as a failed but heroic effort.

Statues throughout the world depict Scott facing death and are inscribed with his last message:

> I do not regret this journey, which has shown that English-men can endure hardships, help one another and meet death with as great a fortitude as ever in the past.[2]

In fact, some have argued that Scott's misadventure resulted from severe deficiencies in his personal style and leadership ability. Roland Huntford, for example, in his book on the Amundsen-Scott race, *The Last Place on Earth*, is merciless in describing Scott's flaws. The book's index entries[3] include the following list of Scott's "characteristics": "absentmindedness; agnosticism; command, unsuitability for; depression, bouts of; emotionalism; impatience; improvisation, belief in; inadequacy, sense of; insecurity; insight, lack of; irrationality; isolation; jealousy; judgment, defective; leadership, failure in; literary gifts; panic, readiness to; recklessness; responsibility, instinct to evade; sentimentality; and vacillation."[4]

Others have charged that Huntford was excessively biased, and unduly harsh in his assessment of Scott. Sir Vivian Fuchs, who led the British Trans-Antarctic Expedition of 1957–1958, has argued that Huntford used "the full force of his vitriolic pen" to pursue a personal vendetta against Scott.[5]

Huntford may have been hard on Scott, but there is little question that—as a leader—Shackleton was everything that Scott was not. Both men were products of a romantic age of exploration, and both were highly competitive ambitious individuals. But there were fundamental differences in their effectiveness as leaders and, in particular, their ability to create a sense of team unity. Why were these two individuals so different? What created these sharp contrasts?

When you look beneath Huntford's index of "characteristics" and into Scott's limitations as a leader, one thing becomes clear. There is little question that many of Scott's deficiencies resulted from the environment in which he learned to lead: Britain's Royal Navy in the latter part of the nineteenth century. This environment is worth looking at more closely, because in it there are lessons for leaders and for organizations today.

In the 1880s, when Scott attended Dartmouth—the British Naval Academy—the Royal Navy was living in the past. Still basking in Admiral Horatio Nelson's victory over the French at Trafalgar in 1805, the navy was complacent, resistant to innovation, and focused on form rather than function. It was, as Huntford put it so well, "more like an exclusive yacht club than a warlike institution."

Leadership focused on appearances—smart looking ships with obsolete weapons, for example. Another pitfall was the Royal Navy's reliance on hierarchy, strict obedience, and centralized decision making. Scott's limited talent and personal insecurities, then, were mixed with a leadership training regimen that was as ill-suited for Antarctic exploration as it was for naval warfare.

This unfortunate combination played out in Scott's leadership in many ways. Lacking Shackleton's understanding of the positive functions of structure (described in Chapter 1), Scott put the crew to work on tasks that were ridiculously inappropriate. As the commander of the National Antarctic expedition, he directed the crew of the *Discovery* to follow the Royal Navy tradition of scrubbing the decks daily. The crew was ordered to perform this task in subfreezing temperatures. The water turned to ice instantly and had to be shoveled away.[6]

Scott was also fond of holding inspections with all hands on deck, forcing the men to stand in place until their feet were frostbitten.[7] As if this were not enough, Scott was also a terrible communicator. Instead of using information to strengthen the bonds of team unity (Chapter 5), he withheld the most basic information. Even the officers were kept in the dark about their destinations and how long they would be staying.[8]

All of these behaviors created anger, resentment, and depression among the crew. Scott's greatest flaw, however, may have been the "classist," hierarchical view of the world that he learned in the Royal Navy. It is true, of course, that other British naval officers had much the same training and were still able to be effective leaders. The combination of Scott's personality and his rigid training, though, was a toxic mix.

In assembling the crew of the *Discovery* expedition, for example, Scott resisted the involvement of anyone who was not a member of the Royal Navy, because he doubted his ability to deal with "any other class of men."[9] The organization of the *Discovery* maintained the strict separation between officers and enlisted men, between the wardroom and the mess deck. Scott seldom even spoke to ordinary seamen, except during inspections. This caste system was wholly unnecessary on a merchant vessel and a liability in the snow and ice of Antarctica. It created a fragmented, dispirited group that could hardly be considered a team.

Shackleton's approach to leadership was a night-and-day contrast to Scott's. Shackleton's father, unable to afford the high cost of a Dartmouth education and a cadet training ship, sent young Ernest to sea on a full-rigger named the *Houghton Tower*. Shackleton literally "learned the ropes"—all 200 of them on the ship—from the bottom up.[10]

Not only did he learn basic seamanship, he also lived in a world far different from the rigid Royal Navy. To be sure, there were status distinctions between officers and seamen, but they were nowhere near as rigid as those of the navy. In this environment, the gregarious Shackleton made friends among all factions—officers, engineers, and apprentices alike.

When Shackleton joined Scott as a member of the *Discovery* expedition, he brought with him more than an outgoing, ebullient personality. He also carried a view of people and relationships that was fundamentally different from Scott's. While Shackleton was a strong leader, he saw no value in unnecessary trappings that differentiated team members. He saw the need for decision-making authority, but it did not take a form that created a superior, elite class.

On the *Discovery* expedition, the fundamental differences between the two men surfaced again and again. When expedition members were learning to ski, Scott looked on while Shackleton and the rest of the expedition floundered in the snow. When Scott bullied Hartley Ferrar—the expedition geologist and youngest member of the wardroom—Shackleton stood by Ferrar because he felt Scott's anger was misplaced.[11]

It was on the Imperial Trans-Antarctic Expedition, however, when Shackleton was given full latitude to lead, that the striking contrast became so clear. In particular, Shackleton's ability to eliminate the damaging effects of unnecessary hierarchy was clearly illustrated. On *Endurance*, everyone pitched in, regardless of station. Scientists, physicians, and seamen alike worked side by side to do the work. A photograph from the expedition, for instance, shows Macklin, the surgeon, on his knees vigorously scrubbing the deck.

Not everyone understood and initially embraced this egalitarian view. Thomas Orde-Lees, who was brought up in the Royal Navy system, wrote in his diary:

I am able to put aside pride of caste in most things but I must say that I think scrubbing floors is not fair work for people who have been brought up in refinement.[12]

Over time, however, this "caste free" system became part of the culture of the team. Unlike Scott, who observed while others labored, Shackleton was an integral part of the team.

This egalitarian spirit had two critical benefits. First, it ensured that every member of the expedition would do his utmost to accomplish whatever work needed to be done. Second, it served to minimize the resentments that inevitably rise when, under conditions of stress, hardship, and deprivation, there is a perception that some are more equal than others.

One way in which Shackleton maintained this sense of equality was in his scrupulous fairness about distributing resources. Shortly after *Endurance* broke up, for example, the crew was faced with the dilemma that there were not enough reindeer-skin sleeping bags for every member. These bags, specially made by expert furriers, were perhaps the best insulating protection against the cold available at the time. Their original plan required reindeer-skin bags only for the sledging party, so there were only eighteen. Now everyone was out in the cold, and ten of the twenty-eight would have to make do with Jaeger woolen bags. To ensure equal treatment, the desirable reindeer bags were distributed using a lottery, in which Shackleton did not participate. As an "old hand," he decided to make do with wool.

As important as protection from the cold was, food was even more central to the life of the crew. Feelings ranging from wild exuberance to deep depression would turn on the size of the rations. Even the appearance of favoritism would have created conflict and resentment. Here is how the Boss described the Solomonic process used to ensure impartiality:

All is eaten that comes to each tent, and everything is most carefully and accurately divided into as many equal portions as there are men in the tent. One member then closes his eyes or turns his head away and calls out the names at random, as the cook for the day points to each portion, saying at the same time, "Whose?" Partiality, however unintentional it may be, is thus entirely obviated and every one feels satisfied that all is fair, even though one may look a little enviously at the next man's helping which differs in some especially appreciated detail from one's own. We break the

Tenth Commandment energetically, but as we are all in the same boat in this respect, no one says a word.[13]

To reinforce this norm of equal treatment, Shackleton made sure that he, as the leader, got no special privileges. He wore the same clothing, ate the same food, and took his turn with the daily chores. He assumed, for example, the role of "Peggy," carrying the "hoosh pot" from the galley filled with their daily fare—a yellow-brown mixture of lard, oatmeal, beef and vegetable protein, salt, and sugar. When Shackleton learned that the cook had given him special treatment, he quickly put a stop to this violation of the law of equals.

Another of Shackleton's characteristics that helped him retain authority while maintaining a sense of equality was his ability to apologize, to admit when he was wrong. He had strong ideas, of course, and he could be bullheaded. But when it was clear that he had made a mistake, he was quick to own up to it.

On one such occasion, Worsley and Shackleton disagreed about the amount of ballast needed for the *Caird* to make it to South Georgia. Knowing that the crew and stores would weigh 1,000 pounds, Worsley argued for a relatively small amount of extra weight. Shackleton, fearful that the *James Caird* would capsize in heavy seas, insisted on nearly a ton of ballast. This caused the *James Caird* to ride low in the water and handle badly, making the ride worse that it needed to be. When Shackleton realized his mistake, he spoke directly to Worsley:

Skipper, you were right. I made a mistake about the ballast. Had I listened to you, I think the journey would have been shorter, the boat wouldn't have been so stiff or so jumpy in her movements and we should have shipped very few heavy seas.[14]

This admission, made after the *James Caird* had successfully completed the passage, could have been omitted. Others might have glossed over the mistake. But Shackleton did not, and it only served to increase his credibility as a leader.

Lessons for Leaders

All organizations have hierarchy, but some are more explicit about it than others. In his thoughtful book, *From the Ground Up*, Ed Lawler describes a German corporate headquarters with an unusual design.[15] The building is shaped like a pyramid, and each level of the building houses one level of management. Every employee knows his or her position in the hierarchy, and moving up in the organization means exactly that: Those who are promoted relocate to the next higher floor.

This degree of rigid stratification is hardly conducive to teamwork at *The Edge*. Hierarchy itself, however, is not the problem. People understand the need for legitimate authority and for differences in salaries, roles, and titles. What fragments a group is the perception of an elite "upper class"—a sense of superiority conferred on a chosen few. Thus, the critical leadership challenge is to create an environment in which each person experiences a basic sense of respect regardless of his or her role in the organization.

To illustrate this point, here's a story from my own experience: After graduating from the Harvard Business School, I continued my career journey by taking a job in Washington as an assistant to the Commissioner of the Office of Education, John Ottina. I arrived at work my first day, eager to attack the problems of education in America. I found, however, that the other new assistants and I were jammed into an office area so small it was difficult to have a conversation or to think deeply enough to do analytic work. It was not a matter of survival, but it was a very poor work environment.

John saw us jammed into the office, sized up the situation, and then acted quickly. He immediately moved out of his big corner office reserved for "the Commissioner" and set up shop with a table and some filing cabinets in a much smaller space. He did not make a production of it; he did not brag about it; he just did it. That simple move said it all: We were all in this effort together and—regardless of our titles—we were going to work as one to do the formidable job faced by the team.

Willingness to admit mistakes is another way of minimizing status differences, and I am always impressed by leaders who can say they were wrong. Scott Sklar is co-CEO of TravelSmith, an outfitting catalog business specializing in products designed to withstand the rigors of the road. Sklar once took a career course I taught at Yale, and we met on one occasion to catch up. During our conversation, Sklar took great pleasure in recounting the story of "the little black dress."[16]

Natalie Carlson, at the time the head of women's apparel, had proposed including a black knit dress in the TravelSmith catalog. Sklar resisted the concept. It was something the company had never done before, he knew little about dresses, and TravelSmith was taking "baby steps" in women's apparel. But Carlson persisted. Her husband was working for a company in France, and she frequently spent long weekends in Paris. Without the right wardrobe, and surrounded by chic Parisian women, she often felt out of place. So Carlson went on a protracted hunt for the perfect black dress that packed well, didn't wrinkle, and looked stylish. She had so much difficulty finding the perfect dress, that she designed and developed her own. Carlson knew that this was a dress that could be important—not just for her, but for other female travelers as well.

Sklar had reservations, but he listened. Persuaded by Carlson's arguments, he finally agreed. The results surprised him. The black dress turned into one of the most successful products in the history of TravelSmith. As Sklar reflected:

> It's been the number-one product in the catalog ever since. And it was probably one of the most successful products we could have conceived of running. It's become our trademark. What it illustrated for me was that you don't have to be an expert in everything to be an effective leader. But you have to be an expert in understanding people's talents and how to motivate and manage them.

Carlson is now vice president of merchandising, and the "indispensable black dress" is part of the TravelSmith culture. Through his retelling of the story, Sklar makes it clear that he does not pretend to be omniscient as a leader. And he has encouraged Carlson and others to stand up for what they believe in.

Insist on Mutual Respect and Courtesy

It is not possible to force one human being to have genuine feelings of concern about another. But it is possible to create an environment in which taking care of others becomes a normative behavior and—over time—these caring behaviors help forge emotional bonds.

From the beginning of the Trans-Antarctic expedition to its end, Shackleton consistently encouraged behavior that emphasized respect and caring. His extraordinary attitude of self-sacrifice, plus his ability to act in the service of others, created a foundation for teamwork. These obvious manifestations of caring for his comrades help explain why the crew felt such a strong pull of personal loyalty to Shackleton. It explains why First Officer Greenstreet would be moved to say:

> [Shackleton's] first thought was for the men under him. He didn't care if he went without a shirt on his back as long as the men he was leading had sufficient clothing . . . you felt that the party mattered more to him than anything else.[17]

This sense of connection meant more than fidelity to the Boss. It became, over time, a force that created enormously powerful bonds of loyalty among every member of the expedition.

Shackleton's nurturing behaviors—including his demonstrations of Strategy 2, setting a personal example—were often simple things. On one occasion, after the destruction of *Endurance*, Shackleton and Wild heated hot milk for the crew and went from tent to tent with the "life giving" drink. After the sail to South Georgia, when the exhausted crew had landed, Shackleton took the first watch, which he kept for three hours instead of the usual one.

Just as Shackleton avoided scapegoating, the way in which he cared for the crew reflected his absolute commitment to team unity. Again, on the sail to South Georgia, he took great pains to avoid singling out those in special need. During the bitter night, Shackleton made sure that, every four hours, a drink of hot milk was served to stave off the cold. The men drank the liquid scalding hot, willing to endure the pain to get extra warmth inside their bodies.

As a result of this nurturing drink, no one died on the journey. But it was close. Worsley remembers that:

> Two of the party at least were very close to death. Indeed, it might be said that [Shackleton] kept a finger on each man's pulse. Whenever he noticed that a man seemed extra cold and shivered, he would immediately order another hot drink of milk to be prepared and served to all. He never let the man know that it was on his account, lest he become nervous about himself and, while we all participated, it was the coldest, naturally, who got the greatest advantage.[18]

What is important to realize is that Shackleton's behavior as a leader had ripple effects beyond his individual concerns. Crewmembers often performed acts of caring and self-sacrifice for each other, showing a concern that rarely occurred in accounts of other expeditions I have studied. `

One of the most dramatic moments in the *Endurance* story occurred at Patience Camp, just before the launching of the boats. The food supply had dwindled to dangerously low levels. Less than a week's supply of blubber remained, and the small ration of seal steak normally served at breakfast was eliminated. The waste meat generally used to feed the dogs was examined for any edible scraps, and several of the crew had tried eating frozen, raw penguin meat.

Under these desperate conditions, and after a wet sleepless night, an argument broke out among Worsley, Macklin, Orde-Lees, and Robert Clark, the biologist. Caught in the middle, Greenstreet spilled his tiny ration of powdered milk and shouted at Clark. It was a tragic moment. In his book on the *Endurance* expedition, author Alfred Lansing described the scene:

> . . . Greenstreet paused to get his breath, and in that instant his anger was spent and he suddenly fell silent. Everyone else in the tent became quiet, too, and looked at Greenstreet, shaggy-haired, bearded, and filthy with blubber soot, holding his empty mug in his hand and looking helplessly down into the snow that had thirstily soaked up his precious milk. The loss was so tragic he seemed almost on the point of weeping. Without speaking, Clark reached out and poured some of his milk into Greenstreet's mug. Then Worsley, then Macklin, and Rickenson and Kerr, Orde-Lees, and finally Blackborow. They finished in silence.[19]

Thus, others emulated the caring behaviors that Shackleton modeled. In the face of death and starvation, the bonds of teamwork held.

Another important method for creating mutual respect comes from insisting on common courtesy, even under stressful conditions in which it may seem unnecessary. Of course, conflict under extreme conditions is inevitable and—as will be discussed in the next chapter—it can even contribute to the health of the team. But living at *The Edge* does not mean ignoring civility. Frank Wild was known to remind the crew that, as Shackleton later put it, "a little thanks will go a long way." And so will "please," "excuse me," and the other familiar phrases that lubricate social interaction.

This point was brought home to me in a personal way early in my service in Vietnam. During one of our first operations, my battalion encountered heavy resistance from the North Vietnamese. One unit—India Company—walked into an ambush and was hit by devastating mortar and automatic-weapons fire from an entrenched enemy force. After the attack, a third of the company lay killed or wounded. It took only a few minutes to cripple the unit.

The company made it back to battalion headquarters, a hastily constructed command post on a just-captured, blackened ridge. The hill, still smoking from the air strikes that had preceded the American assault, looked like something out of hell. The battalion intelligence officer, or S-2, was questioning the India Company commander, who was still in a state of shock. The two officers knelt facing each other in the dirt, several feet apart, as the S-2 fired questions about the strength of the enemy, their weapons, and possible countermeasures.

Above, helicopters flew forward firing machine guns, while others flew back carrying casualties. Jet aircraft dropped napalm yards away. I had no idea whether we were about to be overrun or whether the North Vietnamese had disengaged. In the middle of this chaos, and without thinking, I ran directly between the two Marines, bent on my mission of carrying a message to the battalion commander. As I ran by, I heard the S-2 snarl, "Excuse you."

Excuse me? I thought. *Where the hell do you think we are?* Then it struck me. In this surreal situation, I had been rude. I had insulted the company commander, who was struggling to recover from shock. I had angered two members of my team. Under these conditions, common courtesy was one of the few vestigial elements of civilization left. It was an important lesson, one that I never forgot.

Lessons for Leaders

Leaders who want team members to care about each other need to model that behavior themselves. It is not something that can be delegated, and it cannot be feigned. If it is modeled and reinforced, though, over time it will become part of the culture of the team.

Michael, the CEO of a large media company, took over an organization that one close observer described as "political, competitive, and nasty." People were regularly ripped apart in public. Insulting, abusive, and demeaning behaviors were commonplace.

Michael soon came to realize that, under these conditions, the collective intelligence of the team could not be brought to bear on the pressing competitive issues the company faced. In collaboration with other members of his senior team, he developed a code of conduct that laid out the behaviors that would be expected of leaders in the organization. Fundamental to that code were respect for others and courteous behavior.

In the beginning, skeptics suspected that this was a paper exercise, designed for appearances but without "teeth." It was not. This became clear when, after repeated, visible, and well-verified violations of the code, two senior executives were asked to leave the organization. The message soon reverberated throughout the organization, and a company once described as a "magnet for obnoxious behavior" transformed its culture. In doing so, it replaced an antiquated, individualistic society with a team prepared to move into the digital age.

Expedition Log

1. When you look at the structure of your team and organization, what are the special distinctions that create differences in class or status? Are there policies or procedures that create fragmentation? If so, are they really necessary? How can these differences and special privileges be minimized or eliminated?
2. How, specifically, are resources divided among members of your team? Are there ways the team can share resources or deploy some to others with greater need? Does the process for distributing resources support perceptions of equity and fairness? Consider making this a topic of an agenda item for a team meeting.
3. If you asked members of your team to assess your leadership, would they see you more as a Shackleton or more like a Scott? Would they describe you as "above the action," "looking on," or "in the trenches" with them? Are there physical or psychological barriers that separate you from your team?
4. Have you ever spent some time doing a team member's task? Make a plan to spend time this month actually doing some task assigned to the team. This hands-on experience can have multiple benefits. First, it will show that you are willing and able to perform the same duties as others. Second, you will have a better understanding of the challenges and kind of work that your team must perform, so you'll be empathetic to the needs of the team. Finally, it can provide insights that will contribute to process improvement.
5. When was the last time you made a personal sacrifice for the benefit of the team? Have you ever done the equivalent of "serving tea and milk"?
6. Does the culture of the team reinforce courtesy and mutual respect? Are there explicit or implicit "rules of the road" that create expectations about the way team members will deal with one another?

7

Conflict

Strategy 7

Master conflict—deal with anger in small doses, engage dissidents, and avoid needless power struggles.

> . . . Such were the usual psychological hazards of an isolated community. Cliques, quarrels and tension hung in the background. There was the irritation of all too familiar faces, and no hope of escape . . . Above all, however, it was essential to believe in the leader, and Shackleton possessed the power of forestalling trouble without actually appearing to do anything.[1]
>
> Roland Huntford

*C*onflict: The very mention of the word can raise feelings of anxiety. Competent executives who fearlessly enter the competitive marketplace often go to great lengths to avoid interpersonal friction. Yet conflict is a predictable component in the volatile mix of attitudes and emotions found in organizations at *The Edge*. It comes in many forms: direct arguments, disagreements, sabotage, and passive aggression.

If handled ineptly or suppressed, unresolved tension can be incredibly destructive. At the *Survival Edge*, it can result in loss of life, either through physical attack or breakdowns in teamwork. For organizations in which physical survival is not the issue, conflict can mean decreased productivity, increased stress, wasted energy, and diminished problem-solving ability. It can also result in an unhappy workplace, loss of revenue, vulnerability to competition, and ultimately, organizational death.

This chapter looks at cases in which conflict has spun out of control and resulted in the loss of lives, along with examples in which conflict was managed effectively under the most stressful conditions. It illustrates how proactive leaders can skillfully use conflict to their advantage in creating and sustaining higher performance.

Deal with Anger in Small Doses

The *Karluk* expedition (described in Chapter 1) suffered from a gaping leadership hole created by Stefansson's abrupt departure, and by the subsequent inability of Captain Robert Bartlett—who was left behind with the ship—to create a cohesive team. The fatal effects of this fragmentation became magnified as the months wore on and conflicts erupted unchecked among the members of the ill-fated expedition.

In a sledge march even more grueling than that faced by Shackleton, Captain Bartlett managed to lead the remainder of the *Karluk* expedition across the ice from the trapped ship to land. Having reached the relative safety of Wrangel Island, however, Bartlett saw no alternative but to leave the exhausted survivors and set out for help.

Leaving fifteen surviving members behind, Bartlett and his Eskimo guide, Kataktovik, began their journey to Siberia in a snowstorm on March 18, 1914. It was a treacherous 200-mile journey across the floating, unstable sea ice. On April 5, 1914, the two exhausted travelers reached land and were soon taken in by a party of friendly Siberian Inuits.

Bartlett and Kataktovik rested for two days with the Inuits, but—concerned about those left behind on Wrangel—set out once again with their weary dogs. On April 25, 1914—thirty-seven days after leaving Wrangel—Bartlett and Kataktovik arrived at the Siberian settlement of East Cape. They had covered about 700 miles of ice and shoreline and had averaged almost twenty miles a day, in what has been called the "most dangerous ice journey ever made by human beings."[2]

As heroic as this effort was, it was not until May 1914, when the ice had broken up, that Bartlett was able to find a ship to take him to Alaska. After arguing with a telegraph operator who refused to send a message without advance payment, Bartlett was finally able to send out messages telling of the plight of the Wrangel Island castaways.

While Bartlett tried frantically to mount a rescue effort, the already-shaky community of the Wrangel Island survivors continued to deteriorate. Quarrels broke out constantly. The responsibility of leadership had passed to Chief Engineer Munro, who was placed in command on the island. Munro, who had earlier developed strained relations with a number of his shipmates, was no Frank Wild.

Further undermining a sense of unity, the party split into four subgroups, each of which was free to do as it pleased. The rationale for this arrangement was that it would increase hunting opportunities. However, it also had the effect of increasing the centrifugal forces that were pulling the group apart.

McKinlay, the expedition meteorologist, observed that:

> . . . [I]n our very mixed community we had all the seeds of future disaster. In normal circumstances we might have got by as very ordinary chaps, our frailties and idiosyncrasies unnoticed by any but our nearest and dearest. A good leader might have brought out the best in everybody. . . . But on our own, the misery and desperation of our situation multiplied every weakness, every quirk of personality, every flaw in character, a thousandfold.[3]

Biscuits became a major source of dispute. The men shouted obscenities in arguments over an eighth of a biscuit. Crewmembers accused each other of plotting to hide hunting spoils. When game was shot, the fortunate hunters gorged themselves rather than share their bounty, or lied about what they had shot.

At times, conflict escalated to the point where there were threats of violence. One enraged member of the party threatened to shoot another, and Breddy, the fireman, was found shot dead. Although the incident was apparently suicide rather than murder, a search of his effects uncovered numerous items Breddy had stolen from his comrades.

Attempts to talk through the disagreements momentarily helped dampen the conflicts, but the truces were only temporary. Incredibly, people became so argumentative and preoccupied that they forgot Bartlett's last instructions: to meet a rescue ship at Rodgers Island. This oversight almost cost them their lives.

On September 7, 1914, the nine surviving members of the *Karluk* were rescued by the schooner *King and Winge*. The castaways were so dazed that they first ignored the rescuers, then—finally—stumbled across the ice to the ship. Eleven of their comrades had died: eight on the ice, two of malnutrition, and one of a gunshot. Conflict and lack of unity had destroyed the ability of the team to function at *The Edge*.

The *Karluk* is but one of many survival accounts in which an inability to deal with conflict played a destructive role. The infamous Donner Party is another tragic example in which petty disagreements escalated into violence and disaster.

In 1846, the eighty-seven members of the Donner Party left St. Louis, Missouri, for California. One of the pioneers, Milt Elliott, was driving a team of oxen and attempted to pass in front of another member of the party, John Snyder. They became entangled on a narrow path. An enraged Snyder began beating Elliott's oxen furiously with his whip. John Reed, the leader of the party, rushed over to try and stop him. Snyder was further angered by this act and lashed out at Reed and his wife with his whip. Reed, now himself overcome with rage, drew his hunting knife and subsequently murdered Snyder.[4]

The fight lasted only seconds, but the disastrous event had a terrible outcome. First, it fractured whatever sense of unity existed among the families:

> ... [T]he evil feelings that had been loosed that day ... were
> not to be again confined. The emigrants were no longer a
> "company"; they were only a number of family groups each
> for itself, some of them ready to cooperate only where manifest good was to be gained for themselves. Hatred and inhumanity walked beside the wagons.[5]

Second, precious time was wasted dealing with the aftermath of the murder. The train encamped. A council was created to deal with the event. Written depositions were taken. People called out for vengeance. Further shooting was threatened, as the pioneers took sides.

Finally, a compromise was reached, and Reed was allowed to leave without firearms. The resentment remained, however, and the delay was to prove tragic. The Donner Party reached the summit of the Sierras only to be trapped by blinding snow. The horror, cannibalism, and unbelievable suffering that followed can, once again, be traced to the inability of the party members to deal with conflict.

The destructive conflict seen in the Donner Party and the *Karluk* expedition stand in stark contrast to the way conflict was handled by the crew of *Endurance*. In part, Shackleton's effectiveness in dealing with conflict may have come about because he knew—at first hand—just how destructive conflict could be. On the earlier National Antarctic Expedition, Shackleton's relationship with Robert Scott disintegrated to the point that the two men barely spoke to one another. They quarreled about almost every crucial issue, including diet, discipline, and dogs. Scott's impatience and quick temper, his ineptness at decision making, and his often-pessimistic attitude were constant annoyances to Shackleton. This tension was a steady drain on their efforts to reach the pole and was only eased by the intervention of Edward Wilson, the third member of the team.

Shackleton, however, had more than direct experience. He had also studied the records of other explorers and accounts of previous expeditions, including the fate of the *Belgica*. The *Belgica*, which carried the Belgian Antarctic expedition, was caught in the ice in 1898 and drifted for more than a year in the ice of the Bellingshausen Sea. The *Belgica* was the first ship to winter in the Antarctic, and the experience was not a happy one.[6] Boredom, paranoia, hopelessness, and dissidence affected most of the crew. One man drowned and three went insane before they were able to break out from the ice and return to South America.

Determined to avoid the fate of the *Belgica*'s crew, Shackleton viewed teamwork as critical to the survival of the *Endurance*'s crew and effective conflict management as one of his most critical leadership tasks. As in other aspects of his leadership, Shackleton was first and foremost a role model. He knew that it was critical for him—as the leader of the expedition—to set an example in dealing with the inevitable tensions and strains caused by the close quarters and by the physical and emotional stress suffered by the crewmembers.

Shackleton was not a man without emotions—in fact, he was known to have a quick temper. He worked, however, to maintain his composure, to step back and assess difficult situations, and to help his men find a resolution. This was especially true in times of ambiguity or stress when he "appeared to drop his moods . . . and stretch out a soothing hand."[7]

Shackleton also encouraged his men to keep him informed of any disagreements so that he could keep abreast of mounting tensions or damaging alliances. During the first months of the expedition, for example, the eccentric Orde-Lees had a number of encounters with the other men on the ship. He was one of the few who had spent time in the military, and he continued to adhere to many of the protocols of service life.

This was often a source of conflict. On one occasion, in his role as storekeeper, he asked a sailor for a receipt for some Heinz chutney. The practice of asking for receipts was common in the Royal Navy, but it offended his mate, who complained to Shackleton. According to Orde-Lees's diary, Shackleton "said that it was contrary to the spirit of . . . the Merchant Service . . . he was very nice about it . . . but I could see he was displeased."[8]

Shackleton used instances such as these to communicate what he found acceptable and unacceptable behavior. He was also able to be proactive and defuse problems that could distract the men or sap their much-needed energy. Furthermore, resolving a problem early on prevented it from becoming a larger issue.

In spite of all this attention to conflict, there were times when tensions ran high. The most serious conflict took place during the first July, when *Endurance* was beset in the ice. John Vincent—an able seaman and by all accounts a bully—began exchanging words with several other crewmembers. In Hurley's words, Vincent began to call the men "evil names" and he "struck them."[9] When Shackleton got wind of the altercation, he made it clear that this behavior would not be tolerated under his command. Vincent was demoted and that was the last recorded incident of physical violence.

Perhaps this incident, early on in the journey, reinforced in Shackleton a view that the men needed to be able to release on a daily, if not hourly, basis the stress and negative feelings they felt. Small arguments took place throughout the day. The men would argue about which way the wind was coming from, or how far they had floated in the previous week. A person who stepped on another as he left a crowded tent was subjected to fierce reproach. A man who failed to close the tent flap when going out in the middle of the night to relieve himself heard about it from everyone. If snow were knocked into shoes or chores were not done correctly, people would be reminded of their transgression in no uncertain terms.

This norm of releasing anger in small doses did not depend solely on Shackleton's skillful leadership. It continued under Frank Wild, who was left in charge of the party on Elephant Island. In fact, Wild had a superb ability in knowing just how to orchestrate the conflict dynamics of the men under his charge:

> For men growing heartily sick of the same faces around them, bizarre, lurking conflict was a part of daily life . . . Everybody at some time wrangled with neighbors in the hut about encroachment on their floor space. Wild would allow them all to let off steam and then, just when they appeared on the verge of blows, would defuse the situation with sweet arbitration.[10]

The daily life of the *Endurance* crew, then, was an endless stream of small arguments and minor disagreements. They were sometimes good-humored and sometimes not. But there were few hostile or serious interactions. This culture of letting off steam defused conflict, and it prevented incidents from gaining momentum and becoming serious. Said another way, a series of small tremors prevented a major earthquake.

Lessons for Leaders

Conflict is a pervasive element in any organization, particularly in those that press their performance limits. The challenge is not how to eliminate conflicts, but rather how to manage them in productive ways that strengthen bonds among team members.

Ironically, the emphasis on teamwork in today's corporate culture can serve to drive conflicts underground. In this subterranean state, unresolved issues become latent sources of tension. How often, for example, have you attended a "polite" meeting that ended with smiling faces—only to hear subsequent hallway and rest room discussions about the "real" issues? Or seen deep differences of opinion devolve into a lukewarm compromise that no one truly supports?

There are several reasons why conflict, anger, and negative feelings need to be dealt with directly and in small doses. First, conflict not expressed means that problems are not being confronted. Second, conflict not expressed directly surfaces in other, nonproductive ways. Unnecessary arguments erupt over peripheral issues, and team members sabotage others in subtle and not-so-subtle ways. Finally, as in survival situations, conflict not expressed and resolved can escalate out of control, with disastrous business consequences.

In spite of the importance of managing conflict, being proactive about dealing with disagreements can be difficult for many leaders. In an honest but misguided desire to promote harmony, otherwise skillful executives avoid the tough issues or fail to create a climate in which conflict is freely expressed.

Perhaps the first step in promoting healthy conflict is to understand—and really to internalize—that conflict and caring are not mutually exclusive. The extraordinary example of Shackleton's crewmembers sharing their milk in the middle of a heated argument makes this point vividly.

The second step in dealing with conflict is to create an effective process that encourages team members to surface their differences and to identify those lurking problems that need to be addressed. An approach that I have found quite effective for this purpose comes from an unusual source.

Some years ago, when I first began to work with senior leadership teams, I encountered a great deal of difficulty and frustration in getting executive teams to confront sensitive issues, and that affected their performance. At the time, I was teaching a course at Yale in which I used a "family systems model" as a lens for looking at the dynamics of organizations.

With this approach, I analyzed organizations as if they were families to see what insights this perspective might generate. While I understood that organizations were not really families, I thought this metaphor might provide a fresh perspective on organizational dynamics. I also thought it might help explain the persistence of organizational problems that defied rational analysis. After all, no one expects families to be rational!

One aspect of the family-systems theory that proved to be particularly valuable was the notion of the "family secret." Family secrets are emotionally charged, taboo topics. In family life, they often center on drug or alcohol dependencies, marital difficulties, and personal idiosyncrasies of various kinds. Most family members are aware of the "secrets," but these forbidden subjects are never openly discussed. When conversation moves in the direction of a secret, the anxiety level rises palpably.

The executive teams I was dealing with seemed to resist sensitive issues in much the same way that families avoid confronting secrets. So I decided to try an experiment and approach these taboo team topics as if they were "family secrets." The next question was how to surface the issues.

Family systems therapists use a number of images to represent secrets, but none of them seemed quite appropriate for use in an organizational setting. After some thought, I chose a metaphor I thought would work: the Moose on the Table.[11] It seemed to me that the image of a large, hairy, ungainly moose—sitting in the middle of a table and blocking communication—vividly symbolized the issues being avoided by the group. And, while imposing, the moose was a goofy-enough critter that it would add an element of humor to otherwise tense situations.

With some trepidation, I began to use the Moose on the Table in my consulting work. Although the metaphor initially raised some eyebrows, I was amazed at the ability of the Moose to surface issues that had long been ignored. In one leading technology organization, for example, the CEO and his team were struggling with their inability to create and manage new businesses successfully. They knew this was a fundamental problem, but they were unsure of why it persisted.

As part of a study organized to unravel the mystery, I presented the family systems model and conducted a "Moose round-up." The results were astonishing. The "Moose List" included in the team's final report included the following issues:

> ➢ We approach every new product as if it must be a home run, achieving the same level of success as our earliest successes.
> ➢ We are, in fact, becoming a technology-averse company.
> ➢ The revenue plan drives our resource allocation and decision-making process.
> ➢ We have developed a tolerance for mediocrity.
> ➢ We are looking for a "magic product" to save the company.
> ➢ We have no real competitive marketing competence.
> ➢ The operating plan cycle is not flexible enough to allow timely response to business initiatives.

The report (Figure 7-1), along with a stuffed moose, was presented to the CEO, who accepted it with a smile. The conclusions were not ones he was delighted to hear, but he knew that—once identified—the issues were ones that could be systematically attacked.

Over the years, my colleagues and I have brought the Moose on the Table to scores of organizations throughout the world. There are times in which substitute animals are needed: For example, the Water Buffalo on the Table made an appearance in Asia. Whatever the form, however, the image has always succeeded in getting conflict out in the open where it belongs.

Why is the Moose metaphor so effective? I believe that this ungainly animal does a number of things very well. First, it legitimizes and rewards people for being open, and it provides a shared vocabulary for doing so. "In the spirit of the Moose, I'd like to say . . ." becomes a common phrase. Second, the comic image takes the edge off issues that can create tension and divisiveness. Third, identifying an issue as a Moose provides psychological distance. It reframes the issue from an internal conflict to an external problem to be solved. Once the conflict becomes a shared problem, team members can work together to find solutions.

Engage Dissidents

The men of the *Endurance* spent countless hours, day after day, talking or sleeping in their crowded tents to avoid the elements and pass the

Figure 7-1. The Moose on the Table.

Why New Business Initiatives Fail

time. Shackleton recognized that these close quarters could be breeding grounds for discontent, and his keen awareness of the difference in people's personalities and needs was vital in minimizing destructive conflict among the crew.

Shackleton studied everyone and appeared to know when he, or others, may have gone too far. Macklin, the surgeon, described Shackleton as someone able to ask you "little things about yourself, how you were getting on . . . and all that sort of thing. . . . Sometimes when you felt he'd been perhaps a bit ruthless, pushing you round a bit hard, he seemed to have the knack of undoing any bad effect . . . with these little intimate talks."[12] Shackleton clearly recognized that hurt feelings needed immediate attention to prevent anger or resentment from building.

During the crew-selection process and early in the expedition, Shackleton identified individuals whose attitudes or behavior could either adversely affect morale or be seen as a challenge to his leadership. Instead of limiting his contact with these men, he brought them closer into his fold.

The photographer, Frank Hurley, for example, always needed to feel that others saw him as one of the leaders of the group. If he felt slighted of the attention he thought he deserved, he would become aggressive and difficult. Hurley's need to be recognized earned him a place in Shackleton's tent, and the Boss consulted him on key decisions. This supported, in Hurley's mind, his own prominence among the ranks, and thus helped ensure his support.

Shackleton saw value in selecting certain other tent-mates as well. He bunked with the physicist, Reginald James, out of concern that his "withdrawn academic manner" would cause him to be teased by the other men. Shackleton did not want to expose one person to excessive ridicule for fear it could escalate into a full-blown altercation.

When Shackleton had to choose his crew for the open boat journey from Elephant Island to South Georgia Island, he was again mindful of allowing potential troublemakers unlimited access to the emotionally and physically worn-out crew. Shackleton felt that McNeish's skills as a carpenter could prove invaluable on a wooden boat, but he also wanted McNeish to accompany him for another reason: Shackleton was concerned that, left behind, McNeish could stir up discontent.

He also selected Vincent to make the trip. Because of Vincent's reputation as a bully, Shackleton thought better of leaving the seaman behind to create trouble for Frank Wild. Finally, Shackleton chose Crean, who was less of a team player and was also likely to create problems for the marooned castaways.

In retrospect, Shackleton's foresight and his willingness to deal directly with dissidents is rather astounding. When he needed to select a team for the most difficult challenge he had yet to face—the crossing to South Georgia—more than half of his crew consisted of potential troublemakers. Shackleton's willingness to maintain close relations with these questionable characters, however, undoubtedly mitigated the conflicts that occurred on Elephant Island, and it helped Wild with his formidable task of maintaining morale among those left behind.

Lessons for Leaders

In difficult leadership situations, we are often tempted to ignore or isolate individuals whose personalities rub us the wrong way or who have a knack for stirring up trouble. While this is an understandable reaction, it is the wrong one. It only creates space for further problems, and rejecting dissidents is ultimately detrimental to the organization. A more productive response—however counterintuitive it may seem—requires doing just the opposite:

> ➢ Identify those individuals or groups that may be undermining your leadership.
> ➢ Be proactive and keep troublemakers close by.
> ➢ Find ways to minimize the negative impact of their behaviors.
> ➢ Make sure these people are engaged, in some way, in the decision-making process.
> ➢ Treat everyone, including dissidents, with respect, even when they are antagonistic.
> ➢ Be willing to set limits, and make it clear that this works both ways. Inappropriate, rude, or bullying behavior cannot be tolerated.
> ➢ Avoid the temptation to denigrate malcontents and keep your personal opinions about people to yourself—and your closest advisers.

Leaders who are proactive in dealing with individuals who have the potential to be dissidents can avoid antagonistic relations further down the road. Henry Schacht, former CEO of Lucent Technologies, provides an example of how a leader can turn a potentially conflictive relationship into a collaborative one.

In 1995, AT&T Chairman Bob Allen announced that Schacht—former chairman and CEO of Cummins Engine Company—would become chairman and CEO of a new $20 billion communication systems and technology company, later known as Lucent Technologies. Richard McGinn, then CEO of AT&T's Network Systems Group, was to become president and COO of the new organization.[13]

McGinn, a highly capable executive with a strong track record, was a strong contender for the position of CEO. Schacht's appointment, therefore, came as a surprise. McGinn could have easily challenged Schacht's leadership. But Schacht went out of his way to reinforce the importance of McGinn's role and to send the message that he and McGinn would manage as equals.

Schacht made it a point to ensure the two men would be seen together constantly. Before the initial public offering, the two men led a thirty-city road show that emphasized the organization's depth of talent. At one point, *The New York Times* wanted a photograph of Schacht, the new chairman. Schacht insisted that McGinn be flown by helicopter from New Jersey so they could be photographed together. As a result of these efforts, what could have been a disaster turned into a complementary relationship. Together, they led the company in creating a new culture, a solid friendship, and an exciting new venture. McGinn is now Lucent's CEO.

Avoid Needless Power Struggles

In December 1915, more than a year after the *Endurance* crew had set sail from South Georgia, there was still no prospect of rescue and no end of the journey in sight. Shackleton could feel the morale of his men slipping. He had heard grumbling that, since the ship had been destroyed and they could not carry out their mission, the men would not be paid. Some began to believe that they were enduring these torturous conditions for nothing, and they worried for the safety of their family members at home who were depending on the income.

Shackleton believed that he had to act. He could not let his men continue to feel sorry for themselves and wallow in anger or frustration. He thus decided that they would make a second march across the ice toward land. On December 22, the party celebrated Christmas early, eating as much as they wanted to fortify themselves for the journey ahead, then they started out at four-thirty the next morning.

As before, two teams of fifteen men each pulled the boats and sledges weighing over 1,000 pounds. As in the previous march, they would sink to their knees in the soft, wet snow. Their progress was excruciatingly slow. They were averaging just two miles a day. Four days into their journey, McNeish, who was close to collapsing from the combined effects of exhaustion, starvation, and exposure to the elements, simply decided that he would no longer go on.

Worsley ordered McNeish to pick up his section of the rope and continue. McNeish refused, arguing the march was useless. Worsley, himself on the verge of exhaustion, called for Shackleton, who stood facing the angry and frustrated carpenter. McNeish argued that the march over the ice was not in their best interests because they would never be able to cover the distance they needed to reach their destination.

Shackleton stood quietly by while McNeish lashed out. The carpenter declared he did not have to obey any orders, because the ship's articles were not enforceable. He argued that he was no longer obligated to follow orders, since the articles he had signed were to serve "on board," and they were no longer aboard the *Endurance*.

With all of his men watching the first real challenge to the Boss's authority, Shackleton turned his back on McNeish and walked away. He knew that he could not reason with the carpenter, and did not want to waste energy on a pointless argument. Shackleton simply left the carpenter standing in the snow—giving him time to come to his senses.[14] After weighing his options, McNeish took his position at the rear of the sled when the expedition set out again. The one-man mutiny had been put down without further conflict.

Lessons for Leaders

It is vital to decide which battles are worth fighting and which are not. The battles worth fighting should be engaged with all available resources; those not central to your mission should be let go.

When a situation cannot be resolved immediately, you may, like Shackleton, choose to leave your "McNeish" standing in the snow until you can assess the situation realistically. It is better to wait until you are prepared than to respond in haste and further escalate the problem.

It is particularly important to avoid creating situations in which people feel trapped, causing them to escalate conflicts because they see no way out. The Roman general Scipio advised giving opponents a "Golden Bridge," an avenue of retreat, arguing that an enemy with no way out will fight with unprecedented ferocity.

Scipio's maxim applies to nonmilitary situations as well. A Golden Bridge resolved a business conflict among three colleagues—Tom, Elizabeth, and Patrick—who were at loggerheads over a dissolving partnership. Their hopes of maintaining a profitable business with strong friendship had not been realized and—after months of trying to revive the firm—it became clear that there was no chance of solving their differences.

Patrick, in particular, felt aggrieved and rejected. He responded by making financial claims that Tom and Elizabeth found unreasonable. The haggling continued, lawyers were called, and the careers of all three were stalled. Finally, Elizabeth came up with an idea.

All three had made an initial investment in the company, and the amount remaining in the partnership bank account included this investment, plus a small additional sum. Elizabeth proposed that the partners each withdraw their initial investment and that Patrick receive the remainder. Although the leftover money amounted to only a few hundred dollars, Patrick accepted the offer. The proposal provided a Golden Bridge, a way to end the stalemate. A needless power struggle was avoided and the three partners moved on with their lives.

Expedition Log

1. What are the norms about conflict in the culture of your organization? What is the level of openness? Do team members share their opinions openly and deal with problems directly, or do they raise conflict in oblique, indirect, or passive-aggressive ways?

2. What changes can you make that will allow anger to be dealt with productively and in small doses?

3. How many Mooses are there in your organization? Are there taboo topics that affect performance but are never discussed? Consider a Moose roundup, or some other proactive way of initiating a discussion about these off-limits topics.

4. What is your characteristic style of dealing with troublemakers, skeptics, and malcontents? Do you engage them or push them away? Is there a dissident you could "pull into your tent" and engage productively?

5. Are you, or others, engaged in any nonproductive power struggles? Is there anyone who is your "McNeish in the snow"? If so, how can you move your expedition forward without compromising your authority and position of leadership?

8

Lighten Up!

Strategy 8
Find something to celebrate and something to laugh about.

> The disappearance of the sun is apt to be a depressing event in the polar regions, where the long months of darkness involve mental as well as physical strain. But the *Endurance's* company refused to abandon their customary cheerfulness, and a concert in the evening made the Ritz a scene of noisy merriment in strange contrast with the cold, silent world that lay outside.[1]
>
> Ernest Shackleton

This strategy incorporates what is probably the most counterintuitive behavior of all the ten strategies for leading at *The Edge*. In stressful circumstances, when times are grim, celebration is usually the furthest thing from anyone's mind. Under survival conditions, laughter is an unnatural act, and in tough business situations, humor can seem frivolous, inappropriate, or out-of-touch.

Yet, under extreme pressure, the ability to lighten up, celebrate, and laugh can make all the difference. It can break a spiral of depression and stimulate creativity. It can enable people to step back and get psychological distance on their problems. It can cut through fear and tension. Finally, it can enable a team to refocus, reenergize, and surmount daunting obstacles.

This chapter shows how these behaviors influenced the outcome of the Shackleton saga and the course of other survival situations. It also illustrates how effective leaders have used these qualities to make their businesses successful. Above all, it makes the case that, at *The Edge*, celebration and humor are neither superfluous nor luxuries. They are imperatives.

Find Something to Celebrate

From the very beginning, Shackleton's expedition had a certain celebratory atmosphere that characterized the life of the group. It created an upbeat mood and a way of thinking about life that sustained the men through the grimmest of times.

This atmosphere of celebration contributed to the sense of cheerfulness and optimism, as described in Strategy 3, but it was more than simple cheerfulness. It reflected the complexity of Shackleton's leadership and his ability to be both deliberate and spontaneous in shaping the culture of the team.

Shackleton grasped any excuse—some rather far-fetched—in finding things to celebrate. On May 24, 1915, for example, they marked Empire Day, an occasion originally created as an opportunity to encourage patriotism among British children. To celebrate Empire Day, the crew of the *Endurance* sang songs in the Ritz, seizing the occasion to honor their native land.[2]

Later, while still aboard *Endurance*, Shackleton continued the festivities by calling for a "Dog Derby." In this twilight celebration, dogsled races stimulated merriment, laughter, and heavy betting involving chocolate and cigarettes.[3] The following week, on June 22, they celebrated Midwinter's Day. It was an occasion that gave the physicist, Reginald James, an opportunity to display his "witty and truly unintelligible" acting ability with a tongue-in-cheek "Dissertation on the Calorie" by Herr Prof. Von Schopenbaum.[4]

In those early days, when times were not so bad, celebration came easily. What is most impressive, however, is that the spirit of celebration continued throughout the darkest of days, when cheerful rituals could easily have turned to deep despair.

The day of December 5, 1915, marked one full year since the crew had left civilization. Their ship had been crushed two months earlier, and they had been carving out a harsh existence on the ice floes. According to the original plan, they would have been heading home by now, so this anniversary might have turned into a gloomy reminder of their predicament.

Shackleton, realizing the significance of the day and the potential for disappointment, decided to be proactive. Exemplifying the aphorism "If you can't fix it, feature it," the Boss declared a holiday to celebrate the anniversary of their departure from South Georgia. What could have been a day of depression turned, instead, into a day of celebration.[5]

Later, at Patience Camp, the living conditions continued to deteriorate. Food was in such short supply that discarded seal heads and flippers had to be dug from the ice in a desperate search for any last scrap of blubber. They lived hand-to-mouth, relying on the few penguins and seals that could be snared. All of the suet had been used, so any meat that was brought in had to be fried in fishy seal blubber.

These were not times that cried out for celebration. Yet Shackleton still found occasions for festivities:

> On Leap Year day, February 29 [1916], we held a special celebration, more to cheer the men up than for anything else. . . . The last of our cocoa was used today. Henceforth water, with an occasional drink of weak milk, is to be our only beverage.[6]

The living conditions of the expedition continued to worsen, but the commitment to celebration did not. By June 1916, the abandoned castaways were living in the desolate squalor of Elephant Island. Blackborow's foot, which had been frostbitten on the open boat journey, got progressively worse. It was clear that an amputation had to be performed to save his life, and Macklin and the other surgeon, James McIlroy, went about their business.

A blazing pile of penguin skins created enough warmth to vaporize the chloroform needed as an anesthetic. McIlroy removed the bandage from Blackborow's foot and systematically severed each of the gangrenous toes at the ball joint. At the end of the fifty-five-minute operation, the stowaway opened his eyes, smiled, and asked for a cigarette, which the surgeon rolled using a page from the *Encyclopaedia Britannica*.[7]

These were not the hopeful, fun-filled early days of the expedition. This was life at its harshest, most severe, and frightening limit. And yet, a week later, a second Midwinter's Day celebration was held. The occasion was marked with a concoction of nut pudding, biscuits, sledging rations, and powdered milk.

Amazingly, the castaways summoned up enough energy to put on a program of twenty-six different acts, including poetry and music. Although the members of the audience lay in their sleeping bags, the event was spirited. Not only did Hussey play the banjo, but James also sang a clever song about Frank Wild and their primitive living conditions.

The celebration ended with a toast to Shackleton and the crew of the *James Caird*, followed by the only available libation: "Gut Rot, 1916."[8] The concoction—made with stove alcohol, water, ginger, and sugar—was not Dom Perignon, but it served its purpose. They had celebrated together and broken the endless monotony of waiting for rescue. Shackleton's ability to use celebration and ceremony to boost team morale seemed to come naturally. It is surprising, though, that many leaders fail to understand the importance of ceremony—or conduct them so ineptly that spirit is diminished rather than enhanced.

The story of the *Karluk* provides numerous illustrations of failures in leadership. The sinking of the ship, for example, served as an occasion for Captain Bartlett to indulge himself in a unique and bizarre ceremony. Although the rest of the crew had abandoned the doomed vessel, Bartlett stayed aboard. He built a roaring fire in the galley stove and proceeded to play all the gramophone records aboard the ship, one by one. As each record was finished playing, he threw the disk into the galley fire . . . save one. He played Chopin's Funeral March, then set it aside for later.

When the end finally came and water reached the deck of the *Karluk*:

> Captain Bartlett placed the Funeral March on the Victrola. With the water running along the starboard side of the deck and pouring down the hatches, he waited at the rail until it came down level with the ice. Then he stepped off. . . . The Canadian Blue Ensign fluttered until it cut through the water. Captain Bartlett, deeply moved, stood right alongside her until she was gone.[9]

Watching the *Karluk* sink to the strains of Chopin's Funeral March undoubtedly served some need of Bartlett's. But imagine the effect of this lugubrious scene on the twenty-two men, one woman, sixteen dogs, and a cat that watched the funeral event. It was not a ceremony likely to build hope, confidence, and morale.

Lessons for Leaders

Effective leaders find ways of building celebration into the culture of their organizations. The annual "Vision Event" of Hartford Life provides an excellent example of how celebration can be used effectively in building organizational spirit and business success.

Hartford Life, one of the nation's largest life insurance groups, is now a market leader in annuities, mutual funds, retirement savings vehicles, group disability coverage, and life insurance. The company, based in Simsbury, Connecticut, enjoyed phenomenal growth in the 1990s, but it entered the decade as the twenty-third largest insurance company—a relatively minor player in a business category long dominated by Prudential, MetLife, Aetna, and other household names.

In 1991, Hartford Life's senior management team, led by CEO Lon Smith, crafted and adopted a vision statement that has served since then as a blueprint for cultural change and organizational growth. From that time on, the company has experienced a string of successes. Looking back on the journey, Smith noted in a letter to his employees:

> In 1991 . . . we had big thoughts of growing to be a major contender, of being a force within the financial services industry. . . . Since that time, we've grown to become the nation's fourth largest life insurer. There are lots of reasons for that. I believe our willingness to "go for the Vision" is one of them.[10]

Since 1992, the company (now the third largest life insurer) has held a series of annual events—each designed to celebrate the work that has been accomplished during the year and to recommit to the vision of the organization. These celebratory events have taken a number of forms, including the creation of a "vision quilt," outdoor team-building events, and company picnics. In an industry in which light-hearted events rarely come naturally, Smith and his team have made a commitment to celebration. These celebrations, combined with business vision, have produced noteworthy results.

Celebrations can be held on a smaller scale and still be effective. Amy Pizzarello, head of the American Express market research department, incorporates something called the MARTHA awards into her annual planning and midyear meetings. MARTHA (Market Researchers That Have Accomplished Something) awards are presented to employees who have accomplished something unique in their personal or professional lives over the prior six-month period.

The Dazzling Diva award was bestowed on an employee who had auditioned for her first leading role in an opera and got the part. The award took the form of a large sparkling star with her name on it for her dressing room door. The Life Savers award, including flowers and rolls of Life Savers candy, was given to an employee who frequently came to the rescue of her coworkers. Other awards took a similar tone.

None of these awards was particularly expensive, but they were obviously heartfelt, with elements of humor and deservedness. In addition, great care had obviously gone into their selection and preparation. Amy had personally created the Dazzling Diva star and—in the process—covered her home with sparkles, which she jokingly said had risked a domestic disturbance. It was clear that MARTHA awards, while simple, were thoughtful and personal. They meant something, and that was the point.

Find Something to Laugh About, Too

Shackleton and Wild set aside specific times for special celebrations, but humor, banter, and merriment were constants in the life of the expedition. Shackleton, in particular, went to great lengths to make sure that the mood of the group would be as lighthearted as possible under the circumstances.

In a dramatic gesture (described in fuller detail in Chapter 2), Shackleton threw gold sovereigns into the snow to emphasize the absolute necessity of ridding themselves of extra weight during their sledge journey. In a surprising move, however, the Boss went back to the wreckage of *Endurance* and retrieved Hussey's treasured "zither banjo." He presented the twelve-pound instrument to Hussey, who recalled the incident as follows:

> "It's rather heavy," I said dubiously. "Do you think we ought to take it?"
> "Yes, certainly," was the chief's prompt answer. "It's vital mental medicine, and we shall need it."[11]

Shackleton made the right decision, and the banjo contributed in important ways to the continued positive morale of the expedition. Although Hussey had a limited repertoire—six tunes to be exact—many nights were spent listening to the "cheery twang" of the banjo.

Hussey's music was supplemented by another favorite form of entertainment: good-natured banter. Captain Frank Worsley recalled:

> Hussey was a brilliant wit, and his keen repartee was one of the few joys left to us. Often we would combine to provoke him just for the pleasure of hearing his clever retorts, and invariably he would emerge the victor, no matter how

many of us tried to best him. On an ice-floe any little diversion is more welcome than people living in civilized conditions perhaps can imagine.[12]

Hussey was not the only one to lighten the atmosphere. First Officer Greenstreet was also noted for his ability to "fool around" for a laugh. And then there were the inevitable impersonations. Impersonations were one of the most encouraged forms of amusement. They had the effect of lightening the mood while, at the same time, alleviating tension and subsurface conflict. Some of the more annoying characteristics of crewmembers were often the focus of these short expositions.

Orde-Lees, for example, had a habit of being a little too anxious to please Shackleton. McIlroy, the surgeon, thus saw an opportunity to mimic an interaction between the two, and Orde-Lees described the impersonation in his diary:

> "Yes sir, oh yes certainly sir, sardines sir, yes sir here they are (dashes to pantry and back) and bread sir, oh yes sir, bread sir. . . ." (Another dash to pantry and much groveling effusion. . . .) "And may I black your boots sir," and so on.[13]

Banter and impersonations broke the monotony, but humor also had its place in sustaining the crew through the darkest crises. The loss of *Endurance* was one of the lowest, most demoralizing points in the journey. When the ship finally succumbed to the unbearable pressure of the ice, Shackleton ordered all hands onto the floe. As they were going over the side, Shackleton turned to Orde-Lees and said:

> "We've got it in the neck all right this time, haven't we?"
> "Well, no, I don't think so," [Orde-Lees] ventured. "You wouldn't have had anything to write a book about, if it hadn't been for this."
> "By Jove, I'm not so sure you aren't right," [Shackleton] remarked (at) which we both had a good laugh.[14]

The Toga Party

Humor is a consistently effective tool for dealing with adversity, and a Navy pilot related a more recent example. I had the opportunity to present the Shackleton story and the ten *Leading at the Edge* strategies to then–Secretary of the Navy John Dalton. The meeting, held at the Pentagon, was attended by a number of the Secretary's staff members, many of whom had their own personal experiences at the Survival Edge.

The discussion that followed my presentation was a stimulating one, and it expanded my understanding of the ten strategies. Afterward, a naval officer wearing pilot's wings approached me. He said that he had enjoyed the presentation and asked whether I had heard about the "toga party."

I remembered the toga party in the movie *Animal House,* with John Belushi. These were not the kinds of parties sanctioned by the Naval Academy, so I had no firsthand experience with such events. The officer's comment did, however, raise a vivid image of John Belushi hosting a fraternity toga party, wearing only a sheet and a mischievous smile. So I knew exactly what he was talking about, but just how it related to leadership was completely obscure.

It became clear, however, when he told me the story of *Alfa Foxtrot 586,* a Navy patrol plane that left Adak, Alaska, on October 26, 1978. The plane, a four-engine turboprop, had taken off with its crew of fifteen on a routine ocean-surveillance and antisubmarine mission. What was to be an uneventful flight turned into a crash landing at sea and a fight for survival. Their plight—desperate though it was—sheds light on leading at *The Edge.*

After my conversation at the Pentagon, I gathered every piece of information that I could about the crash. Although I found literally hundreds of pages of information about the incident, I was unable to make direct contact with any of the survivors. The information about this story comes from U.S. Navy incident reports; from written sources, including the Patrol Squadron Nine web page; and from the details related by other Navy pilots.[15]

> As the flight continued over the North Pacific, the weather worsened and winds increased. Of greater concern, however, was the performance of a propeller on the left wing of the aircraft. The engine was running erratically and was stopped, but the 1,200-pound propeller began to increase the speed of its rotation, from 103.5 percent of normal to 110 then 120, and finally 129.5—the maximum that could be recorded. The prop was on the verge of shearing from its mount and causing great damage. Had this happened, the inevitable outcome would have been a nonsurvivable crash and the death of all aboard.
>
> The pilot, Jerry Grigsby, climbed to slow the prop. At 1,100 feet, however, its speed was still much too high. Then,

without warning, the engine burst into flames. The runaway prop was out of control.

The flight engineer, Harold "Butch" Miller, was able to extinguish the blaze with fire-fighting compound, but the action depleted the limited supply of the compound. There were sure to be other outbreaks, and the situation was grim. They were now 800 miles from Adak, an impossible distance in their current state, and 337 miles from the Air Force station on the island of Shemya—still light-years away for the crippled aircraft.

Anticipating an explosion, Grigsby brought the plane down to 1,000 feet. Then the fire alarm went off again. Miller used the last of the fire-fighting compound to douse the blaze. Grigsby continued to descend, to 500 feet, and they limped toward Shemya.

Anticipating the worst, the crew donned life vests and survival suits. The fire alarms went off again, smoke streamed from the crippled engine, and Matthew Gibbons, the flight's tactical coordinator, radioed the plane's coordinates and added, "This is five eight six. Out."

With those final words, Grigsby landed the aircraft in the frigid twenty-five-foot swells of the North Pacific. As the plane hit, the right wing came off, fuel tanks ruptured, and the engines exploded in balls of steam. The fuselage cracked open and water flooded in, but the plane was down.

In the jarring crash, many crewmembers had been buried in debris and caught in the wreckage. But the radar man was able to launch two life rafts, one large and one small. Grigsby stayed on the aircraft, counting his crew, until he was certain that everyone had made it off. Then he swam for the large raft.

After repeated efforts, Grigsby failed to reach the raft, and he was lost in the swells. The pilot then tried for the second raft and was within twenty-five feet of it when those aboard threw him his last hope—a rope anchored with an emergency radio. It fell short by a few feet, and Grigsby disappeared from sight.

Four men huddled in the large raft, which was designed to carry twelve, while nine men jammed into the smaller raft, designed to carry seven. The small raft, with no tarpaulin cover, was awash with breaking waves from the freezing ocean. In their desperate attempt to bail with the boat's metallic survival blanket, an air valve was inadvertently opened.

The rafts drifted helplessly in the heavy seas while planes from Shemya searched for survivors. In the bitter cold and rain, the men—seasick and in a state of shock—began to lose their alertness and coordination. Finally, one airman in the seven-man boat realized that something was desperately wrong. The raft was deflating, and they were slowly sinking. This startling observation jarred the others from their near-comatose state, and they began a frantic search for the leak. Finally, the loose valve was discovered and closed.

As the hours went by, water entered the torn survival suit of Technician Gary Hemmer, and his eyes began to close. Master Chief Garland Shepard slapped Hemmer's helmet until he regained consciousness. James Brooner, a sonobuoy technician who had gone into the water in an effort to save Grigsby, slowly slid into the water sloshing around in the raft. Soon only his head was visible. Three others pulled him up, talked to him, slapped him, and shook him. But they were all at *The Edge* of death.

Then, in this grimmest of moments, the pivotal event occurred. Someone suggested they sing. And, slowly, the chant started: *To-ga . . . To-ga . . . To-ga . . . To-ga.* Somehow, from the foggy depths of despair, the comic image of John Belushi dressed in a sheet at a fraternity party had entered the consciousness of one of the survivors. Others joined in. The chant, feeble at first, grew in strength and rallied the survivors, just as Belushi had rallied his despondent fraternity brothers. This strange combination of humor and determination breathed a last element of life into the group, which was finally rescued by the Soviet fishing vessel *MYS Synyavin.*

This story of survival does not have a Hollywood ending. One crewmember went down with the aircraft, three others died of exposure, and the pilot Jerry Grigsby was lost at sea. He was later awarded the Distinguished Flying Cross. But the ten who survived the crash of *Alfa Foxtrot 586* owe their deliverance to perseverance, the support of their comrades, and—ironically—to the humorous spirit of the toga party.

Lessons for Leaders

Humor is one of the most effective leadership tools. The ability to use humor skillfully has served American presidents with political views as disparate as John Kennedy and Ronald Reagan. The absence of humor also undermined the effectiveness of Richard Nixon, who often appeared grim or mean-spirited.

The multipurpose nature of humor makes it a sort of leadership Swiss Army knife. Kidding that is truly good-natured—not hurtful—can strengthen interpersonal bonds. A joke can break the monotony of routine work, some of which is inherent in any job. Laughter can create a relaxed atmosphere and stimulate creativity. Humor, even dark humor, can cut through tension, fear, and anxiety.

Herb Kelleher, CEO of Southwest Airlines, is one leader who understands the power of humor in creating organizational success and bottom-line profitability. In *Nuts! Southwest Airlines' Crazy Recipe for Business and Personal Success,* authors Kevin and Jackie Freiberg outline Kelleher's formula.[16]

The playful attitude encouraged by the airline begins with casual clothing, or "fun ware," which is designed to engender a lighthearted perspective. Kelleher himself has appeared at meetings dressed as Elvis, General Patton, and Corporal Klinger from the "M*A*S*H" television show.

A tabloid-style internal publication titled *Southwest Airlines Plane Tails* contains stories of employees who have developed innovative solutions to problems, along with humorous, tongue-in-cheek articles. One piece, for example, discusses the nuances of eating Southwest Airlines Peanuts.

This sense of playfulness permeates the organization. It affects the way employees interact with both customers and one another. The "Southwest Way to a Sense of Humor" includes these guidelines:

> ➢ *Think funny.* Look for the flip side of situations, and make outrageous thoughts fun.
> ➢ *Adopt a playful attitude.* Stay open to silly or nonconformist thoughts and behaviors.
> ➢ *Be the first to laugh.* Try to be the first to find humor in stressful situations.
> ➢ *Laugh with, not at.* Promote healthy, constructive humor.
> ➢ *Laugh at yourself.* Take work seriously, but not yourself.

In reading this list, I was struck by how well these guidelines fit the norms of the Shackleton expedition. Almost a century later, they still work.

Expedition Log

1. Do you celebrate the major successes and achievements of your team?
2. Do you look for opportunities to celebrate the "small wins" as they occur?
3. How would you characterize the culture of your organization: grim and serious, or playful and spontaneous?
4. Do those you manage feel free to be themselves and to find humor in work situations? If not, what can be done to promote a relaxed atmosphere?
5. Do people joke with others in healthy, constructive ways?
6. When things go wrong, do you use humor to defuse tension?
7. Can you laugh at yourself?

9

Risk

Strategy 9
Be willing to take the Big Risk.

> . . . Shackleton was (paradoxically enough) an exceedingly cautious man. It may sound fantastic to call an Antarctic explorer of his caliber cautious, but I claim that it was true of him. He was brave, the bravest man I have seen, but he was never foolhardy. When necessary he would undertake the most dangerous things, and do so fearlessly; but always he would approach them in a thoughtful manner and perform them in the safest way. He was proud of his reputation for carefulness, and therefore, the nickname that he had won on his first expedition, that of "Cautious Jack," which tickled him immensely.[1]
>
> Frank A. Worsley

I recently presented my perspective on leading at *The Edge* to a group of senior executives in the insurance industry. These executives, many of whom were actuaries, raised a number of thoughtful questions about this strategy. Their business, one commented, was not one in which taking "the Big Risk" is viewed favorably.

Risk taking for its own sake, however, is not the subject of this chapter. Needless risk taking is a form of bravado that endangers organizational stability, or even lives. Clearly, there are times to stay the course, and there are situations in which risk should be minimized. Unfortunately, there are also times in which taking what appears to be a safe course is actually a dangerous move. This chapter explores both dimensions of risk.

Never Take an Unnecessary Chance

The very nature of Antarctic exploration involves risk. Nevertheless, Shackleton was incredibly disciplined in his ability to avoid taking unnecessary chances, and there are numerous examples of this restraint.

He severely disapproved of any carelessness that might tempt fate. Soon after the loss of *Endurance*, for example, Macklin and Greenstreet decided to combine seal hunting with a joy ride on a small floe. Poling along merrily, they were as happy as college students punting on the river. Then they sighted the Boss and, like "guilty schoolboys," promptly ended their excursion. When the two returned the camp, Shackleton's "awful look" made it clear that this was their last bit of reckless horseplay.

Shackleton's caution was tested again and again. By March 9, 1916, the crew on Patience Camp had drifted far enough north that the crew began to feel a slight movement caused by the swells of open water. The motion broke through the apathy that had set in among the crew, who were eager to launch the lifeboats at the earliest opportunity. Two days later, the pack opened up and a large stretch of open water appeared. They prepared to launch the boats, but the Boss hesitated. Something inside him signaled caution, and he gave the order to remain on the floe. He had been wise to trust his intuition as the ice closed soon after.[2]

The pressure to launch the boats continued to build. It peaked again on March 23, 1916, when the party sighted land—the northernmost point of Antarctica. The expedition had been drifting for five months of claustrophobic monotony, and the thought that they might escape the floe sent shock waves of excitement through the camp. Here was a chance to make a sledge journey that would put them on dry land.

Shackleton and Worsley climbed to the top of a hummock to assess the situation. They scanned the horizon with binoculars, and Worsley posed the question foremost in everyone's mind: Would they attempt to make it across the ice? Worsley describes what happened next:

> [The Boss] did not reply at once, and I could see by his ex-
> pression that he disliked having to say the word that would
> disappoint all of us. At length he said shortly: "No . . . I
> can't risk the danger of crossing ice that will be opening and
> closing rapidly under the influence of the tides and currents
> between us and the land. The boats might get crushed. We
> might get separated. Many things could happen. But if we
> keep on as we are for another hundred miles or so, we are
> bound to drift to open water, and then we will make for the
> nearest whaling station."[3]

Shackleton could not foresee the dangers that lay ahead. But he
was sure that, having safely brought the expedition 2,000 miles since
they were first trapped in the ice, he was not going to make an impetu-
ous move that would risk the expedition.

When a Risk Is Justified, Do Not Hesitate

The landing on Elephant Island had given the crew a brief respite, but
it was only a temporary sanctuary. Anyone searching for the crew of
the *Endurance* would expect them to be somewhere in the south of the
Weddell Sea, far from the expedition's current position, so there was
absolutely no hope of rescue from Elephant Island.

In addition to this grim fact, there was another more immediate
problem nagging at Shackleton: their food supply. Clark had managed
to add variety such as limpets to their menu, and Green, the cook,
continued to make hot meals, but the hard reality was that the food
supply would not last forever. Worsley recalled:

> . . . [T]he day dawned when Shackleton had to face the fact
> that he would not be able to feed his men through the win-
> ter. I remember that day. He asked me to walk with him to
> our usual lookout promontory, and there he confided to me
> his ever-growing anxiety. "Skipper," he said, "we shall have
> to make that boat journey, however risky it is. I am not
> going to let the men starve."[4]

This was not a time for wishful thinking about rescue, or for imag-
ining that the food supply would be sufficient to sustain the men. It
was a time for carefully calculating the odds, and for having the cour-

age to do what no one had ever done before: risk the 800-mile sail to South Georgia.

It is hardly possible to exaggerate the dangers involved in the boat journey, but Shackleton's logic in choosing this course was impeccable. Sailing in subfreezing temperatures across 800 miles of stormy ocean in an open boat was extremely hazardous, but he reasoned that the venture would add nothing to the risks of the men left on the island. First, there would be six fewer mouths to draw on the limited food supply at Elephant Island. Second, Shackleton planned to take only a small amount of rations—one month's provisions—for the crew of the *James Caird*. He knew that if they had not made South Georgia in one month, they were not going to make it at all.

The Boss balanced the odds and concluded:

> The risk was justified solely by our urgent need of assistance. The ocean south of Cape Horn in the middle of May is known to be the most tempestuous storm-swept area of water in the world. The weather then is unsettled, the skies are dull and overcast, and the gales are almost unceasing. We had to face these conditions in a small and weather-beaten boat, already strained by the work of the months that had passed.[5]

The lifeboat *James Caird*, only twenty-two feet, six inches long, was hardly built for such a voyage. The passage was one of extreme danger and hardship, a constant battle against the seas and the gale-force winds. Those men not on watch sought protection from the bitter cold, but there was no respite. Every part of the small vessel was soaked by the relentless waves.

Space was so cramped that Shackleton had to direct the movement of each man during watch changes to avoid collisions and bruises. Boulders that had been taken for ballast had to be moved constantly to trim the boat, a "weary and painful" task. Their clothes and reindeer-skin sleeping bags were always wet and, as the bags disintegrated, the reindeer hair contaminated their drinking water.

The *James Caird* was often in danger of swamping. The tiny boat took water with each cresting wave, and one man bailed furiously at all times. They were often forced to crawl forward on the decking to chip the ice that was weighting down the boat. Each effort meant a risk of life: If a man had gone over the side, he would have been lost forever.

The ice continued to accumulate and the boat became "more like a log than a boat." To regain buoyancy, they discarded everything not absolutely essential for survival, including spare oars and two of the wet frozen sleeping bags, each of which weighed some forty pounds.

By the sixth day of the journey, each man suffered from frostbite and showed blisters on his hands. They ate, treated their wounds, and prayed for better weather. Good weather meant more than relief from the cold. To navigate accurately, they needed to see the sun. The sky had been so cloudy that they had no way to fix their location.

On the seventh day, the sun eventually came out, and Worsley—hanging on the mainmast with his sextant—was finally able to get a shot at the sun and determine their position. The news was good: They had covered more than 380 miles and were almost halfway to South Georgia. Still, the emergence of the sun showed clearly how tiny the *James Caird* was in the vast ocean. Shackleton recalled:

> So low in the water were we that each succeeding swell cut off our view of the sky-line. We were a tiny speck in the vast vista of the sea. . . . For a moment the consciousness of the forces arrayed against us would be almost overwhelming. Then hope and confidence would rise again as our boat rose to a wave and tossed aside the crest in a sparkling shower. . . .[6]

On the tenth night, Worsley was so cramped from his turn at the helm that he could not straighten his body. He had to be dragged below and massaged until he could crawl into his sleeping bag.

The next day, Shackleton was at the tiller when he saw what he thought was a line of clear sky. As he called out the good news to the others, Shackleton realized he had not seen an opening in the sky. What he had seen was the foam on the crest of a wave—a wave larger than any he had seen in his life.

As Shackleton called out, "For God's sake, hold on!" the wave lifted the boat like a cork. The *James Caird*, half filled with water from the giant wave, was still afloat, but just barely. Fighting for their lives, the men bailed with anything that they could find. Slowly the boat regained its stability, but the voyage had almost ended in disaster.

If conditions had previously been severe, now they were horrible. The food and cooking stove were soaked, and drinking water was running low and was contaminated by salt. With dry mouths and swollen tongues, they strained for a sight of land. Finally, on May 8—fourteen days after their departure from Elephant Island—they sighted the dark cliffs of South Georgia.

They were desperate to land and find water, but the forbidding coast offered no safe haven. Waves broke over the rocky coast and splashed thirty and forty feet into the air. They had no choice but to stand off and search for a better landing point.

As dawn broke the next day, they found themselves being driven onto the shore, which was a sheer wall of rock. In the treacherous seas and hurricane-force winds, the *James Caird* was shipping water heavily. It was agonizing to have come this far and face disaster. Then fate turned. The wind shifted and freed them to maneuver. Shackleton recalled:

> . . . [J]ust when things looked their worst, they changed for the best. I have marveled often at the thin line that divides success from failure and the sudden turn that leads from apparently certain disaster to comparative safety.[7]

As the wind stopped, the pin that held the *Caird's* mast fell out. If the pin had given way earlier, during the hurricane, the mast would have "snapped like a carrot" and they would have been driven onto the rocks to a certain death. Once more, they searched for a landing point, tired to the point of apathy and dehydrated to the point of death from thirst. Their last water—strained through gauze to separate the liquid from reindeer hair—had long been used.

Finally, on May 10, they found a gap in the reef. Fighting shifting winds, they tacked again and again to hit the opening and, on their fifth try, navigated the narrow opening to the safety of the cove beyond. Shackleton sprang ashore with a line and held the *James Caird* against the outgoing waves. After narrowly escaping a twenty-foot fall to the rocks below, the Boss secured the line and the crew came ashore.

As they stood on the beach, they heard a gurgling sound and turned to see a freshwater stream. They fell to their knees and drank the ice-cold water. Safe at last, they had risked the Southern Ocean, and they had triumphed.

In retrospect, Shackleton's decision to leave the ephemeral safety of Elephant Island was the right one. He gambled and he won. But knowing that a risk is called for and actually taking it are two different things. My own experience in Vietnam brought that point home clearly, and one particular day forever shaped my perspective on the issue of risk. Although the events of that day are not happy ones, I will relate them now in the belief that there is significant value to the underlying lesson in the story.

Toward the end of my tour in Vietnam, I was the commanding officer of a Marine rifle company—an infantry unit of about 200 men.

My company, India Company, had been given the task of providing security for a convoy of forty vehicles traveling north from the Marine airstrip at Chu Lai to the base at Da Nang.

The distance, about fifty miles, was relatively short, but moving any distance along Route 1 was potentially treacherous. Appropriately named "Rough Riders," convoys traveling along the elevated road were much like moving ducks in an amusement-park shooting gallery. They followed a fixed, predictable route, and they were exposed and vulnerable to enemy fire at numerous points. In addition, much of the road's pavement had been destroyed, creating opportunities for the Viet Cong to plant mines and other explosive devices.

The convoy left Chu Lai early in the morning. Each truck was filled with either cargo or Marines from my company. I was in one of the lead trucks, surrounded by my radio operators and a forest of antennas. We sat on layers of sandbags placed as protection against explosions from mines. Their value was more psychological than real.

Included in the convoy were several armored vehicles, including a peculiar Marine contraption called the *Ontos*. The *Ontos*, from the Greek word for "thing," had a great deal of firepower but often broke down. In addition to this problem, the *Ontos* was armed with six recoilless rifles that, when fired, create a dangerous back-blast from the explosion. Nothing can be behind an *Ontos* in action.

We were escorted by a helicopter gunship that would provide immediate air cover. We also had the capability to call in "fast movers"—jet aircraft that could deliver additional air support in case of significant trouble. In theory, we had a lot of firepower that could balance the odds in case of an ambush.

Like so many days in Vietnam, things started to go wrong early. I had been given the wrong frequency for the gunship, which circled the convoy repeatedly trying to raise us on the radio. Unless we could communicate, the helicopter could not be used, so I had no choice but to stop the convoy until the problem was fixed.

Finally, the exasperated pilot landed the chopper so we could talk in person and straighten out the problem. The incident would have been just another annoyingly comical moment, but the delay had cost time. Time meant losing daylight, and getting caught out in the open at night meant losing the ability to use aircraft effectively—a situation I did not want to think about.

As the convoy moved north, there was another delay at the small town of Tam Ky. The Viet Cong had planted a large mine set to detonate when a very heavy load—such as a military truck or tank—went over it. An unfortunate Vietnamese farmer, in a small truck filled with heavy bags of rice, had detonated the mine. The farmer had been killed and his truck blocked the road until it could be removed.

Throughout the day there were delays at each point in the road where pavement had been destroyed. Each of these sections had to be swept by a combat engineer team using mine detectors. The team, led by Naval Academy classmate Bill Gleeson, used the most sophisticated detectors available to methodically examine every square inch of dirt for buried explosives. The engineers also went into the water to check for wires and explosives that might be planted in culverts. It was a tedious task, but it could not be rushed.

After several hours on the road, I received a radio message that a battalion of the North Vietnamese Army (NVA) was operating in the vicinity and was warned to be on the alert. Intelligence reports were frequently wrong, but the news raised my level of vigilance another notch. It meant that an ambush, if it occurred, would be a serious fire-fight with the NVA, not a limited skirmish with the Viet Cong.

With all these delays, it was getting to be late in the afternoon, and I was becoming more and more concerned about still being on the road when night fell. Still, there was no way of avoiding the time-consuming process of sweeping for mines. At one stretch of road, the driver of a lead truck refused to move forward—even after the road had been swept. Gleeson waved him across from the far side, but the driver pointed at himself and shook his head, "No." Unconvinced that the road was clear, the driver thought he was being used as a human mine detector. Gleeson walked back to the truck, flashed his signature smile, climbed in beside him and said, "Let's go!"

The convoy rolled forward and the lead trucks, including mine, passed safely. But as I looked back, a truck exploded in an inferno that instantly killed the two Marines aboard. A mine, fashioned from several hundred pounds of high explosives, had been buried so deep that it could not be detected. It apparently had been "command detonated" by a nearby enemy soldier who was trying to hit my truck marked with antennas, but had hesitated and hit a vehicle following behind. The delay cost lives and time. The burning truck had to be pushed off the road, and medevac helicopters brought in to take out the casualties.

We cleared the wreckage and the convoy moved on. As we passed through another small village, we were hit by sniper fire and lost another Marine. Another life, another delay, and it continued to get dark.

We finally began picking up speed and made it to a small village about twenty miles from Da Nang. The village sat at the entrance to a long bridge across one of the many rivers in the area. A large wooden gate at the entrance to the bridge controlled traffic movement.

The lead vehicles with the minesweeping team crossed the bridge, and my truck approached the gate. When we were about twenty-five yards away, the gate slammed shut. The village erupted with a series of explosions that was unlike anything I had ever experienced in Vietnam. Hundreds of tracers streaked across the road like strands of a fiery spider web.

As soon as the ambush was triggered, the *Ontos* ahead of my truck turned ninety degrees to return fire. This meant that the road ahead was now blocked by the back-blast from its six recoilless rifles and by the closed gate. We were now caught in the withering fire of the NVA battalion, armed with mortars, rockets, automatic weapons, recoilless rifles, and other heavy weapons. The closed gate and the back-blast had stopped the convoy; the trucks were fixed targets. Marines piled out of the trucks to take cover and return fire.

The sustained din of explosions and small-arms fire was so great that it was impossible to hear someone shouting only a few feet away. I tried to raise the rear of the column on the radio, but could hear nothing but the thumping of the .50 caliber machine gun mounted on my truck. As I crouched by my radioman trying to decide what to do next, I came to the sudden, chilling realization that we were in the killing zone.

Every ambush is carefully designed with an area of entrapment appropriately called the "killing zone"—and we were in it. The NVA had driven the civilians out of their homes, and the entire village was now a free-fire zone designed for death. If we stayed where we were, we would all die.

I should have realized this sooner. The immediate action in an ambush situation is to move forward, no matter what. But the blocking of the road by the closed gate and the back-blast of the *Ontos* had taken me by surprise. In addition, I am sure there was a part of me that wanted to engage, not run, but this was not a time to fight.

I got the Marines back onto the trucks and we broke through the gate. As we approached the bridge, the NVA troops began firing at my truck with a recoilless rifle. If they had hit my lead vehicle, every other truck would have been stopped on the bridge and the situation would have been hopeless.

Then the firing from the recoilless rifle stopped abruptly. I later learned that Gleeson, whose engineer team had made it safely across the river, had risked his life to come back and silence the weapon with a grenade launcher. We moved onto the bridge and were now fully exposed to enemy fire.

Tracers were everywhere, and it seemed impossible that the convoy could make it across the full length of the bridge. There was no choice, however, but to keep moving. As the lead trucks rolled onto the bridge, the rear of the convoy was heavily engaged. The NVA troops were attacking with fixed bayonets prepared for close combat. The last truck in the convoy was on fire, and its wounded driver was rescued only through the courageous efforts of one of my men. He ran back to the truck, threw the driver over his shoulder and—firing an M-60 machine gun from his hip—carried the driver to safety.

When the convoy reached the far side of the river, we regrouped. Every vehicle was riddled with bullet holes, and two had been destroyed. There were wounded, but no one had been killed. As I look back, it still seems unbelievable that the company survived the ambush without loss of life. We reached Da Nang late that night.

I have since thought a great deal about that day. There was great risk for everyone in driving across the open bridge and being directly exposed to the full force of the ambush. The greater risk, though, was standing in place, taking what cover could be found and eventually— inevitably—running out of ammunition and being overrun. In the killing zone, there is only one course of action: *Move, move, move.*

Lessons for Leaders

Henry David Thoreau once noted that "a man sits as many risks as he runs." There are times when doing nothing, or making a "safe choice," actually entails greater risks than a bold gamble. Shackleton could have avoided sailing 800 miles across the Scotia Sea, and it is possible that, by some miracle, the expedition would have been rescued. It is far more likely, however, that they would have all suffered slow starvation on Elephant Island.

The situation Shackleton faced was analogous to being caught in the killing zone of an ambush. In both cases, the crucial leadership decision is whether to stay in a deteriorating situation or risk greater immediate danger to reach a position of ultimate safety. Under these circumstances the decision that appears to be the safe choice is often the one that carries with it the greatest risk.

These life-and-death situations, while extreme, are metaphorically similar to those faced by leaders in a number of adverse business situations. In their book *The Profit Zone,* for example, Adrian Slywotzky and David Morrison point out that information technology, global competition, and business design have combined with other forces to create changes in the old economic order. As a result of these changes, market share and volume growth no longer guarantee business success. Yet many managers cling to the illusion of the security they provide. In doing so, they stay pinned down in the "no-profit zone":

> No-profit zones are the black holes of the business universe. In a physical black hole, light waves go in, but never come back out. In an economic black hole, investment dollars go in, but the profit dollars never come back out.[8]

A business that stays caught in the no-profit zone will, like a military unit in the killing zone, meet with disaster. Getting out of the zone requires, first, recognizing the danger and, second, taking the risk of doing things differently—of reinventing the business.

There are some situations in which the economic danger is difficult to ignore. Egghead.com, for example, made its name as one of the first software chain stores. Faced with mounting losses, the firm needed to do something to turn the tide. Egghead chose to close completely its bricks-and-mortar operations and focus entirely on the Internet.

The short-term results of this decision have been increasing revenues, increased gross margins, and narrower losses than anticipated by analysts. The long-term results of this decision have yet to be seen, but Chairman and Chief Executive George Orban understood the company's vulnerability and took the risk.

Under these conditions—a losing situation with little hope of a turnaround—it makes sense to take major risks because there is little real alternative. In other instances, risk aversion may not result in disaster, but neither does it create change. Risk takers make things happen.

Randy MacDonald, for example, has been unusually effective in using his staff role proactively to lead many of the transformations that have occurred at GTE. MacDonald, now senior vice president for human resources, first joined GTE in late 1983. I worked with MacDonald on one of his first initiatives—an employee-opinion survey—and have since observed his willingness to take risks in order to promote change.

MacDonald's ability to take on tough issues has influenced GTE's internal operations, but he has also had a wider impact. He was asked, for example, to serve on the President's Advisory Commission on Health Care. The commission was composed of a diverse group of academics, business people, lawyers, union leaders, and representatives from the Clinton administration. After extended debates over a number of controversial issues, the commission finally delivered its report.

MacDonald was pleased with the report because he felt that it contained a Patient's Bill of Rights that was fair and balanced. The day after the report was submitted, however, and an hour before President Clinton's press conference on healthcare, a concerned staff member came in with an announcement: Clinton was going to propose legislation to enact the Patient's Bill of Rights.

MacDonald and others in the company felt that legislation was unnecessary, however, and that voluntary compliance was the preferred course, so this news came as an unpleasant surprise. MacDonald thought for a second and then made a decision:

> We're going to have to preempt the President. Let's put together a press release right now, and we'll announce it prior to the President's press conference. We'll give the President a heads-up that GTE is going to comply voluntarily with the Patient's Bill of Rights. GTE will also lead the effort to enlist big business to comply voluntarily.

Many staff members were taken aback at this bold move. Government and public affairs people proposed calling Chuck Lee, the CEO of GTE, to get his approval. Less than an hour remained before the President's press conference and there was no way of contacting Lee, but MacDonald was not dissuaded. They wrote the press release and called the White House to tell the President's staff what GTE planned to do.

The President was delighted. At the press conference, he congratulated MacDonald and GTE for their leadership on healthcare. MacDonald knew, though, that not everyone would be as pleased. Later, Chuck Lee was challenged by other CEOs who resisted the Patient's Bill of Rights. When MacDonald explained his rationale, Lee responded, "Randy, if you think it's the right way to go, I'm behind you 100 percent." MacDonald's ability to be decisive, and to take a major risk, was facilitated by the knowledge that Lee supported and trusted him.[9]

David Pottruck, co-CEO of the brokerage firm of Charles Schwab, is another leader who was willing to take a risk. In 1996, Pottruck established e-Schwab as an online brokerage arm that offered customers trades for $29.95 rather than Schwab's regular $65-per-trade fee. Rather than maintain this awkward two-tiered pricing structure, Pottruck decided to make all trades $29.95, despite the risk to company revenues and profits. Essentially, there would no longer be a difference between the traditional brokerage and the online brokerage.

When the price cut took effect in January 1998, Schwab's stock lost almost a third of its value. However, it would only be a short-term loss. Since the price cut, the number of new accounts has soared, the stock has recovered, assets under management have increased dramatically, and the firm has earned a 42 percent market share in the online brokerage market.

To communicate this dramatic change to the firm, Pottruck staged an event he called "Crossing the Chasm." At this event Pottruck and his top managers walked across the Golden Gate Bridge to symbolize leaving one business model behind and establishing a new one.

Rather than remaining entrenched in the firm's established position, Pottruck risked losing short-term revenue and profits for long-term gains. Pottruck stated: "You can't steal second with one foot on first."[10]

Clearly, leaders at *The Edge* need to be comfortable with the discomfort of risk. Unnecessary risks should be avoided, but there are times for bold moves. Understand the risks you face and evaluate them carefully. Then balance risk and return, and have the courage to step up to those calculated risks that are worth taking.

Expedition Log

1. Think about a risk you might take to improve the effectiveness or profitability of your organization. Using the Risk Assessment Matrix (Figure 9-1), list the best- and worst-case outcomes you anticipate. What does this analysis tell you about whether or not to take the risk?
2. Is your assessment of the risks involved consistent with the views of others on your team?
3. If you are anticipating taking a significant risk, have you developed a plan for communicating this risk to others? Have you made a compelling, logical case that will facilitate understanding and commitment?
4. Is there a risk you might take to improve your own effectiveness as a leader? Use the Risk Assessment Matrix again, writing out the best- and worst-case outcomes, to analyze this opportunity.

Figure 9-1. Risk Assessment Matrix.

	Best Case	Worst Case
Do It! Take the Risk		
Don't Do It! Don't Take the Risk		

10

Tenacious Creativity

Strategy 10
Never give up—there's always another move.

> Without a sea anchor, the boat bobbed and squirmed and shipped
> plenty of green water. The compass glass was broken, but repaired
> with sticking plaster from the medicine chest.[1]
>
> Frank A. Worsley

Finding creative solutions to daunting problems is a difficult task under the best of circumstances. It is even more challenging at *The Edge*. Fear, physical exhaustion, and psychological weariness are integral parts of the journey faced by those at the limits of survival—or by organizations striving to achieve the highest possible levels of performance. Yet it is precisely in these stressful situations that the ability to solve problems becomes most critical and that the need for innovation is the greatest. This chapter explores tactics for approaching this formidable challenge.

Encourage Relentless Creativity at *The Edge*

The survival accounts in this book have emphasized teamwork under adversity. Self-leadership, however, is an important element in leading

139

others, and there are numerous accounts of individuals who have demonstrated exceptional resourcefulness. One of the most colorful stories I have encountered involved a Texan who was bitten by a poisonous coral snake. He saved himself by biting off the snake's head, slitting its body lengthwise, and using the skin for a tourniquet until help arrived.

Less bizarre than the coral snake story, the adventure of Steven Callahan is an individual journey that exemplifies tenacious creativity in the face of enormous challenge. Callahan was sailing his small sloop, the *Napoleon Solo*, from the Canary Islands bound for the Caribbean when the boat sank during a heavy gale. Apparently rammed by a whale, the *Solo* went under in a matter of minutes. Callahan escaped in a small inflatable raft, the *Rubber Ducky III*, and embarked on a remarkable 1,800-mile journey that lasted seventy-six days.

Each day of the ordeal that followed was a continuing fight for survival. The solar stills intended to produce freshwater malfunctioned. Sharks attacked the small, five-and-a-half-foot raft, rubbing their backs against the floor and biting at the ballast pockets underneath. Ship after ship—nine in all—passed by without seeing the sailor in distress.

Short of water and slowly starving to death, Callahan finally managed to spear a triggerfish, and its nourishment brought him back to life. His equipment continued to deteriorate, however, and waves crashed into the small craft. Every day was a delicate balancing act:

> I must work harder and longer each day to weave a world in which I can live. Survival is the play and I want the leading role. The script sounds simple enough: hang on, ration food and water, fish, and tend the still. But each little nuance of my role takes on profound significance. If I keep watch too closely, I will tire and be no good for fishing, tending the still, or other essential tasks. Yet at every moment that I don't have my eyes on the horizon is a moment when a ship may pass me. If I use both stills now, I may be able to quench my thirst and be in better shape for keeping watch and doing jobs, but if they both wear out I will die of thirst. . . . It is a constant struggle to keep control, self-discipline, to maintain a course of action that will best ensure survival, because I can't be sure what the course is . . . all I can tell myself is, "You're doing the best you can."[2]

On day twenty-three, Callahan lost the power strap to his speargun while attempting to capture a dorado, a powerful fish that reaches sixty pounds. This one, skewered in the tail, thrashed through the water dragging the raft until it finally broke free.

The speargun was Callahan's only means of gathering food and was thus essential to his survival. Lashing the arrow to the shaft with codline, he created a jury-rigged weapon now powered only by his arms. This new limitation demanded what seemed like endless, motionless waiting—like "an ancient bronze statue of a bowless archer"—until his prey reappeared.

Lacking sugars, starches, and vitamins, Callahan's body withered. Saltwater sores began as small boils and soon burst, leaving dozens of open sores. Remarkably, he forced himself to perform yoga exercises in the early morning, at dusk, and at night. The routine was slow and painful: It took an hour and a half to do what could normally be accomplished in a half-hour. Through sheer force of will, however, he did what he could to maintain his strength.

After forty days at sea, Callahan noted ironically that he had reached the maximum amount of time that his raft was guaranteed by the manufacturer. Nevertheless, he had cause for celebration. Callahan estimated that he had, by that time, drifted more than halfway toward the Caribbean. He had also managed to seal the leaking distillation stills and—by acting as a "human bellows"—to keep them inflated. He had also improved his rainwater collection system. Callahan used the awl of his knife—a Cub Scout model he had found when he was twelve—to bore holes in a Tupperware box he mounted on top of the raft.

His situation was momentarily stabilized, but disaster struck again on day forty-three. A speared dorado ran the sharp tip of the spear into the lower tube of the raft, creating a gaping hole four inches long. Huge air bubbles rushed through the hole until the tube was completely deflated. The *Rubber Ducky*, now kept afloat only by her top tube, floated a mere three inches above the water.

Callahan's life now depended on repairing the lower tube. If he failed, he would not be able to spear fish, and even if he caught them, he could not dry them for food. Sleep would be impossible, and his legs would hang down as the lowest point on the craft. Harassing sharks would now attack his legs rather than the ballast tubes.

The plugs from the raft repair kit were useless—they were much too small. Thinking quickly, Callahan looked at the gaping hole in the raft as if it were an open mouth. Into the mouth he stuffed a "tongue" made of part of a foam cushion salvaged from the *Solo*. Holding the torn edges of the raft, he wrapped light line around the foam until he had created a seal.

This first effort was only a momentary success. Fifteen minutes after it was inflated, the tube was flat again. Callahan tried for five hours to fill the gaps in the seal, but it was still leaking badly. He calculated that 3,000 pumps a day would be required to keep the raft afloat. That amounted to about two hours of strenuous exercise—far more than he could manage.

For eight days, Callahan tried to patch the leak. It had to be repaired if he were to survive. As calmly as possible, he thought the problem through:

> You've got to come up with something. . . . Go back. Identify the problem . . . lashings working off. I have to keep them on. What equipment have I got? Space blanket, flare gun, useless lighter, plastic bag. . . . What else have I got? First aid kit, bandages, scissors, twine, and line. And the stuff I've already used—spoon, fork, radar refl . . . The fork! Of course, why you stupid bloody idiot! "It's the fork!"[3]

Energized by the hope that the fork would provide the answer, Callahan lay awake all night planning the repair. When morning came, he carefully broke the tines off the fork and inserted the fork handle through the foam tongue. Then he rewrapped the plug with lines of various sizes.

In his weakened condition, Callahan was forced to rest between each stage of the operation. It was mid-afternoon before the repair was completed and he could begin pumping. What would normally have been a five-minute job took a half-hour. After the exhausting work of pumping, the tube finally inflated, but not for long: In an hour and a half, the air was gone.

Depressed but determined, Callahan tried once more. Tightening the tourniquet and adding a second, he again painfully inflated the bottom tube. This time it worked:

> *Ducky* gorges on air, picks herself up out of the water, and drifts forward again like a lily pad cut free from its roots. . . . Twelve glorious hours pass before *Ducky* needs another feeding. . . . My body hungers, thirsts, and is in constant pain. But I feel great! I have finally succeeded![4]

The raft continued to drift—slowly, but inexorably—westward toward the Caribbean. Each day presented new problems and renewed demands for improvisation. Callahan devised a water collection cape from part of his space blanket. He scraped the sticky gum from the back of repair tape to create a goop that would plug a hole in the solar still. He lashed three pencils together to make a "low budget" sextant that allowed him to determine his latitude.

Sharks continued to harass the boat, and replenishing his food supply was a daily challenge. His spear, damaged by the thrashing of the dorados, needed constant repair. During one ferocious battle, a fish unscrewed the point and swam away.

Callahan repaired the tip with a thin knife from a Boy Scout utensil kit made of flat stainless steel. But the tip bent too easily, so he contrived a new spear tip by lashing the butter knife together with another small knife he had salvaged from the *Solo*. Both were weak, but together they provided enough strength to spear a fish when thrust at just the right angle.

The restricted diet and exposure continued to take their toll on him, but Callahan's creativity enabled him to adjust to his surroundings:

> By now the habitat in which I live, Duckyville, has become a neighborly suburb. The fish and I are so familiar I can chat with them individually . . . I recognize a dorado's nudge, a trigger's peck, or a shark's scrape the way you recognize different neighbors' knocks on the back door. Often I know which individual fish is whacking the raft with its tail or butting it with its head . . .[5]

On day seventy-five of the journey, Callahan sighted a soft glow of light, first to the south, then to the north. Then a beam of light swept the horizon—a lighthouse! Dancing up and down in the small confines of the raft, he hugged an invisible companion, shouting, "Land! Land ho!"

On the following day, a small white boat carrying three astounded fishermen sighted the *Rubber Ducky III*. After being hauled on board the rescue craft, Callahan calmly opened his water tins and drank five pints of hoarded water. He was soon safe ashore on the island of Marie Galante, near Guadeloupe. Through determination, creativity, and force of will, he became the only person in history to have survived more than a month at sea in an inflatable raft.

Although Shackleton's journey was of longer duration than Callahan's, the crew of *Endurance* had an advantage: Its members were able to draw from each other. This support and creativity enabled them to persist when, individually, each might have given up. The story of the

Imperial Trans-Antarctic expedition is replete with examples of tenacity, and it is impossible to look back over the journey and not be impressed by the remarkable resilience and dogged perseverance of the crew.

At each critical point in the journey, the crew could have given up—when *Endurance* was crushed; when the two sledge marches failed; when they found themselves marooned on Elephant Island; when they faced the glaciers of South Georgia; and when repeated attempts to rescue the castaways had failed. Each time, however, the party persisted and its members eventually found their way to safety.

The expedition's ability to reach safety was due to more than simple persistence. The success of Shackleton's crew also depended on the ability to stand in the face of death and think creatively about potential solutions. Interestingly, many of these out-of-the-box ideas came from the photographer, Frank Hurley, and the carpenter, McNeish, both of whom Shackleton had labeled as potential troublemakers.

As Shackleton contemplated taking the fragile *James Caird* through the roaring waves and gale-force winds of the Drake Passage, he called on McNeish to make the boat more seaworthy. McNeish fashioned a makeshift decking of canvas, lids of cases for equipment and supplies, and four sled runners that had been saved for overland travel.

The canvas was frozen stiff and had to be thawed out over the blubber stove before it could be sewn, nailed, and screwed into position. The nails were salvaged from packing cases, another improvisation. They were a bit short, but they did the job. Although the result was not pretty, the *James Caird* could never have survived the voyage without it.

Another invaluable tool was the bilge pump that Hurley had made from the Flinders bar used to adjust the ship's compass. This iron cylinder, moving in a brass tube, was exactly what was needed to create a pumping action, but no one—other than Hurley—saw the connection.[6]

It was not surprising that Hurley was the one to come up with the idea. He was an experienced metal worker, but he also had a record of ingenuity. He had earlier, for example, constructed a superb camp stove out of the ash chute from the wreckage of *Endurance*. Since most of his tools had been lost, he had chipped the quarter-inch steel with a blunt chisel.[7]

As the *James Caird* made its way through heavy seas, the compass glass was broken. Because the instrument was critical for navigation, the loss of this essential navigational tool was potentially devastating. The problem was solved, however, with sticking plaster from the medicine chest.

The crew responded with creativity in the face of adversity

throughout the remainder of the journey. After the *Caird* had arrived safely at South Georgia, Shackleton and his crew were still some 150 miles by sea from the safety of the whaling station at Stromness. Because of the condition of the boat, and the weakened state of several of the men, there was little alternative but to attempt an overland crossing of the island.

Shackleton believed that they could shorten the journey by sailing further up bay, but the *Caird* had lost its rudder in the surf. So they contrived another rudder with an oar that had survived the passage. As they launched the *James Caird* once more, the lost rudder miraculously appeared floating in the water—a sign they all took as a good omen.

When the men reached their point of departure for the overland journey, they had to contend with the fact that they were wholly unprepared for a climbing expedition. Once again, McNeish's inventiveness came in handy. The carpenter removed screws from the *Caird* and put eight in each boot, point down. The makeshift crampons were especially important for Shackleton. With characteristic generosity, he had given away his heavy Burberry boots and was now wearing a light leather pair in poor condition. Shackleton's rule, as cited by Worsley, was "that deprivation should be felt by himself before anyone else."[8]

Shackleton, Worsley, and Crean began the assault of South Georgia on Friday, May 19, 1916, at 3:00 A.M. To minimize the pain of separation from the others, the crossing party left quickly and moved out with a minimum of equipment: two compasses, fifty feet of rope, and a carpenter's adze that would have to substitute for an ice axe. The only map they had was incomplete and showed no details of the mountains.

Traveling by moonlight, they sloshed through knee-deep snow, skirting precipices that fell hundreds of feet into blackness. The terrain was confusing in the darkness, and they often had to backtrack. Retracing their steps was exhausting and demoralizing.

At one point, they encountered a deep pit in the ice, as though made by a huge meteorite. In the fog, each feared the other had fallen into the gaping hole. Thereafter, they roped themselves together to ward off such a tragedy.

Meals were eaten while perched precariously in the snow, each man taking turns using his body to shield the Primus stove and prevent it from blowing out. When the rations were warm, they took turns scooping out a spoonful of the life-giving food. The good-natured banter that had become so much a part of the life of the expedition continued: Shackleton accused Crean of having a bigger spoon, and Crean accused Worsley of having a bigger mouth.

As the journey continued, the weary team explored one pass after another, never knowing quite what was on the other side until they reached the summit. Each time, they found themselves blocked by impassable chasms and were forced to retreat over hard-won terrain. These return trips, made in bitter cold, were horribly discouraging. Having unsuccessfully attempted to negotiate three passes, only one more remained. As they struggled to this fourth and last pass, heavy fog rolled in from the sea. It obscured everything around them and was so heavy that the climbers had difficulty seeing each other.

Their position was truly desperate. As they sat perched at the top of the fourth pass, some 4,500 feet high on the glacier, fog had cut off their retreat, and darkness cloaked the way forward. It was a steep descent, but how steep? If they waited for moonlight, they would freeze to death. Even with light, the tedious process of cutting steps with the adze would still take too long. It had taken them a half-hour to descend a hundred yards, and they had thousands of feet to go.

They needed a creative solution, a way out. Sitting on a large step he had cut out on the mountain, Shackleton thought for a moment and then said:

> I've got an idea. We must go on, no matter what is below. To try to do it this way is hopeless. We can't cut steps down thousands of feet. . . . It's a devil of a risk, but we've got to take it. We'll slide.[9]

The prospect of sliding down the steep slope into uncertainty was indeed daunting. Anything that lay in their path—a rock, a crevasse, anything at all—would have meant the end. Yet this was the only hope for them, and for their shipmates waiting on Elephant Island. Worsley recalled thinking that "if we were killed, at least we had done everything in our power to bring help to our shipmates." Then he recounted what happened next:

> We each coiled our share of the rope until it made a pad on which we could sit to make our glissade from the mountaintop. We hurried as much as possible, being anxious to get through the ordeal. Shackleton sat on the large step he had carved, and I sat behind him, straddled my legs round him and clasped him round the neck. Crean did the same with me, so that we were locked together as one man. Then Shackleton kicked off.
>
> We seemed to shoot into space. For a moment my hair fairly stood on end. Then quite suddenly I felt a glow, and

know that I was grinning! I was actually enjoying it. It was most exhilarating. We were shooting down the side of an almost precipitous mountain at nearly a mile a minute. I yelled with excitement, and found that Shackleton and Crean were yelling too . . . To hell with the rocks![10]

Whether Shackleton and Crean shared Worsley's excitement, or whether they were yelling out of sheer terror, is not entirely clear. When they reached the bottom of the steep slope, they all shook hands and the Boss remarked, "It's not good to do that kind of thing too often."

Nevertheless, they had successfully tobogganed some 1,500 feet down the mountain without crashing into a rock or creating an avalanche. The slide, which had taken about three minutes, provided a creative alternative to freezing to death on the mountain. And it embodied the spirit of Strategy 9 (Be willing to take the Big Risk) and Strategy 10 (Never give up—there's always another move).

This was not, however, the last time they would need to be creative on the journey across South Georgia. As they neared the whaling station, the trio once more found itself in a precarious position on a nearly vertical ice precipice. Again, they attempted to cut steps with the adze, and again the process was too slow. The threat of a blizzard loomed large, and had they been exposed to gale-force winds on the open mountain, they would have been carried into the void.

In this untenable position, able neither to walk nor crawl, Shackleton made a discovery: The slippery ice was, in fact, covering a layer of snow that had been deposited by the winds. As Shackleton negotiated the descent, the possibility occurred to him the heel of his boot could be used to smash through the ice crust, thereby forming a small step. He tried it, and it worked! The others followed suit, and the three weary climbers descended the mountain, literally walking on their backs!

With the factories and ships of the whaling station in sight, the exhausted travelers shouted and waved, but they were much too far away to be heard. As they stumbled onward, one last obstacle emerged: A glacial waterfall blocked their path. With nothing to secure the rope, Worsley held the line fast while Shackleton and Crean slid down the waterfall. Wedging the frayed rope into the rocks and holding his breath, Worsley followed. The rope was left dangling in the waterfall.

At three o'clock in the afternoon of May 20, 1916, the three exhausted explorers reached the whaling station at Stromness. Halting only to eat, and with no map to guide them, they had crossed the uncharted glaciers of South Georgia in thirty-six hours.

The men walked up to the station manager, Thoralf Sørlle, who stared at the disheveled trio with disbelief. Sørlle, who knew Shackleton as a friend, found him unrecognizable. "Don't you know me?" Shackleton asked. "I know your voice," the station manager replied. "My name is Shackleton," the Boss responded.[11]

It is said that Sørlle turned away with tears in his eyes. And at that, the three grimy, bearded "ruffians" were welcomed inside to food, hot baths, and clean clothes. Their heroic journey across South Georgia had saved their shipmates. It remains a tribute to unremitting effort— and to tenacious creativity at *The Edge*.

Lessons for Leaders

Chapter 3 stressed the importance of maintaining an optimistic attitude when leading organizations in challenging situations. But having an optimistic outlook does not mean creating rosy, unrealistic expectations of smooth sailing. Optimism at *The Edge* means believing that somehow, someway, the team will succeed—in the long run. In the short run, however, problems are inevitable.

It is somewhat paradoxical that, in everyday life, we are seldom surprised when things go wrong. Keys are lost, cars do not start, people forget appointments, and computers crash. But when organizations are at *The Edge*, these expectations can change. I have seen leaders become furious at the small problems and "normal accidents" that inevitably occur when people and machines are stretched to the limits.

Rather than expecting things to go right, successful leaders under these conditions should be prepared for things to go wrong. In fact, when at *The Edge*, a realistic expectation is that things will go wrong with greater frequency and magnitude than ever before. Once this reality is accepted, daunting problems become a normal part of the journey. Then the leadership challenge becomes one of mobilizing the collective creativity of the team to find a solution.

Scott McNealy, CEO of Sun Microsystems, Inc., typifies this approach.[12] McNealy has always been an iconoclast. Rather than being confined by conventional wisdom, he has consistently chosen to steer his own course. According to industry analyst Laura Conigliaro of Goldman, Sachs & Co., "there have been times when Sun seemed way out of sync, . . . yet two years or three years later, we see the rest of the industry moving in their direction."

McNealy has continually reinvented Sun around his vision. From the start, Sun's workstations had built-in networking capabilities. The company introduced Java, a common language for Internet programs that will run on any type of device. Sun also designed Jini, a set of software tools intended to simplify the installation of new devices on a network. The firm's vision expanded to provide all the hardware and software needed to create what McNealy calls Internet "webtone," the equivalent of the telecommunications network's dialtone.

Facing crushing competition from such companies as Microsoft and Intel, Sun has continually redefined itself under McNealy and been able to survive in the rapidly changing world it helped to create. According to Charles Fitzgerald, a Microsoft group product manager quoted in *Business Week*, "Sun appears to have nine lives. . . ."

Tenacious creativity such as that displayed by McNealy demands flexibility, and it requires recognizing what works and what doesn't. When a strategy fails, acknowledge it and find another one. When the obvious moves are exhausted, keep looking for new ones. Do not dismiss any idea, no matter how farfetched, without thoroughly considering it. Think the unthinkable, and encourage others to do so as well. The unshakable belief that there is always another move will give you the energy to search for solutions, and creativity will give you the ability to find them.

Expedition Log

1. How would you characterize your core beliefs about problems and obstacles? Do they always come as unpleasant surprises, or do you expect them to occur?
2. What are your typical reactions when things go wrong? What is your tolerance level for potentially frustrating events?
3. Do you have a systematic process for identifying problems and finding solutions? Do you involve all members of the team—including your "troublemakers"—in a search for creative solutions?
4. What are the "breakthroughs" that would need to occur for you and your organization to reach *The Edge*? Have you demonstrated tenacious creativity in making them happen? What "other moves" would enable your expedition to reach its full potential?

PART TWO

Case Studies in Leading at *The Edge*

11

Introduction to the
Case Studies

In Part One of this book, the Lessons for Leaders sections in each chapter include a number of examples designed to illustrate how the ten strategies have been applied in business situations. The case studies in Part Two are more comprehensive. They provide greater detail about the nature of the organizational challenges, and they show how leaders have used multiple strategies in leading at *The Edge*.

The cases do not deal with every aspect of the organizational challenge. They do not, for example, address broad issues of strategy or specific issues such as portfolio analysis or capital efficiency. Rather, they are intended to provide a "leader's eye view" of what it was like to be at *The Edge*—to portray the way each leader thought about the challenges faced and to capture the nature of his or her leadership journey.

The leadership cases were selected with several considerations in mind. First, I wanted to find situations that involved exceptional performance under truly formidable conditions of challenge or adversity. None involved physical survival, but all required dealing with the ambiguity, uncertainty, and change associated with leading at *The Edge*.

Second, I looked for diversity in the nature of the challenges and in the characteristics of the leaders. As a result, the cases reflect differences in time span; the size of the organizations involved; the organizations' products or services; and the gender and experience of the leader.

Finally, although there are many differences among the cases, there is one common theme. They all involve leaders who, in my view, exhibit genuine respect for others, and who are passionate about pressing the limits of organizational performance.

There is no suggestion that the cases portray "perfect leaders." Each was quick to point out his or her own shortcomings, and none of the leaders described in the book—including Ernest Shackleton—is without limitation. The leaders I have chosen, however, have impressed me with their competence, their ability to motivate, and their genuine concern for others. I believe they are exceptional individuals.

Case One

The first case deals with the leadership of Pat Russo, who became president of AT&T's Business Communication Systems (BCS) division—which now is part of Lucent Technologies. I first met Russo when she spoke at an offsite meeting of the Delta Consulting Group. I was so impressed by her presentation that I took some ten pages of notes. Some were indecipherable, because her ideas came so quickly, but I scribbled madly. I was excited by her obvious passion for her job, by the way she thought about the role of the leader, and by the down-to-earth way she described her personal journey. I thought at the time that if I ever wrote a book, I wanted her story to be in it. She graciously agreed.

Case Two

The second case, Rice Health Systems, deals with a serious financial and service quality problem in a major division of a national healthcare organization. Anna Mahr, the leader who was brought in to resolve this crisis, has since moved to another organization. Because of the severity of the problems described in the case—and Mahr's concern about the possibility of negative impact on colleagues who remain with Rice—she asked that the case be disguised. Consequently, her name and the name of the organization are fictitious.

I first met Mahr in her role as president of the alumni board of an innovative midwestern college. Although she was then working full-time at Rice, Mahr devoted a great deal of time and effort to this voluntary position. At the time, the alumni board was dealing with a set of extremely complex and volatile issues, and I was called in as a consultant to help the board deal with them.

I was immediately impressed by Mahr's ability to mobilize the board and to help its members systematically work through a series of knotty, frustrating problems. Her soft-spoken, thoughtful approach was extremely impressive, and I was struck by the way she was able to focus on win-win solutions in a conflict-laden environment.

Later, when Mahr left Rice's national headquarters, I continued to follow her career. As we began to discuss the challenges she was facing in her new position, it became clear to me that her leadership experiences in general, but especially her experiences with Rice, fit the criteria for the book. She agreed to share her story with me, and it appears as the second case study.

Case Three

The third study, which focuses on Jack Creighton's leadership of Weyerhaeuser Company, is a story that encompasses almost a decade. I first met Creighton in 1990, as an associate of the Delta Consulting Group. At that juncture, he was assuming the role of president and CEO of Weyerhaeuser. In our first meeting, Delta colleague Jeff Heilpern and I explored the possibility of helping Creighton with the large-scale changes that he envisioned for the company.

The meeting went well, and Jeff and I worked with Creighton from that point until his retirement in 1998. Over time, I came to know him as an exceptional leader who was capable of translating his perception of a "one-company vision" into reality. I saw how he modeled collaboration and how he infused the organization with a team orientation previously unknown. I also saw how his self-effacing manner and humor engendered loyalty and dedication.

The Weyerhaeuser case is not an account of a crisis, but it is a story about *The Edge.* It describes a company that pressed the limits of performance with a sustained effort to effect fundamental changes in the culture of the organization. It also illustrates how a leader can combine business acumen, respect for people, and strong interpersonal skills to achieve superior financial performance.

Case Four

The Malden Mills story surfaced during early meetings of our "book team." Paul Kessler had read about CEO Aaron Feuerstein's efforts to rebuild the Malden Mills textile factories that had been destroyed by fire in December of 1995. We were all impressed by Feuerstein's tenacity—and by his commitment to his employees and the community. The more we learned about the situation, the more it seemed to exemplify the spirit of leading at *The Edge*. We pursued the possibility of developing the case, met with Feuerstein and other members of the organization, and documented the rebirth of the company from the ashes of the fire—a story that became known as the "Malden Miracle."

⬙ ⬙ ⬙ ⬙ ⬙

All of the case studies involve leaders facing *The Edge*, but each case places a different emphasis on the ten strategies. To assist in linking the cases to Part One of the book, points at which a particular strategy is applied are marked by sidebars. These strategies, either in large or small measure, are the key lessons of the case studies.

12

Business Communication Systems (AT&T/Lucent Technologies): Back to the Future

At *The Edge*

> I believed that we had to meet the goals we had set or the long-term viability of the business was in jeopardy. This was not practice. This was real! We were at *The Edge*—it was survival, and this was the last chance to get this business healthy. I felt it personally because I had been promoted to lead this business, and I knew others were watching me and the business. Certainly, my reputation was on the line.
>
> Pat Russo

The Situation

The deregulation of parts of the Bell System in 1984 heralded significant changes in the telecommunications industry. This was a dramatic period of transition for AT&T in some of its businesses. These changes in the industry caused some AT&T divisions to struggle as their monopolies came to an end.

One such division was Business Communication Systems (BCS). BCS was the arm of AT&T that had the charter to design, develop, manufacture, market, sell, and support communication systems for large and small enterprises around the world. It was the market leader in these services, but it faced several organizational challenges. In 1993, Pat Russo was named president of BCS. Personally and professionally, she faced *The Edge*: She knew that the scope of change and the responsibilities involved were enormous. For example:

> ➤ By the early 1990s, with the impact of deregulation and declining revenues as competition increased, the division had not been profitable for years. Several attempts to turn the business around had failed.

> ➤ A 1991 survey found that fewer than four in ten employees expressed positive views about the business. Much of their dissatisfaction was driven by years of forced reductions that had caused many employees to disengage or experience low morale.

> ➤ Customers were increasingly unhappy with the services provided by BCS. Meetings in which managers addressed customer product and service issues had become battlegrounds. Faced with these severe problems, senior management was considering selling the business.

Russo had joined AT&T in early 1982, as part of a large recruiting effort to help the company get ready to enter a deregulated market. She held a number of line and staff assignments including sales, marketing, operations, and customer service. In the process, she had gained invaluable experience interacting with a diverse customer population across different business units.

When Russo was named to head the division's North American sales and service operations in 1990, she and others believed the business could be turned around. They worked to design a realistic plan for success. They knew that any plan had to be extremely aggressive, because of growing impatience at AT&T's corporate headquarters with the continual financial bleeding of the business. Whatever plan was proposed, it had to have a true chance of achieving its goals to be accepted.

Part of the challenge faced by Russo and her team was to help senior management grasp the size and complexity of the change effort. As she remembers:

> This was a huge business that had lots of people supporting what was a monopolistic, regulated entity. Think of the

magnitude of change that had to occur on almost every front to transition from a regulated world to a deregulated, competitive world. There were some really tough decisions that had to be made. People had to be laid off, the organization had to shrink, and products had to be discontinued. Things needed to change, but our culture was deeply rooted in the "tyranny of the status quo"—the pressure to keep everything the same. There was resistance to change because with change comes uncertainty and anxiety. People begin to ask the questions: What will happen to me? What if I don't like the change? It is always tough to help people accept change.

The Actions

Establishing a Vision and Leveraging the Talents of Others

When she assumed her new position as president in 1993, Russo focused on her vision for the business. She believed that as the market-share leader in the industry, there was no reason why BCS could not be a healthy, profitable, growth-oriented business. She saw three instrumental steps to reaching this goal:

> **Strategy 1**
> *Never lose sight of the ultimate goal, and focus energy on short-term objectives.*

1. The financial health of the organization needed to be restored.
2. The organization needed to achieve the highest level of customer satisfaction possible.
3. All employees at BCS would need to feel that they were both valued and valuable to the success of the enterprise.

Although sure of her convictions, she knew that she would need to rely on the assistance and expertise of others to help her realize this vision.

I wanted everyone to share insights and perspectives. I wanted everybody to have the information and the insight and the knowledge so they could all speak on behalf of the business. Early on my model was to leverage the strengths, perspectives, and experiences of the senior ex-

> **Strategy 5**
> *Reinforce the team message constantly: "We are one—we live or die together."*

ecutive team of the business. I told them, "I know better than anyone that I don't know everything. We've got a lot of talent and expertise in each and every one of you, and, collectively, we can do incredible things in this business. Individually, we're all limited." My whole philosophy was to leverage the team. Leverage the strengths; acknowledge that nobody's perfect, but everybody brings a perspective to the table; and—when you have it all—you can solve the toughest problems.

Mobilizing the Leadership Team and Focusing the Organization

Russo believed that strong teamwork was crucial to the success of BCS. At her first meeting with her senior team as president, she talked with the managers about the challenges they faced. She was extremely clear in her expectations for each of them to "lead the parade on change." Russo knew that if they were unwilling to work together and to provide a consistent message, they would not reach their goals.

She asked each of them individually—in a clear, direct manner—whether they believed in and could endorse the kind of cultural environment and change she wanted to create. Those who could not commit to being part of a unified team moved on. Those who were willing to make the commitment stayed.

Once the team was set, its members were able to work together and deal with the organizational obstacles they faced. For example, some fundamental business decisions needed to be made about the portfolio. BCS had to eliminate the lowest-profit items in order to play to its strengths and abilities. Furthermore, there was a need for fundamental reengineering of many of the major processes of the business: manufacturing, strategic planning, and the "quote to cash" processes of configuring a system for a customer, installing the equipment, and collecting the revenue for the project. As Russo described the situation:

> Our business processes were broken. They were costly; they were inefficient; and they were unresponsive to customers. We did a lot of external benchmarking, and we shaped our initiatives in a way that had us focusing on the biggest hitters that helped both improve our productivity and performance and the way we served customers. I don't think there was a major process in the business that did not have an initiative around fundamental-process reengineering.

In addition to these initiatives, Russo believed it was critical to create an operating environment that was fundamentally different from the culture that had grown out of their monopolistic history. This new culture would change significantly how people behaved and were treated, and it would emphasize the effective use of everyone's talents and capabilities. Russo recalled:

> **Strategy 6**
> *Minimize status differences and insist on courtesy and mutual respect.*

We could not afford to have a culture that was hierarchically focused—where people kept looking up and saying, "What do you want me to do today?" We couldn't have middle managers believing that people who worked for them should leave their brains at the door so managers could tell them what to do. No, we needed a culture that called for accountability and responsibility on everyone's part. A culture where it was okay to say what you think—where it was okay to push back, ask tough questions, and challenge the leadership of the business. We needed a culture that would push decision making much closer to where decisions ought to be made rather than in the Taj Mahal of headquarters. We knew our success depended on having a culture that was willing to take risks.

Opening Lines of Communication

This cultural change came about through a massive communication effort on the part of Russo and her senior team. Committed to a cultural change as much as they were to a financial turnaround, they found themselves dealing with the pressing need to open up lines of communication.

Regular employee broadcasts were held to disseminate information and to reinforce open communication. Countless written materials, audio broadcasts, and large and small group meetings consistently emphasized the value of candid feedback and the importance of each individual voicing his or her unique perspective about how the business could be improved.

> **Strategy 5**
> *Reinforce the team message constantly: "We are one—we live or die together."*

The message that every single employee was critical in helping BCS survive was sent through these various channels. Individuals were made to feel they had a responsibility to express their views and to work to remove the real or perceived obstacles in the organization that blocked open dialogue. As president of the division, Russo took a prominent role in supporting this initiative. She gave out her office number and had a separate line installed in her home so that people could reach her around the clock.

> I returned the phone call of anybody who called me. That took a lot of time. Why did I do that? Because you can't say "call me" and not call people back. I constantly was reaching into the organization to underscore the importance of communication. I wasn't trying to undermine the people who reported to me, or the layers of management that were between them. I was trying to role-model the behavior of communicating beyond your direct reports. I wanted to get rid of this "level consciousness" that existed in the organization, to give people an opportunity to say what they thought, and to be willing to listen. What was important was that they perceived that I, in my role as president, was accessible to everyone.

Strategy 2
Set a personal example with visible, memorable symbols and behaviors.

Breaking Down Barriers

One of the goals of the emphasis on communicating and breaking down barriers was to gain the best thinking of every employee. Initially, there was some skepticism, but the tide began to turn. People started contributing and looking for improvement solutions.

One such employee was Beverly, who worked as a customer-service representative in the Atlanta Customer Care Center. She left Russo a voice mail one day saying, "You told us that if we had a problem that we could not get resolved

Strategy 6
Minimize status differences and insist on courtesy and mutual respect.

or that was not being addressed by our management that we could call you. So I'm calling you."

When Russo returned her call, Beverly outlined the problem. The BCS sales structure consisted of headquarters in several cities across the country, each of which served specific geographic territories. Each regional headquarters was supported by a customer care center that handled—among other responsibilities—customer calls, order taking, and invoicing. Recently, a new headquarters had been established in Dallas and executives there were drawing upon the customer bases of different regions, including the Atlanta area, to establish the Dallas sales territory.

Beverly told Russo that she did not believe it made good business sense to move the Atlanta customers into the Dallas region. The customer base had been assigned to the Atlanta region only nine months earlier, and the service representatives had developed relationships with these customers and understood their needs. In short, Beverly felt that another reassignment would cause great disruption for the customers and severely impact customer service.

Russo told Beverly that she appreciated the call and that it sounded like a good point to raise with the management team. Careful not to commit to any changes, she called the executives and said, "Hey, I understand there is some discussion about creating a customer care center in Dallas and moving accounts again. Can you help me understand how you think that's going to improve customer service?"

Russo asked them to present a strong rationale for making any moves that risked or resulted in the disruption of customer relationships. She reminded them that decisions should not be based solely on the new organizational structure. Shortly thereafter, the sales executives concluded that the Atlanta people could easily support the Dallas customers and simply charge the Dallas office. The accounts were never moved, and this action undoubtedly prevented an interruption in customer service that could have resulted in lowering customer satisfaction for many of the Atlanta clients. Russo looks back on the incident and says:

> A woman who saw a very real and legitimate issue had an avenue to articulate her concern, which is important. But the most important thing that happened was a different decision—the right decision—got made because of her insight about the need to support customers. When she called to thank me, she admitted that she did not believe I would return her call, let alone do anything about it. I told her she made a good point—by the way, not everybody who calls in with an issue will see it turn out the way they want it to turn out. That's not what this is about. This is about creating the conversation. That woman has never forgotten that. That center has never forgotten that.

Another way Russo made herself accessible and available was by instituting an *Ask the President* program. The goals of the program were to create a vehicle to communicate with others and to establish a "listening post" for individuals. Individuals at any level of the organization could fax in questions, raise issues, and get answers to questions with which they were grappling. As Russo put it: "I sought out the tough questions. I made it clear that, within the bounds of civility and respect, I was willing to deal with any issue."

The *Ask the President* program served as a direct link to gather information and to provide feedback as initiatives were rolled out or incorporated into the changing organization. It also allowed Russo and her team to track trends and spot difficulties in serving customers, and it resulted in more proactive and informed decision making.

Fostering an Environment to Support Creative Solutions

Russo and her team knew that if they were going to be successful in turning around the culture of BCS and improving bottom-line profitability, they needed to remove the obstacles that stood in the way of achieving their strategic goals. Many of these obstacles were seemingly intractable problems that had resisted repeated attempts to find solutions.

> *Strategy 10*
> *Never give up—there's always another move.*

To deal with these barriers, Russo and her team devised a plan that highlighted the conditions that needed to be satisfied in order to reach their goals. These projects were called Breakthrough Projects.

> By using this methodology of *breakdowns and breakthroughs,* we could say, "Let's put an audacious goal on the ground— such as reducing by half the amount of time it would take to develop new products." We started with goals and objectives that nobody knew how to reach, but we had to go for it. We had to think in breakthrough terms because we knew that incremental improvements weren't going to get us there. We knew from the start that we had to think totally out of the box. We had to do something radically different. We started out by creating the sense that a team had to come together and think in breakthrough terms in order to achieve a goal that nobody had a clue how to reach.

Using this methodology, they were able to reach their goals for product development, as well as for reducing inventory levels, while still meeting customers' needs. Again, Russo credits their earlier efforts to encourage others to take chances and to think big for the success with this initiative.

> I always argued to take the jump. You know, if I jumped five feet previously and you give me a goal to jump eight feet, I'm going to have to think differently about the challenge. When you set aggressive goals and accept the fact that you can fall short, you really think out of the box. You do things differently, and you get further than when you set goals that you know how to make. We tried to create a mind-set around aggressive goals that said, "It's okay to fall short." What you really want to measure is how far you get.

> **Strategy 9**
> *Be willing to take the Big Risk.*

Celebrating Success . . . Even If Things Aren't Coming Up Roses!

With so many initiatives and changes taking place at every level of the organization, Russo and her team needed to be sure that they kept motivation levels high. In their fight for survival, people had to be energized and focused on overcoming the obstacles they faced on a daily basis.

Celebrating wins and victories of all sizes was a key aspect of keeping people's energy and spirits high. There were cakes in the cafeteria, along with videos and broadcasts of the results produced by the collective hard work of everyone. Celebration was a part of the culture.

> **Strategy 8**
> *Find something to celebrate and something to laugh about!*

On one occasion, Russo and her senior team announced their strategic intent: "We will be the leader before, during, and after the communications industry transformation." The announcement was launched with a *Back to the Future* theme. Russo arrived onstage in front of a packed audience in the car from the movie, and she interacted with Doc Brown, a character from the movie, on a couple of sequential videos to keep the theme alive and create some fun. Russo recalls:

> You can be in a business that's losing a ton of money and be on a turnaround plan and still have fun and celebrate progress. You have to have fun and celebrate progress.

Being Positive but Holding People Accountable

Russo believes that if you act with confidence and speak with confidence, you will project confidence. In her mind it is that simple. She found it crucial to recognize accomplishment and help individuals feel proud of the goals they had already reached, but she balanced this optimism against three additional "reality checks":

One [reality check] is progress. How are we doing against what we did last year? The second is accountability. How are we doing against what we committed to? The third is quality—how are we doing against the best-in-class benchmarks?—because that's where we need to get to. So you could be doing very well against how you did last year, and very well against what you said you were going to do, but you can still be a long way off from the best in the business. I tried to remind people to measure the various projects against these three dimensions to recognize progress, but also to acknowledge, in a turnaround situation, that we still have a long way to go to be best-in-class.

> **Strategy 3**
> *Instill optimism and self-confidence, but stay grounded in reality.*

Instilling Confidence and Dealing with Mistakes

One of the most challenging leadership tasks is to give others the confidence that the organization will succeed while, at the same time, dealing with personal doubts. Russo comments:

I believe that, in times of great challenge, people cry out for strong, visible, approachable leadership. Of course, I'm just another human being, and I have questions and anxieties. But you have to have the courage of your convictions.

How you speak and what you say are crucial in leading an organization through difficult times. The words that come out of your mouth are important. People really hang on them, and I am very careful about word choice. I used to use words like "I hope." Now I say "when." What people want is to know where you stand.

> **Strategy 3**
> *Instill optimism and self-confidence, but stay grounded in reality.*

This is not to say that every goal will be achieved, or that execution will be flawless. Russo's perspective on making mistakes is that they are an expected part of bringing about radical changes in an organization and within an industry:

> You need to be willing to stop trying to defend decisions. When mistakes are made, you need to say, "We make the best decisions we can make at the time with the information, insights, and data we have. Hopefully, most of them will be right. But every now and then, we're going to make a decision that, in retrospect, we'll wish we didn't make." When that occurs, you just try to prevent it from happening again, and move on. You move on and, hopefully, don't make the same mistake twice.

Strategy 4
Take care of yourself: Maintain your stamina and let go of guilt.

This advice is easier in some situations than others. Russo recalls an occasion soon after she became president when she and the senior team made some difficult decisions that resulted in the resizing of the organization. She received letters from unhappy employees and their family members who were directly affected by the decisions to eliminate jobs or product lines.

Russo felt weighed down by the burden of the changes they had to make. While watching the New Jersey gubernatorial election results one night with her husband, he asked her why she was taking the negative feedback so personally.

> "Well, it's hard not to take it personally," I responded. I mean, these people are writing letters to me. They say, "Dear Pat." Right? The buck stops with me. The responsibility for the decisions stops with me, and I had this naive belief and desire that everybody would think that what we were doing was right. Well, I learned quickly that everybody doesn't think what you're doing is right, and I was initially discouraged by that fact. At that moment, my husband pointed out that Christie Whitman had just won the governorship of the state of New Jersey, and 49 percent of the people didn't vote for her!
>
> That was a real breakthrough for me personally in appreciating my leadership role. Everybody is not going to agree that what you're doing is right or that the choices you

make are right. And that's okay. When you have 25,000 people in an organization, the chances are that some people are going to say you're wrong . . . you're making bad decisions. Some will even tell you that directly. What you have to do is get yourself focused on the 90 percent or more who think you're doing the right thing and are with you. You've got to concentrate your energy there.

Recognizing and Acknowledging Your Limits as a Leader

Having experienced considerable success in her career, Russo has a clear vision of her role as a leader and of the qualities and characteristics she believes have played a role in her success. As the examples throughout this case study make clear, Russo finds real value in making herself approachable and accessible as a leader. Her approachability and her ability to connect with others seem to come from her willingness to be open—to be human:

I have found that when the people you support see that you are a human being like they are—that you have more to learn, that you have vulnerabilities, that you aren't per-

> **Strategy 6**
> *Minimize status differences and insist on courtesy and mutual respect.*

fect, that you struggle with issues—you will engender amazing loyalty. Some people in leadership positions seem to be wrapped in this impenetrable package—maybe it is because of their titles or their positions—but they feel they are always supposed to have the right answers and to know the right thing to do all the time.

The Emergence of Lucent Technologies

Russo considers the years from 1991 to 1995 as those spent at *The Edge*, fighting for the survival of the business. The turnaround plan for BCS was, in fact, a four- to five-year plan that remained on course and on track once it was implemented. In 1995, AT&T announced that it would divide itself into three independent corporate identities within a year—the largest voluntary breakup in commercial history.

AT&T continued as the long-distance communications service business. NCR, a computer company, regained the independent status it had held before being acquired by AT&T several years earlier. Five other divisions of AT&T—Bell Laboratories, Network Systems, Consumer Products, Microelectronics, and Business Communications Systems—became Lucent Technologies.

While the initial announcement was met with the expected uncertainty and anxiety that comes with any organizational change of this magnitude, BCS had clearly turned the corner and had achieved the goals the initial turnaround plan had outlined. Realizing the opportunity this restructuring presented, Russo and the members of her organization set their sights on new goals. Throughout these changes, Russo remained in the leadership role of president until 1997, when she became Lucent Technologies' executive vice president for strategy, business development, and corporate operations.

In November 1999, Russo was named executive vice president and chief executive officer of Lucent's Service Provider Networks business. This organization is the largest of Lucent's four core businesses, and generates approximately $25 billion in annual revenues.

The Results

By the end of Pat Russo's four years as president of BCS, the organization had gone from the brink of being sold or dismantled to becoming a successful business. BCS experienced great increases in customer satisfaction. Survey results that measured employees' sense of empowerment moved from 43 percent favorable to 63 percent. Satisfaction scores increased similarly. Employees now felt that they were part of the success of the business. BCS won a Chairman's Quality Award for Improvement in 1995 and 1996 and was granted a site visit for the prestigious Baldrige Award.

Financially, the revenue decline was reversed and BCS met its revenue-growth, profit, and return-on-assets goals. Over the turnaround period, Russo and her team had successfully swung the bottom line of the business hundreds of millions of dollars in a positive direction and had achieved all of the goals they had set for the business. There was a significant gain in market share, and the overall business grew from $50 million in 1991 to hundreds of millions by 1995.

13

Rice Health Systems: Healing a Sick Organization

At *The Edge*

I felt a tremendous amount of pressure: pressure to save the organization, pressure to gain the trust of the local leadership—all of whom were skeptical about my abilities, given that I was a lawyer, and therefore not as schooled in the business as they, a woman, and a corporate type from another part of the country. [Then there was] pressure to succeed for the benefit of the corporation's leaders, who had taken a big risk by entrusting me with this position. I also felt the pressure to figure out a way to earn the trust of an incredibly broken and understandably disenfranchised employee population.

Most profoundly, I guess, I felt alone. There was no one at work to talk with about my fears and frustrations because I couldn't risk having them give up what little hope they had remaining. My family had faith in me and wanted to support me, but there was no way they could fully understand or appreciate what I was facing.

On the bright side, I figured there was an enormous upside opportunity and probably very little downside risk. It was going to take some doing to make it much worse than I found it.

Anna Mahr

The Situation

A Regulatory Crisis

After ten to twelve years of unsatisfactory administrative audits, followed by Rice Health Systems' submission of elaborate corrective action plans, the State Regulatory Agency (SRA) found that Rice rarely implemented its submitted plans. The SRA announced that it was on the verge of issuing a cease-and-desist order that would have forced Rice Health Systems to discontinue its business operations in the state. (As indicated in the Introduction, the names in this case study are fictitious.)

With a reputation for unflappable problem solving, Anna Mahr was called from Rice's national headquarters to help deal with this organizational disaster. Originally brought in as chief counsel, she was made acting president after a year and then was selected as the division's president. In many respects, Rice was as beset by solid pack ice as Shackleton's Trans-Antarctic expedition was.

The SRA conducts two audits for healthcare organizations: one for finance and administration and one for operations. In their finance and administration review, the SRA auditors had uncovered serious problems. They found, for example, that there was no person in the organization who could describe clearly how the organization worked. They were unable to get straightforward answers to a number of basic questions: How does money flow through the system when you charge a premium? How and where are decisions made? What are the checks and balances within the system? As Anna recalls:

> There was nobody who could do the math for them. That was, in part, because no one person really did understand the complete process. And it was partly because the organization had never taught people about how to deal with an audit situation, and how to bring teams of people together so that you could get the collective vision.

The quality of care being delivered to patients by physicians was never in question. The problem was that in pursuing its mission of rapid growth and expansion, the healthcare organization had lost some of the foundational process pieces along the way. For example, an effective system had never been developed to track physicians' signed medical records. Physicians were, in fact, creating the records and reviewing them, but the law requires a mechanism be in place to ensure that the doctor has reviewed and signed it. That mechanism did not exist.

There were also problems with service standards, such as the time required to get an appointment with a doctor and the responsiveness to telephone calls. Ironically, Rice was authorized to set its own standards. There was nothing in the law that required that an urgent-care appointment, for example, be handled within a specific period of time. Once an organization established standards, though, it was expected to meet them, and Rice was failing to do so.

Because there was such preoccupation with growth and just getting through the audits, the key people in the organization failed to focus on actually meeting the standards that had been set. When the next audit report came out, they discovered that they had not complied with their own standards. Mahr summarized the problem as follows:

> No one had stepped back and asked the key questions: Did we set the right targets in the first place? Should the targets be readjusted? What in the process is keeping us from achieving these targets? We didn't do any of that. Over the course of roughly twelve years we got audited every two years and got cited for repeat violations each time. Each time we submitted corrective action plans that were never implemented, never communicated, and never monitored. By the time I became chief counsel and then president, there was a twelve-year history of noncompliance. The SRA said, "We've told you every two years over the course of the last twelve years, and you've never taken it seriously. A cease-and-desist order is the only action we can think of to get management's attention."

Service Problems

The organization's problems extended beyond the SRA. Once considered the Cadillac of healthcare services, Rice could charge more because it delivered more. This was no longer the case within the state. In a dramatic downturn, Rice found itself ranking close to the bottom in member-, physician-, and provider-satisfaction surveys of all competitors in the marketplace.

In fact, matters had reached the point that about twenty of Rice's largest accounts in the state had frozen their "book of business." These companies had chosen Rice as a carrier years before, and many of their employees were covered under Rice plans. To avoid disrupting their healthcare, these employees continued their membership. However, no new employees were allowed to enroll in Rice programs.

In the healthcare insurance world, this situation creates what is known as a "death spiral." The population is a closed population that keeps getting older and sicker. It's a no-win situation if new, healthier, and broader-based populations cannot be moved into the covered pool. Over a period of years, an organization in the death spiral will lose a significant amount of money with no hope of recovery.

Financial Problems

The financial impact of these problems was serious. Rice's flagship division was losing nearly $20 million a year, and a major cause of these losses was the lack of a coherent, focused business strategy that was broadly understood and embraced by its employees.

This lack of a clear strategy was illustrated in a number of ways. Over the years, Rice would buy or lease a building, hire staff, and make benefits decisions without a view toward the collective, long-range vision of the organization. The organization ended up with some extremely expensive real estate, and yet it was not always located in areas where there were opportunities to grow membership or expand business operations.

The company had established, for example, a healthcare center on a spectacular site with beachfront property and a beautiful building. It was their single most expensive real-estate commitment. But the geographic circumstance of that decision meant that half of the available service area was the water—automatically limiting by 50 percent the size of the membership that could be attracted.

The company continued to expand into new areas in the hope that there would be business there. But lacking a clear strategy, the pieces did not come together. Often, the company failed to coordinate the opening of a healthcare center with a complementary marketing effort or sales strategy.

Rice had also made a series of short-term decisions about attracting and retaining people, but these decisions ignored the competitive marketplace. The result was a generous but paternalistic compensation-and-benefits program. Everybody wanted to work for Rice, but there were no internal mechanisms for market adjustment and no meaningful way of tying performance and compensation together.

The cumulative effect of these decisions was that the business was financially unsound. Employees sensed the depth of the trouble, and fear and paralysis engulfed the organization. People were leaving in a state of panic. It was during this chaotic period that Mahr was named president—Rice's third in one year.

The Actions

Dealing with Anxiety

Taking over an organization in this condition was a daunting challenge. Mahr recalled:

> My insight into the situation was born of a plain old anxiety attack while I was serving as chief counsel. I remember just sitting in my office and feeling almost paralyzed. There were so many competing priorities that it wasn't clear what to do next.
>
> The way I typically deal with that sense of "not knowing where to turn because there's too much on my plate" is that I just pull out a pen and paper and write down everything that I'm thinking about. I might categorize it as personal and professional, but I try to put it all down and then try to make some order of it and think about where I should start. That's exactly what I did this night of the "panic attack."

Mahr came up with a list of some forty-eight items that had been described to her as "number-one priorities," each of which needed to be completed before the end of the year. It was then August. Although she realized that it was humanly impossible to complete forty-eight major initiatives in four months, the process of getting things down on paper had a stabilizing

> **Strategy 1**
> *Never lose sight of the ultimate goal, and focus energy on short-term objectives.*

effect. However, her list raised another troubling issue: If these priorities were hitting her desk, what must be going on in each of the other departments? Additionally, why was the company strategy so unclear that it could result in forty-eight competing number-one priorities?

Mobilizing the Leadership Team and Focusing the Organization

Shortly after developing her list of priorities and trying to bring order to her part of the organization (the legal department), Mahr was asked to move into the role of president. The first action she took was to call a meeting of her senior leadership team.

The atmosphere was tense. The scene was reminiscent of Shackleton's situation, when he faced his crew and proposed marching to Paulet Island.

> **Strategy 5**
> *Reinforce the team message constantly: "We are one—we live or die together."*

Calmly and deliberately, Mahr distributed the list. She explained that these were the top work priorities on her plate and that she could only imagine that those same things were on their minds—plus many additional challenges.

Mahr engaged the group in an open discussion about the obstacles they were facing. The team talked about the pressure the organization was under and the feeling that nobody was doing anything well. They admitted that there was nothing that they could feel proud about and nothing that they could take off their "to do" lists. They talked about the depths of despair across the organization. The conversation quickly moved to the challenges of focusing people's energies, relieving some of the pressure, and communicating with the rest of the organization.

Everyone shared the issues their own departments were facing, and they created a collective "to do" list. Then—as a group—they set about trying to bring some order to the mammoth task ahead. Mahr reflected on the process:

> I wasn't sure of the right way of going about this. I'd never done anything like it before. But I knew that the way I would handle it in my personal life would be to say, "What items on this list are nonnegotiable? What things are critical to keeping the ship afloat?" And then, after identifying those items I would ask, "What are the other things that are high, medium, or low priorities?"

> **Strategy 1**
> *Never lose sight of the ultimate goal, and focus energy on short-term objectives.*

> I first try to identify the issues that are critical, because it's clear the things that are life-threatening have to be done.

Then I try to rank the rest of the items based upon relative order of priority. Once you've done that, you always have the list to go back to—a filter to help you focus on the imperatives.

The senior team went through exactly that exercise. They ranked work that needed to be done in those four categories—nonnegotiable, followed by high, medium, and low priorities—and then agreed on a communication strategy. The strategy was to meet with everyone, customers and regulators alike, to develop personal relationships, to listen and understand their concerns about company performance, and then to develop and deliver on a meaningful corrective-action plan.

The team was now aligned behind three critical, life-threatening issues that had to be resolved: regaining customer confidence, developing a strategic vision, and expanding the leadership team. With this game plan, they were prepared to focus the organization. The release of pressure was almost palpable.

Engaging the Top Customers

Regaining customer confidence was one of the essential actions needed to keep Rice afloat. Mahr personally went with her senior leadership team to each of these accounts and explained Rice management's concern over the situation and its desire to correct it. She and the team invited their customers to tell them what had gone so terribly wrong, asked them what their expectations were of the healthcare delivery system, and urged them to work with Rice to develop solutions.

> **Strategy 7**
> *Master conflict—deal with anger in small doses, engage dissidents, and avoid needless power struggles.*

Establishing a Strategic Vision

The exercise of setting priorities served to quell anxiety in the organization and to give people a sense of direction and focus. Having accomplished that immediate task, Mahr was able to turn her attention to the long-term direction of the company.

It was time to lead the team through the process of developing a three-year strategic plan. This "big picture" document gave the organization a sense of vision beyond the next few months, and

> **Strategy 1**
> *Never lose sight of the ultimate goal, and focus energy on short-term objectives.*

the process enabled employees to set their own priorities in the context of this overall direction. It also rationalized the decision-making process so that investments in real estate, compensation programs, and expansion into new markets were made only after it was clear how these decisions fit into a broader business plan.

> **Strategy 1**
> *Never lose sight of the ultimate goal, and focus energy on short-term objectives.*

Expanding the Leadership Team

With the top of the organization aligned, Mahr and the senior team engaged an expanded group of some seventy people who were recognized as leaders in the organization.

They shared with the expanded team a two-page executive summary entitled the "Strategic Planner." The Strategic Planner laid out the situation. It addressed candidly the threats to survival: the danger of a "cease and desist"

> **Strategy 5**
> *Reinforce the team message constantly: "We are one—we live or die together."*

order, negative public relations, employee distrust of the organization, and lack of employee self-esteem. It also laid out what would be needed to restore the reputation and financial health of the organization.

The decision to share this document broadly was a major risk. Mahr described the rationale:

> When we put pen to paper, we realized that it was a worse situation than any of us had recognized because each of us had a piece that none of the others knew. We shared exactly what the situation was, gave people copies of the Strategic Planner, and told them the risk of doing it.
>
> Obviously, what was in that document—had it been leaked outside the organization—would have been very, very devastating for us. But I wanted to send a message to the organization, particularly the leadership of the organization. The message I wanted to send was a message of trust, of what it meant to be a leader in this organization, and of the candor that we had to have with each other in order to be successful.

> **Strategy 9**
> *Be willing to take the Big Risk.*

This willingness to be honest had a tremendous payoff. It created the opportunity to engage the expanded leadership team in a discussion of the challenges ahead and about ways in which those challenges could be met. And it further solidified the leadership of the organization.

Spreading Teamwork Throughout the Organization

After the broader group refined the strategy, Mahr hosted a series of "all-employee" meetings. Every employee who attended her presentation learned exactly what was in the original strategic planning document.

Mahr went through the document, line by line, and painted a picture of the severity of the crisis they faced. She recalled:

> **Strategy 5**
> *Reinforce the team message constantly: "We are one—we live or die together."*

> What we tried to do was share with all the employees information they had never before seen. Everybody was invited, and every single person in the organization was given the same information. What we tried to do was make it very, very clear. We didn't want to oversimplify it or make it too complex. We had to strike a balance. We gave them a short, sweet, but absolutely candid assessment done in bullet-point fashion on slides.
>
> We dealt with some basic questions: How much money do we have to take in? How much money do we pay out? Where does it go? The answers were depicted in a simple graphic form. Everyone could see from the chart that, when the numbers were consistently in the red and satisfaction ratings were consistently declining, something had to change.

By itself, this stark assessment of Rice's plight could have added to the panic. But the picture that Mahr created did not end with an assessment of their dire situation. It also encompassed the opportunities that lay ahead and the ways in which they could capitalize on those opportunities. It laid out the role that people could play in the turnaround. It recognized and celebrated what was good about the

> **Strategy 3**
> *Instill optimism and self-confidence, but stay grounded in reality.*

past and candidly identified what had to change and why. It delineated a timeline. Ultimately, it instilled a sense of confidence that the organization could get there.

This process created a sense of teamwork, and it gave people a sense of personal and institutional pride. Equally important, people understood how they contributed to the whole and why it was important that they do their part well for the organization to succeed.

The story of Jorge, who ran the mailroom, is a good example of how this turnaround occurred. When Jorge understood that senior managers were genuinely interested in his suggestions about how to do business better, he realized that he was uniquely situated to see how the entire organization functioned. He knew how work flowed from department to department and how different processes could be changed to make the business more efficient.

He began sharing information and generating suggestions based on his observations. He would go from department to department, cross-pollinating ideas and best practices. One of his suggestions dealt with the selection of shipping vendors.

He developed a thoughtful proposal that detailed reasons for recommending one vendor over another. Jorge's process was adopted locally, and it was so successful that it spread to the healthcare division nationwide and then to the whole corporation. He eventually received the National President's Award and was one of a handful of employees honored with his family at a dinner with the national leaders of Rice Health Systems.

The payoff was significant. Jorge's initiative improved the process throughout the company. It ultimately saved millions of dollars. It gave Jorge a sense of contributing to the organization. And it inspired other people to contribute their ideas. People started to participate more, care more, and understand the importance of the linkages between their jobs and those of other people at Rice.

Celebrating Success . . . Without Knowing the Outcome!

Mahr and the leadership team made a concerted effort to communicate both the overall business plan and the successes that were achieved as they moved toward the strategic vision. They gave credit to the teams and departments that had contributed to these victories. As a result, everybody knew that if they were part of a team that had achieved a goal, there would be a public celebration and expression of gratitude.

> **Strategy 8**
> *Find something to celebrate and something to laugh about!*

The unique way that Mahr thought about celebration had an interesting origin. She recalled:

> If you asked me to describe my childhood, one of the clearest recollections that I have was report card day. On report-card-day morning, my mom would ask each of us what we wanted for dinner that night—our very favorite food. Whatever it was, she would make it. So we each got to choose one dish. You named it, and she'd make it.
>
> The important thing was that she asked the question and prepared the favorite dinner item before the report card came out. The reward was there whether you had an A or a D. What I knew was that my parents supported me and believed in me and trusted me. I wasn't afraid to come home with bad news.

Mahr used this same approach in the way she dealt with a critically important national evaluation process. Originally scheduled to follow on the heels of yet another adverse state audit, the national evaluation posed an even more daunting challenge. Believing that she could resolve the most pressing issues if given a little time, Mahr convinced the evaluators to delay their examination of her organization for several months.

Once the breathing space was secured, the organization spent more than seven months preparing for the national review. It was a grueling ordeal and a tremendous workload. The day that the reviewers were scheduled to leave, Mahr invited everybody who had participated in the process to come to her office for a debriefing. The debriefing was, in fact, a pretext for a celebration.

> **Strategy 8**
> *Find something to celebrate and something to laugh about!*

The night before, Mahr moved all the furniture out of her office, except for the desk. She decorated the office, set out hors d'oeuvres, and put up a big "Congratulations" banner. In the marble bathroom in the president's office—a symbol of days gone by—she filled big ice buckets with champagne and sparkling cider. Mahr recalls:

> Part of it was celebrating everybody's contribution, but the biggest part was celebrating whether or not we were successful in the accreditation. People understood that, and they knew that I had to have set up most of this the day before in order to have it ready the minute the reviewers left.

It seemed important to people that I had done the decoration and preparation myself. I didn't have it catered. I served them, and it just broke down some of the

> **Strategy 6**
> *Minimize status differences and insist on courtesy and mutual respect.*

traditional barriers and perceptions. In my mind, I wasn't giving up my authority or my position. I was saying I could still be the leader of our organization and play a different role. It was my turn to serve and celebrate them. It was just a terrific day.

The party in the office involved all those who had directly contributed to the accreditation process: those who had written proposals, done presentations, and/or answered interviewers' rigorous questions. When the accreditation results came, there was an even bigger party. After receiving the news that Rice had been accredited for three years, Mahr immediately left a voice message for everybody in the organization inviting them to join the celebration the very next day.

She rented a large conference room and had banners placed on every floor. The first thing people saw when they walked in the next morning was a banner declaring "Congratulations to the Team!" The intent was to help everybody understand that the celebration was not just for the forty or so people who had participated directly in the accreditation work, but for every person at Rice, each of whom had contributed in one way or another to the dramatic turnaround success.

An event of this sort had never happened before—at least not in anyone's memory. There had been Christmas parties or picnics, but these were viewed as obligatory company activities. This celebration was different. This kind of event historically had been reserved for the leadership team, but now everyone was involved. The sense of organizational pride and renewal was remarkable.

Demonstrating a Commitment to Personal Health

Anna Mahr has been committed to an exercise program since high school and is something of a role model for physical fitness. She loves running, biking, tennis, and racquetball. In spite of the tremendous pressures at work, she made a commitment to take time out for exercise. Her goal was to exercise regularly, even if it meant getting up at 4:30 A.M. or rescheduling her day to fit in a workout.

Mahr made a conscious effort to exercise even during the most demanding periods. She was also vigilant about avoiding bad habits:

eating too much junk food or drinking
too much coffee ("making stupid
choices," as she put it) over a long period
of time. Mahr also used her concern for
others' health as a way of maintaining
her own stamina:

Strategy 4
Take care of yourself: Maintain your stamina and let go of guilt.

> I'm good when it comes to thinking about the well-being of
> my team. If I asked them to work late, I'd make sure that
> I ordered out really healthy food. And that was kind of a
> reminder to me to stop and do those things for myself.
>   It's the same way I approach vacation and time off. I
> firmly believe that it is important for people to take time off
> and just disengage—not to stay hooked up by phone,
> beeper, or e-mail, but to go away and just relax. Really relax.
> It would have been easy for me to let that slip for myself,
> except that I heard myself insisting that my team members
> take time for themselves. It was a good reminder for me to
> do the same and set the example.

When she made mistakes, Mahr had a tendency to rehash decisions excessively, but she developed a humorous antidote. A friend
gave her a spray can labeled "Guilt Away," which she uses as a reminder to keep matters in perspective. She also made a distinction between two kinds of guilt-producing situations: those that involve
interpersonal problems and those that she viewed as organizational or
strategic.
    When guilt resulted from poor judgment in an interpersonal situa-
tion, Mahr dealt directly with the person adversely affected:

> I would explain why I may have made the wrong decision,
> or hurt them, or done something I wish I'd done differently.
> Sometimes they'd just dismiss it and think I was over-
> reviewing it, and sometimes they just appreciated having
> the explanation or the apology. Once I talked with the per-
> son about it, the guilt went away.

She learned to think about organizational or strategic errors in a somewhat different way:

> I tried to look at the decision that I had made and ask:
> Armed with that same information, would I make that same

decision again? If the answer was yes, the guilt often instantly went away. If the answer was no, then I tried to think about how I could handle a situation better next time.

Using Diversity as a Reality Check

With the benefit of number of years in leading organizations, Mahr approached the situation at Rice with a basic sense of optimism. She was confident in her ability to make good decisions and to work through thorny problems. She was also aware of the need to balance her optimism with strong and effective reality checks.

> **Strategy 3**
> *Instill optimism and self-confidence, but stay grounded in reality.*

Mahr made a deliberate effort to avoid surrounding herself with people who saw the world just the way she did. Consequently, she looked for diversity in her leadership team, and that meant diversity in every sense of the word. Mahr described the process as follows:

> When I composed the leadership team at Rice, I tried to think of a gender mix. I tried to think of an ethnic and racial mix. But I also tried to think of an "experience" mix and to make sure that I had touched all the right parts of the organization.
>
> I was running a field operation of a national corporation. The balance that I thought was important was achieved by assembling a team, one-third of which was composed of people who had experience and credibility in the corporate headquarters. Another third knew the state organization and its strengths and weaknesses and how to do its business; and a third came from the outside, so we would have the benefit of the marketplace information and what's new and different, what's going on with the competition.
>
> And if you bring those three pieces together and then get that other mix as well—the gender, ethnicity, and experience diversity—you build a system that does its own reality checks. You don't just have a bunch of mouthpieces. You obviously want people who are complementary, but you don't want them just to parrot your ideas.

For Mahr, the diversity strategy was two-fold. She first thought carefully about where each perspective was needed: marketing intelligence, corporate credibility, and local institutional knowledge. Second, she tried to figure out, within that framework, which jobs needed to be placed in each of those thirds.

The plan worked. The local team began to have more trust in the corporate vision, and corporate began to see that the local team was not a bunch of mavericks. Together they began to understand what the marketplace was doing and to respond effectively.

The Results

At the end of two years under Mahr's presidency, Rice had gone from the brink of being shut down by the SRA to having a full three-year national accreditation, and Mahr was invited to serve on a special advisory committee of the agency that had earlier had such grave concerns about Rice's performance. The financial picture changed from a $20-million-a-year loss to earnings of some $19 million. The major accounts that had frozen new business and refused to give Rice favorable references radically changed their perspective, expressing complete confidence in Rice's new leadership team.

Those who participated in the turnaround remember it as a time of stress and challenge, but also as an experience they can look back on with pride. They had faced enormous challenges as a team, and they had prevailed.

14

Weyerhaeuser Company: Transforming a Culture

At *The Edge*

You've got a company that isn't going to go bankrupt, and it can continue at the current pace. Why do anything? You go to *The Edge* to create change—to push the company over *The Edge* of complacency and comfort into an area of discomfort and dissatisfaction. There were some things that were very good about the culture. But your sense of pride and self-esteem are telling you that things can be better—that we can be the best.

Jack Creighton

The Situation

A Crisis of Confidence

When John W. (Jack) Creighton, Jr., took over as president and chief operating officer of Weyerhaeuser Company in 1988, he faced a challenge of giant proportions. One of the nation's largest owners of timberlands and a world leader in the production of wood and paper, Weyerhaeuser was lagging behind its competitors in the forest-products industry. Although profits had grown, returns on net assets were substandard. Once a high performer, Weyerhaeuser's returns had dropped to the lowest quartile of its competitive peer group.

There were performance problems in most of the basic businesses of the company, and decentralization had created complexity, inefficiency, and divided accountability in all its divisions. Corporate strategy and direction were unclear. Environmental controversies, such as air and water pollution and timber clear-cutting, had undermined the company's reputation as a conscientious steward of forestlands throughout North America.

It was not an acute financial crisis that took Weyerhaeuser's leadership to *The Edge* of radical transformation. It was a far more pervasive crisis of confidence in the corporation's overall performance that triggered change.

Founded in 1900, the Weyerhaeuser Company had a long tradition of founding-family ownership and management. Creighton, a lawyer and certified public accountant who rose through the ranks of the company's real-estate and financial-services businesses, was a departure from tradition. Within months of his appointment, and with the encouragement of then-CEO George Weyerhaeuser, the new president set himself the task of waking a sleeping giant.

The Actions

Refocusing the Organization toward Change

In the spring of 1989, the senior management at Weyerhaeuser launched a corporate-wide, top-to-bottom review of all of the company's businesses and operations. Plans were announced for a major refocusing effort to be led by Jack Creighton. Shareholders were promised "fundamental and permanent improvements" in the company's management of businesses,

> **Strategy 1**
> *Never lose sight of the ultimate goal, and focus energy on short-term objectives.*

operations, and support services—all within three years.

Creighton's team envisioned a radically different company in the future. Its singular commitment to improving performance would increase shareholder value. The company would have more aggressive and more focused competitive strategies. There would be fewer businesses and assets, as well as less diversity, in the portfolio. These objectives—creating a streamlined, more effective organizational structure—would help the team achieve its long-term goal of changing the company into a top financial performer.

Creighton can still recall the risk and uncertainty that attended the new initiatives:

> Coming out of the 1980s, our financial performance was not adequate, but we weren't in danger of going bankrupt. The crisis element, which is a great motivator for change, wasn't there. A lot of people were satisfied with our performance. There were many, many things that were very positive—the ethics of the company, our attention to the environment. I guess if you level a structure and start all over again, it may be easier than trying to remodel something. But you've got to be careful that you don't kill many of those good things that have developed over time.
>
> We were listed as one of the "100 Best Companies to Work for in the U.S." Our employees thought we were the best. We were the best in certain areas, but we were considerably short in others. Over the decade, our financial performance had dropped us into the fourth quartile in our industry. The challenge was to improve the company's profitability, to become an industry leader—not only in ethics and environmental responsibility, but an industry leader in financial performance. And we had to convince Weyerhaeuser people, short of a crisis, that we needed to change.

Strategy 9
Be willing to take the Big Risk.

Searching for Strategies and Preserving Core Values

In meeting after meeting that spring, Creighton urged his managers to think strategically about their company's future course. "This effort is not just another short-term program in response to the external economic environment," he told them. "We are seeking permanent solutions rather than short-term, nonsustained improvements. That means we have to change the way we manage, overcoming old habits and hierarchies and the detrimental parts of our corporate culture. We are talking watershed change!"

Although a major cultural shift was

Strategy 1
Never lose sight of the ultimate goal, and focus energy on short-term objectives.

---

under way at Weyerhaeuser, preserving the best characteristics of the old culture was a high priority for Creighton's team. Given the magnitude of the transition, certain values took on an enduring importance. Weyerhaeuser's orientation toward long-term profitable growth would continue. Pride in the company's standards of quality, service, and customer relationships would not be compromised. The team was determined to reinforce the company's commitment to people—the employees, customers, and communities affected by its policies.

Communicating the Financial Realities

Resistance to change is strong in any organization, especially in the absence of crisis. Often the first task of restructuring is to create a sense of collective urgency among the members of the workforce. At Weyerhaeuser, this meant sharing the financial realities, not just with the top people, but also with the rank and file. It was an unorthodox approach at the time.

> **Strategy 3**
> *Instill optimism and self-confidence, but stay grounded in reality.*

The initial challenge was educational—making employees aware of the company's financial performance without destroying their pride in the company. Creighton took a positive approach as he tried to balance optimism with reality:

> We were embarking on a great amount of change. Change at all levels—from people on the mill floor up through the CEO. How do you convince people the change is needed? We were lucky because, at the same time, we were moving toward a more participatory work atmosphere. We wanted to share with employees the financial results of their particular unit or facility because we wanted them to participate as true members of that team. So first we brought everybody into the loop in terms of what was going on financially.
>
> Second, employees had to realize where we stood in relationship to competitors, both at the corporate level and at the unit level. I can remember a riveting conversation I had with the sawmill manager who had just gone out and benchmarked one of the best facilities in North America. His reaction was, "If I hadn't seen it being done, I wouldn't have thought it could be done. But by God, if they can do it, we can do it!" That's the kind of mental attitude employees need to have. That realism is very important, and if you

do it in the right way, I think you can leverage people's pride—their desire to be the best.

Restructuring the Organization for Top Performance

In 1991, after three years as president, Jack Creighton became CEO of Weyerhaeuser Company. His predecessor, the strong-willed George Weyerhaeuser, had been in place for twenty-six years and remained chairman of the board. It was late in Creighton's career, and there was still much to be done to achieve the goals that had been so carefully crafted during the review process. He recalled his transition into the top job and the decision to place his bets on a new organizational structure:

Strategy 9
Be willing to take the Big Risk.

It was a big risk for me, not having come up through the core businesses of the company. I could have fallen on my face. But it was a wonderful opportunity to learn. Running the refocus effort, I got an inside picture of every part and piece of the company. So it was a firm grounding for me in terms of learning the businesses I didn't know.

There was a significant organizational risk coming out of refocus, and that was organizing the company along business lines. My approach was to break the company down into various pieces and improve those pieces before we started rearranging them. I believed there was more value to be obtained in improving the operations than in trying to wring all the savings out of overhead reduction. I figured that if we could get each business unit to be profitable, it would give us the kinds of returns we wanted.

Restructuring the Senior Team

The Weyerhaeuser culture had long been one of individualistic, one-on-one management. As a result, the organization was more of a loosely knit coalition than a coherent organization. A clear index of this history was that, in Creighton's eighteen years at the company, all the profit center managers were brought together only a few times to talk about the performance of the company.

Insiders jokingly characterized the company as "the wandering tribes of Weyerhaeuser, who sometimes attacked each other." The impact of this fragmentation on the bottom line, however, was not always humorous. As a result of the refocusing reviews, for example,

Creighton learned of a timber auction at which only two people showed up. Both were from Weyer-haeuser, and they bid against each other!

Creighton knew this attitude had to change if the sleeping giant were to rise to its feet once more. At a gathering of the company's key managers in the fall

> **Strategy 5**
>
> *Reinforce the team message constantly: "We are one—we live or die together."*

of 1990, Creighton announced a new management structure and changes in his executive team. Having a cohesive team at the top, he told them, was essential for creating a company-wide unity of purpose:

> I don't mean a committee or a collegial group or assemblage of heads of operating companies. . . . I mean a team—and I mean to lead that team. The first criterion for the personnel in this group is teaming, and if that isn't present or isn't delivered, it's back to the bench or, perhaps, out of the stadium.

Creighton made a commitment to teamwork at the top so this message would become a daily reality and not just a slogan. His senior team would, he said, become the model for teaming throughout the company. To emphasize his belief in the value of teamwork, he made sure that the entire team was pictured together in the annual report and that he himself never ap-

> **Strategy 2**
>
> *Set a personal example with visible, memorable symbols and behaviors.*

peared alone in the report. In ways both large and small, the senior management of the organization showed a level of cohesion that was a dramatic departure from the past.

Creating a Metaphor for Teamwork

As he steered the company on its new course, Creighton found the ideal symbol for his "one company" vision. The Spirit of *Haida Gwaii* is a sculpture of a Northwest Coast Indian war canoe that sits in a reflecting pool outside the Canadian Embassy in Washington, D.C. For Jack Creighton, the sculpture was emblematic of the rich variety of meaning that employees drew from their collective experience during the difficult process of transition. Looking back, Creighton recalled its vivid impact on the company culture:

> The black canoe is a mixture of people, animals, birds, and mythical beasts—characters you'd normally find on a totem

pole, all in similar scale. It symbolizes diversity, which was something we were trying to achieve and improve on: different types of management styles, different types of approaches, both geographical and cultural, and the ethnic and gender mix of the organization.

> **Strategy 2**
> *Set a personal example with visible, memorable symbols and behaviors.*

In a large organization, that kind of symbol is very, very important. It has some sort of special inner meaning for people. To me, it epitomized where we were. A lot of diversity. A lot of uncertainty. A lot of different people, not necessarily with smiles on their faces. And all of these different entities are in the same boat. That was the situation I wanted to portray to the company—that we all had to be paddling in one direction and that we were all working together to move the boat forward.

As we achieved improved financial performance, symbolism continued to be important and we transitioned to a racing shell—a boat that's moving much faster, with a much more coordinated team effort, where everybody is pulling in sync. It symbolized picking up speed, that progression from paddling to rowing, all eight oars moving in unison. It continued to portray visually the message that we were all in the same boat, that we had to work together in a very coordinated way, and that the company's fate would impact us all.

Creighton used the image of *Haida Gwaii* as a powerful metaphor for teamwork. He distributed books showing photographs of the sculpture inscribed with the words, "Thanks for helping to launch the Black Canoe, Jack Creighton." He also invoked the image at meetings and speeches, such as the President's Forum, a gathering of Weyerhaeuser senior managers. Employees throughout the company soon came to identify the symbol of the Black Canoe with the vision of "one company."

Linking the Vision to Company Values

One major lesson that grew out of Weyerhaeuser's eighteen-month refocusing effort was the need for standardization. For years, the company had allowed its managers considerable autonomy in their own plants, facilities, or offices. As a result, communications were compromised and costs increased. By 1990, Weyerhaeuser had more than a hundred payroll systems, twenty-eight different kinds of PCs, and four plant accounting systems in a seven-unit business.

It became clear that without a vision and a set of values for the company as a whole, the notions of teamwork and forward momentum had no place to go. The senior management team spent eight months crafting a vision and values statement (see Figure 14-1) that reflected Weyerhaeuser's commitment to its customers, shareholders, employees, and communities. Then Creighton and his team held informal sessions at the company's major facilities to talk about their objectives and listen to employees' reactions.

Strategy 1 *Never lose sight of the ultimate goal, and focus energy on short-term objectives.*

Creighton recalled that he and his team delivered the message at more than a hundred Weyerhaeuser businesses and plants all over North America, as well as overseas:

> We said individual units could develop their own vision and values; the only caveat was that they had to be compatible with the corporate vision and values. So it wasn't a cookie-cutter approach across the company. I said to employees, "If you look around at what's happening in your office or your plant or your mill or in the forest—and you think things are going on that are not compatible with this vision, or these values or strategies—you need to raise your hand." Employees want to know where you stand. They want to know where the company is going.
>
> This was a fabric that was made up of many, many threads. We had rolled out the vision, we were benchmarking, we were taking a more cooperative approach to relationships with our unions, and we were doing more diversity training. I think it's comforting to employees when they can relate actions by the company back to these values, and to their units and jobs—when we talk about respect for our people, concern about safety, and diversity issues. It gives the Vision and Values life and blood; it isn't just a set of words. And it says, "management is serious about this."

Cooperating with the Unions

Gradual improvements in the areas of communications and employee empowerment at Weyerhaeuser led to a number of changes on the labor front. Respect for people was high on the list of company

Figure 14-1. Weyerhaeuser Vision and Values Statement.

OUR VISION	OUR VALUES

OUR VISION

THE BEST
FOREST PRODUCTS
COMPANY
IN THE WORLD

STRATEGIES
We shall achieve our vision by:

- Making Total Quality the Weyerhaeuser Way of doing business.

- Relentless pursuit of full customer satisfaction.

- Empowering Weyerhaeuser people.

- Leading the industry in forest management and manufacturing excellence.

- Producing superior returns for our shareholders.

 Weyerhaeuser

OUR VALUES

CUSTOMERS
We listen to our customers and improve our products and services to meet their present and future needs.

PEOPLE
Our success depends upon high-performing people working together in a safe and healthy workplace where diversity, development, and teamwork are valued and recognized.

ACCOUNTABILITY
We expect superior performance and are accountable for our actions and results. Our leaders set clear goals and expectations, are supportive, and provide and seek frequent feedback.

CITIZENSHIP
We support the communities where we do business, hold ourselves to the highest standards of ethical conduct and environmental responsibility, and communicate openly with Weyerhaeuser people and the public.

FINANCIAL RESPONSIBILITY
We are prudent and effective in the use of the resources entrusted to us.

values, and the periodic confrontations with unions did not fit well with management's principles of cooperation, inclusion, and teamwork. Creighton knew that there had to be a better way of dealing with organizing campaigns, labor negotiations, and strikes:

> **Strategy 7**
> *Master conflict—deal with anger in small doses, engage dissidents, and avoid needless power struggles.*

> Unions were a fact of life, and we had to develop positive relationships with those unions. We sat down with the leadership of one of the larger unions at Weyerhaeuser, the International Association of Machinists, and came up with a set of relationship-governing principles that we could mutually agree to. The key element was that, in a sense, we were partners; we needed to do a better job of sharing and communicating; we would periodically disagree on certain issues; but that no matter what happened, we would treat each other with respect.

Empowering Employees with Company Ownership

Growing out of the labor principles was the belief that if the company did well, the employees should do well, and that financial performance ought to be tied to rewards in the form of Weyerhaeuser stock. Participation meant ownership, and ownership meant empowerment. Since stock options were already available to those on the senior management compensation plan, the next step was to extend the opportunity for stock ownership

> **Strategy 6**
> *Minimize status differences and insist on courtesy and mutual respect.*

to all salaried employees. And, as Creighton learned to expect, the conscientious alignment of values with policy offered new challenges:

> Initially, we did not extend the stock ownership opportunity to the hourly, unionized employees. Within a year, though, it finally dawned on us that this policy was not in keeping with our goal of breaking down barriers between people—between staff and line, between wood products and pulp-and-paper products, between African-Americans and Caucasians, between men and women, and between union and nonunion employees. We talked about one company, about diversity and respect; but here we had a huge

number of our employees who were not participating in this plan because they were unionized.

> **Strategy 10**
> *Never give up—there's always another move.*

We were a little bit stymied by labor laws and union contracts, but eventually we found a way around the difficulties. We said to the unions, "This benefit is outside the contract and we will never use it for bargaining purposes. Management retains the right to cancel it at any time, but if we do cancel it, we will cancel it for everyone."

Listening to the Community

Long before embarking on its restructuring campaign, Weyerhaeuser had earned a reputation as a caring forester. During the 1980s, however, environmental activists began to complain loudly and bitterly about the company's practice of clear-cutting forests. The subdivision of forest lands, pollution, the threat to salmon runs, and the spotted owl controversy—the list of public concerns continued to grow.

The results of focus groups and polls conducted by the company were surprising: People in the states where Weyerhaeuser did business were convinced that their rights and values were being violated. It soon became clear to Weyerhaeuser's top managers that they were not living up to one of their own values: to communicate openly with the public. The company began a series of town hall meetings in various states and local communities where people were likely to have strong, and mostly antagonistic, opinions about Weyerhaeuser's impact on the environment.

> **Strategy 7**
> *Master conflict—deal with anger in small doses, engage dissidents, and avoid needless power struggles.*

At these meetings, Creighton and one other senior officer fielded questions from legislators, city and county officials, journalists, environmentalists, and ordinary citizens. The experience was often excruciating, but in Creighton's memory, the positive effects far outweighed the discomforts:

> You know, putting yourself up on the stage with a bull's-eye on your chest is not the most comfortable thing to do. The most traumatic experience was in Seattle, where a gen-

tleman got up and said he didn't want to speak from his
seat, he wanted to come right up to the stage and look us in
the eye and tell us what he had on his mind.

He was the epitome of the northwesterner—probably
in his sixties or seventies, gray hair, beard, nice crisp flannel
shirt. He said, basically, "You represent the most despicable,
underhanded . . ." and he just went on and started to cry. I
think some people thought he might physically attack us,
but he was emotionally distraught: He had lost a lawsuit
against Weyerhaeuser for water runoff, and he'd appealed
it twice and lost. He was convinced that we had not only
done the damage, but also bribed the courts. He finished
and walked out of the hall. After this gentleman, all we
could say was, "Thank you." There was no way you could
respond to him.

For people in the audience, it was an opportunity to get
a message to the top of the company. It was very worthwhile. The newspapers loved it. They were very positive
about our willingness to listen and to be open. And as CEO,
I learned a lot. It really sensitized me to people's feelings,
and it reinforced my belief about the importance of listening
and inclusion.

Keeping Perspective and Staying Healthy

Throughout the long and demanding process of leading the cultural transformation, Creighton was aware that his own health had an
impact on the job he was able to do for
the company. On the weekends he hiked
and climbed mountains. During the
week, he played racquetball. These activities helped offset the debilitating effects
of endless meetings, late-night flights,
and difficult decisions:

> **Strategy 4**
> *Take care of yourself: Main-*
> *tain your stamina and let go*
> *of guilt.*

As you make more and more decisions, you come to realize
that you're out in the traffic and you're going to get hit periodically. You're not going to make all the right decisions.
You know, I agonized over closing down a mill, for example. I had to close down our operations in Everett, Washington, where we'd been in business for seventy-five years. I
guess I'm pretty people-oriented, and sometimes your

greatest strength is your greatest weakness. I felt really bad about it and went up and visited the mill. The people weren't happy, but they helped me get over that guilt.

I think it's important to have outside interests and a good family situation. Two great ways to get yourself back on an even keel, if you're feeling really down, are physical exercise and some form of religious activity. You've got to keep your body and your psyche in good shape.

The Results

By the time Jack Creighton retired from Weyerhaeuser in 1998, all the recommendations that came out of the refocus effort had been executed. In 1991, the company's return on net assets (RONA) for its core businesses had ranked in the bottom quartile of the industry. By 1993, it had established itself firmly in the top quartile; and in Creighton's last year as CEO, Weyerhaeuser finished number one. During his leadership, the company divested more than $2 billion of noncore assets. A $600 million acquisition from Procter & Gamble was completed, along with the first ownership of forestlands outside North America.

At the millennium, which also marks the company's 100-year anniversary, the less tangible dimensions that make up the "many, many threads" of Weyerhaeuser's organizational design are strong: safety, customer focus, diversity, communication, empowerment, teamwork, ethics. Recently, the company won recognition on two important fronts: It received the top national Award for Business Ethics and achieved a top ranking in *Fortune* magazine's annual poll on social and environmental responsibility for the forest products industry. Under Creighton's leadership, Weyerhaeuser had made giant strides toward becoming one company—and one tribe.

15

Malden Mills: Rising from the Ashes

At *The Edge*

The wind was blowing from the west to the east and connected the fire among the three buildings so that it seemed like one enormous conflagration. It left everyone with no hope of doing anything about it. All that we had created was destroyed; it was over. Only thoughts of terror and hopelessness and grieving would emanate from the average personality upon seeing the destruction. As I stood there and watched the fire rage out of control, I was at *The Edge*. I could accept defeat and no one would have blamed me for it.

Most people watching the fire would have felt sorry for themselves and the situation. This would have been the normal reaction to what happened, the expected reaction. But that only leads to inactivity and depression and hopelessness. So, crying really doesn't help. In those kinds of situations what you have to do is think as best you can how to creatively improve the situation. I could take the insurance money and retire, but I had an obligation to my employees and the community. I decided that I had to try to save the company. I noticed that the fourth production building was not yet burning. It was close to burning, but if we could save that building, I would figure out how to rebuild the company.

Aaron Feuerstein

The Situation

The Company

Malden Mills Industries, named for the town of Malden where the company had originated, was started by Henry Feuerstein in 1906. The company had prospered in the first half of the century and, when it outgrew its facilities in Malden, moved in 1955 to nearby Lawrence. By then, Henry's son Samuel was president, and he worked hard to instill in his sons the ethic of hard work and the rich tradition of his Orthodox Jewish religion.

The Feuersteins were known throughout the community as generous and kind people who embodied the values of their Jewish heritage and had been responsible for building the Orthodox synagogue that had grown to be the largest in New England. They were also known to be driven and passionate business entrepreneurs who had created one of the most successful private companies in the extremely competitive commodity-based textile industry. As the costs of labor continued to climb in New England, many people speculated that it would just be a matter of time before Malden Mills moved south, where all "sensible" textile companies had relocated to find cheaper labor.

Aaron Feuerstein, however, continued to defy the skeptics. Now seventy years old, he had taken over from his father Samuel as president in the mid-1950s and had been responsible for its exceptional growth and for the development of innovative products that had completely redefined the textile industry. In the late 1970s, Feuerstein pioneered the concept of creating a fabric that had such unique characteristics and was of such superior quality that it revolutionized how clothing fabric was made. Created from recycled soft-drink bottles, the synthetic fabric, called Polarfleece, allowed outdoor enthusiasts to look sharp while staying warm in cold weather. Many of the biggest names in outdoor fashion—including L. L. Bean, Lands' End, and Patagonia—used the product in their popular clothing lines. The synthetic fleece was superior to all other fabrics, and Feuerstein realized that he could create a brand name in an otherwise commodity-based market. This strategy allowed Malden Mills to charge a premium for the product while demand still surged to new records.

During the 1980s, Malden Mills continued to refine its synthetic fleece and in 1991 introduced the next generation of the fabric called Polartec. This newer version was engineered to have the ability to take on numerous combinations of essential characteristics, which are determined during the finishing process. The ability to manipulate these characteristics allowed the fabric to have unlimited applications and to be used for almost any type of outdoor clothing, from winter jackets to wetsuits.

As the fabric's superior quality and characteristics became known to customers, they began to look for clothing that was made from Polartec fabric. Clothing manufacturers found that labeling their products with the Polartec label greatly enhanced sales. Business soared, and in 1995 sales for Polartec were more than $200 million, accounting for more than half of the company's revenues. Malden Mills introduced round-the-clock shifts to keep up with the demand for its products.

The Fire

On a very cold night in December 1995, a bitter forty-mile-per-hour wind swept across the Merrimack River and whipped through the textile factory buildings.

Inside the mill's main buildings, the howl of the wind could barely be heard as the machinery hummed with the sounds of constant production. Three second-shift employees worked along Flock production line two on the first floor of the Monomac building, turning out this fabric. In the production of this fabric, fifty-pound bags of finely chopped nylon particles were emptied into a hopper that sprayed them onto a line of electrically charged cloth. This process yielded fabric of the highest quality, but the combination of dust, heat, and electricity was potentially dangerous. Nobody saw the small fire start, but once the flame reached the dust particles, the fire accelerated through the 250 feet of open space, culminating in a deafening explosion that could be heard miles away.

That Monday evening was a special one for Aaron Feuerstein, who was celebrating his seventieth birthday with his family and close friends. It had been a surprise party, which was the only way that Feuerstein, a private man, would have permitted such an event. When he and his wife Louise arrived home around 11:00 P.M., they were surprised to hear the phone ringing as they walked into their kitchen. Louise watched Aaron's face turn pale as his production manager told him that the entire mill was burning out of control.

As Feuerstein and his wife drove toward Lawrence, still miles away, they were astounded to see the sky lit up with a bright orange glow. By the time they arrived, three of the four main production buildings were engulfed in fire, and the flames shot fifty feet above the roofs. Seeing the flames brought back dreaded memories of a smaller fire in the same building in 1993. That fire had left five workers badly injured, and since that time, Feuerstein had been relentless in his emphasis on safety. He often would show up unannounced to check that all safety procedures were being followed. There were fire drills and safety meetings several times a week, and official inspections showed that Malden Mills was in compliance with all new safety requirements.

But somehow the worst had happened, again. As Feuerstein recalled:

> I arrived there at midnight, and I can't tell you of the enormity of the raging of that fire. My reaction from the first moment that I saw it was that this was total devastation. . . . Our Polartec fabric has a uniqueness in having the finest technical finish in the world, and as a result, we have a quality and performance that is superior to the commodity goods. All the finishing processes were there in those buildings. Whatever technical progress we had made was in those buildings, and whatever specialty processes we had developed were in those buildings. I began to think while I was observing it, "How can I get back into business? How can I save my employees? How can I save the community?"

As he took stock of the situation, his first concern was for his employees. Initially, there were reports that many had died in the fire. As Feuerstein began to take charge, he met with his key managers. After some discussion, he learned that, miraculously, no one had died. Twenty-four workers were injured, and twelve others were badly burned; nine of them appeared near death. Many of the critically burned were being airlifted to nearby hospitals. This was the first glimmer of hope in a desperate situation.

The fire department had determined that there was not much they could do to keep the fire from spreading. Three of the four manufacturing buildings were now engulfed in flames, and it was only a matter of time before the fourth caught fire in the high winds. Although the first three buildings had been built in 1865, the fourth building had been built when Malden Mills relocated to Lawrence and was made from cinder blocks. Feuerstein remembers the scene clearly:

> The fourth mill was beginning to burn. It had some of the finishing equipment in it that was necessary to the production of Polartec. It was smoking and burning, but it seemed

to be not as hopeless as the others, even though it was almost touching the other buildings. So, as the fire raged, I realized that if we could save that fourth building, we might be able to save the whole thing. We could then save the community, the people, the customers, if we have that building. I turned to my director of engineering, who may be one of the best engineers in the country, and I said, "What do you think the chances are of saving that building?" He looked at me and replied, "Aaron, you've always been a dreamer; that building, together with the other three, will be burnt to the ground by 7:00 A.M."

The Actions

Remaining Inspired and Defying the Odds

Feuerstein was not one to give in, even in what seemed like a hopeless situation. He organized his employees and told them the situation. If they wanted to ever work at Malden Mills again, if they wanted to save the company and the community, then they must save the fourth mill. Without it, they could not expect to have a viable business.

> **Strategy 1**
> *Never lose sight of the ultimate goal, and focus energy on short-term objectives.*

Feuerstein inspired his employees to work through the night to save the fourth mill. Under the direction of the head of security, they were able to move equipment, wet down the building, and keep the fire from spreading. When dawn arrived, the fourth building was still standing and the fire was now under control.

> The instructions that I gave them were, "Do anything you need to do, just save that building," and so there they were, twenty-seven of my guys in that building, and they're still in my employ. They were in that building all night, and they saved it, and therefore the company, from certain destruction.

The saving of the fourth mill was an inspiration for Feuerstein and his employees. During the night, he had told many of his employees to go home and get a good night's sleep. He insisted that they would be needed in the days to come to help rebuild the company. As many employees returned in the morning to survey the destruction, they could hardly believe that the fourth mill was still standing.

> **Strategy 10**
> *Never give up—there's always another move.*

Regrouping and Refinancing

Feuerstein had saved the fourth mill but realized that to rebuild he would need capital. He tracked down his insurance manager to find out if they were covered for this type of situation. His manager assured him that they had good insurance and would be covered, but that the cap on the policy was $302 million. This was all that Feuerstein needed to hear. He announced to his employees and the media that somehow, they would rebuild the company and that every employee would eventually be called back to work. He was quoted in *The Boston Globe* as saying, "We're going to continue to operate in Lawrence. We had the opportunity to run to the South many years ago. We didn't do it then, and we're not going to do it now."

Meanwhile, as the employees gathered in the nearby shelters, skepticism continued to grow. Many suggested that there was no way the company would ever emerge from this tragedy. It seemed inconceivable that it could ever rebound from this destruction. Feuerstein was undaunted.

> **Strategy 2**
> *Set a personal example with visible, memorable symbols and behaviors.*

He insisted that by a "miracle," God had given them something to build on and that a new Malden Mills would emerge. Feuerstein displayed great leadership and steadfast courage in the following days, weeks, and months. He visited the injured employees, met with those out of work, and huddled several times a day with his top managers to discuss rebuilding.

Feuerstein moved the families of injured employees into hotel rooms near the hospital so that they could be close to the injured. On Wednesday, two days after the fire, employees lined up for what they thought would be their last paycheck and were surprised to find that 1,400 of the hourly employees had been given a $275 holiday bonus, as well as gift certificates to a local supermarket.

> **Strategy 5**
> *Reinforce the team message constantly: "We are one—we live or die together."*

On Thursday, Feuerstein announced to employees that he would continue to pay their salaries and health benefits for at least thirty days, even though the mill was closed. Slowly but surely, Feuerstein rebuilt his employees' wavering confidence and continued to defy the skeptics with unusual acts of tremendous leadership and great personal example. More important, people were starting to take notice.

Within three days of the fire, the U.S. senators from Massachusetts, John Kerry and Ted Kennedy, announced the award of $3.78 million in Department of Labor money to assist the displaced workers. Within a week, U.S. Labor Secretary Robert Reich promised an additional $3.7 million for job training and counseling. By the following week, the community had started to mobilize. The national Union of Needletrades, Industrial, and Textile Employees (UNITE) donated $50 per employee as part of a $100,000 contribution. Local restaurants began offering half-price meals to workers, while one of Malden's customers donated $20 to each worker for groceries. Many other companies started to follow suit.

Overcoming Setbacks in the Fire's Aftermath

During one of the first of what would become daily crisis meetings with his managers, Feuerstein stated that they would have to be fully operational in thirty days or risk losing customers. He had called his customers and assured them that he could be in production in thirty days. One of his engineers stated that this would be nearly impossible. Feuerstein listened and responded:

> **Strategy 3**
> *Instill optimism and self-confidence, but stay grounded in reality.*

> From this moment on, it is just a question of doing more rapidly what people are used to doing more slowly. We will rebuild in record time; what some consider impossible, we will figure out how to do.

Employees worked around the clock and, inspired by Feuerstein's leadership, began to focus on the number-one priority, which was to get Polartec production up and running. Next, they would focus on the production of Woven goods. These two manufacturing lines were essential because while they lay idle, Feuerstein's mills in Maine and New Hampshire, which supplied unfinished goods to the Lawrence complex, could not resume operations. Once they had these items in production, the plan was to try to rebuild the Flock operation. Even though Flock had been losing money and some wanted to phase it out, Feuerstein felt that too many workers would lose their jobs if this happened.

During peak pre-fire performance, Malden Mills, with its main mill in Lawrence and two smaller ones in New Hampshire and Maine, had been capable of producing about 1.8 million yards of high-quality textiles a week. Feuerstein had employed 3,100 workers—2,320 in Lawrence and the rest in his other mills and warehouses, or in sales offices in five states and two European countries. This was a complex operation with many interdependent parts, all of which needed to be coordinated in the fire's aftermath.

Management set up a temporary operations center in the home of the chief of production. As workers went through the mill wreckage, they made one find as good as a gold mine. In trailers behind a burned-out building, half-buried by the collapsed structure, were five new Polartec machines that had somehow remained undamaged. Workers began installing the new machines in an undamaged warehouse while managers tracked down additional equipment in Europe. They made calls to other manufacturers to outsource the dyeing of the Polartec fabric.

> **Strategy 1**
> *Never lose sight of the ultimate goal, and focus energy on short-term objectives.*

Through sheer willpower, and strengthened by the renewed confidence instilled in them by Feuerstein, the production crew managed to make the first test run of Polartec fabric within ten days of the fire. There was still a tremendous amount of work to do, but this symbolic event made them begin to believe that they might achieve their goals. Feuerstein recalled:

> They called me down and they said that the fabric is coming off of that fourth plant. I went over there and opened the door, and it was a symphony of equipment noise. It took several months to get back to full-scale operation, but they wanted to show me that they could get a fabric out in ten days. The machinery was running, and all my workers were standing there with tears in their eyes.
>
> I went over and shook hands with each one of them, and they were all crying. I let myself cry on that day because it was a cry of joy and satisfaction. One worker said, "Aaron, we're going to pay you back tenfold," and they did.

As the work continued, there were many setbacks along the way. By the end of December, the makeshift mill, called "Finishing Two," was producing 140,000 yards a week of Polartec, which represented 20 percent of normal output. Insurance money, however, was being withheld pending detailed documentation of the losses and a determination of the fire's cause. Only $2 million had been paid, and Feuerstein desperately needed cash to keep rebuilding. He turned to his creditors, with whom he had built strong relationships over the years, and continued to borrow heavily, going tens of millions of dollars into debt.

On January 12, 1996, one month after the fire, Feuerstein shocked the media and surprised his employees again. He announced that he would pay his employees for another thirty days, even though they were not yet back at work. This decision was met with resistance from his management team. The first payment had been a gesture of great generosity and the right thing to do; however, this time, they told him, it was risky financially. By current estimates, the costs of rebuilding were likely to exceed the insurance cap, and that was assuming that they would collect all of it. Feuerstein remembers his response:

> **Strategy 2**
> *Set a personal example with visible, memorable symbols and behaviors.*

> This is the right thing to do and, in another thirty days, I will do it again. These people have worked hard and are the key to our production of the high-quality products that we have become known for. I will not abandon them.

Paying his employees for three months was likely to cost upwards of $15 million, and there was a good chance that this amount would never be recouped. Feuerstein believed, however, that the workers had gained a lot of momentum, even if they still had a long journey ahead of them. He constantly worked to keep his people focused and to maintain their sense of confidence that the company would prevail. He believed that paying them was a powerful example of his commitment to them and that it was essential to keep his employees focused on the short-term goal of rebuilding.

> **Strategy 5**
> *Reinforce the team message constantly: "We are one—we live or die together."*

Tapping Inner Strength and Stamina

Over the weeks that followed, employees who were still out of work showed up each day and asked Feuerstein what they could do this day to help with the effort. He had succeeded in keeping the company and his team of dedicated employees together.

As the daily stress and anxiety continued to mount, many of Feuerstein's managers were becoming burned out. Each day, Feuerstein would meet with those who needed to be shored up and express his confidence in them. He seemed to them to be a pillar of strength and to have an inner calm that was hard to fathom. Each day at 5:15 A.M., without exception, Feuerstein would get up and start his morning routine. He exercised for one hour each day, following a strict regimen to maintain both his physical and mental edge:

> *Strategy 4*
> *Take care of yourself: Maintain your stamina and let go of guilt.*

> I did it through all my financial woes and I did it all through the fire. There is no adversity that can hit me that makes me break down on this commitment to physical and mental exercise because I'm looking for longevity. Besides the physical exercise, about ten years ago I decided that I'm going to do mental exercise every day just like I do physical exercise, to prevent anything from happening to my memory. So while I'm running I am reciting by memory Hebrew poetry. When I do my push-ups and calisthenics, I am reciting English poetry. I do this every day without exception.

Besides keeping up his physical and mental stamina, Feuerstein took other steps to maintain a sense of order in a chaotic world. Each year, it had been his habit to visit the local charitable organizations during the holidays. This year would be no different. On one particular day, he visited the soup kitchen on Newbury Street and a shelter on North Parish Road. After talking with the people inside, he would quietly leave behind a personal check for $20,000. Many could not believe that Feuerstein could remain so focused on others in this time of great personal setbacks.

By early February, the mill was producing more than 200,000 yards of Polartec each week. This production level would do for now, with peak demand still months away. However, this was only 25 percent of the mill's pre-fire capacity, and customers were getting nervous. Feuerstein assured Patagonia, L. L. Bean, Lands' End, and others that Malden Mills would be back in full production by March, and despite competitors' efforts to woo them away, these major customers remained steadfastly loyal, at least for the time being.

Surviving "Sudden Death"

By forty-five days after the fire, Feuerstein was becoming anxious that the company was not recovering quickly enough. The Polartec and Woven lines were working, but by now he had expected to have plans in place for getting Flock production back on line.

On February 10, Feuerstein announced for the third time that the workers who had not yet returned to the mill would again be paid. He regretfully explained that this would be the last payment and that he could no longer continue to pay employees after this month. Feuerstein was, in the interim, arranging for the contractors who were rebuilding the mill to hire temporary workers from his company whenever possible. Feuerstein had worked relentlessly to get employees back to work, but because of delays in getting Flock production on line, there would still be many out of work in the months to follow.

Feuerstein's continued generosity inspired others. One customer, the president of a South Dakota firm, flew to Massachusetts and personally presented Feuerstein with a check for $30,000. *Boston Globe* Publisher William O. Taylor sent a $10,000 donation, and the Bank of Boston donated $50,000 to start a Malden Mills relief fund. Holy Family Hospital began offering free care to victims of the fire, and restaurants started giving free meals to residents evacuated from their homes. Contributions had been flowing in since the fire, but now, inspired by Feuerstein's example, the fund had grown to more than $1 million. This would mean that the workers would continue to receive some support over the next several months.

> **Strategy 2**
> *Set a personal example with visible, memorable symbols and behaviors.*

Feuerstein also visited his customers. He went to San Francisco to shore up his upholstery customers and then to a trade show in Salt Lake City to calm fears of apparel buyers. He had just started a production facility in Munich and went to Germany to assure his European clients that Malden Mills would prevail.

> Our customers are very loyal as long as it does not adversely affect them financially. But the minute they can't get goods and they have to go someplace else, that's it, that is the end of the ball game, and so our ability to get back into business rapidly was key so that customers' financial losses were minimal.

Fortunately, the winter season has the least demand for Polartec, since all cold-weather garments would have been manufactured months before. But this lull in demand would not last long, and Feuerstein found himself racing with time for the next winter season:

> Very often in business there's a situation of sudden death where if I don't meet the financial plan, I'm in trouble and I'll be out of business and if I do [meet plan], I win big-time. People around me at the meetings say, "We can't stand this sudden death, it's just too tense, it's too much, it takes too much out of us!"
>
> I always answer them that this is really what life is all about and that you should figure out the sudden death in almost every situation rather than sit back and think that you've got time. You don't have time. You've just got to do what you've got to do. I'm not afraid of that sudden death period, even though I know it's a risk and that I might not always win it. I am willing to play day in and day out at *The Edge*. That's what makes life exciting.

> **Strategy 9**
> *Be willing to take the Big Risk.*

By the end of February, progress had been made, but there were setbacks, and frustrations remained. The Flock production team had failed to secure a temporary facility, and their initial planning had not revealed that they would have to build a separate steam-generating plant to power the facility. This setback would delay production for at least another ninety days, and time was running out for Malden Mills to maintain a presence in the Flock market.

Meanwhile, the rebuilding was well under way, and Feuerstein could now look out of his fourth-floor window over the twenty-nine acres of Malden Mills and see some progress. The foundation was poured for a new 610,000-square-foot, state-of-the-art textile factory on the site of two of the burned buildings. The existing buildings were starting to return to their pre-fire condition as workers continued to sandblast and repaint their exteriors. On the inside, new equipment continued to pour in, and Polartec production capability was close to 90 percent of the original levels.

Six months after the devastating fire, Feuerstein still faced major hurdles. The mill continued to outsource its fabric dyeing to various facilities across the country, and the daily costs were enormous. To make matters worse, insurance payments had only been about 17 percent, or approximately $51 million, of the total expected amount. Feuerstein worked with fire and safety officials to accelerate their investigation. Money was running out, and he desperately needed an insurance settlement to stay in business. He continued to work with his creditors and to assure them that his business would not only survive but thrive.

The following months proved to be challenging for Malden Mills, but under Feuerstein's leadership, the company continued to make progress. The summer months are the peak demand times for Polartec as the clothing industry prepares for the fall and winter seasons. Production of Polartec was nearly a million yards short of orders as production was just returning to pre-fire levels. The mill could not meet all of its buyers' deadlines and lost critical business in the following weeks. To make matters worse, millions of dollars of much-needed machinery arrived but could not be used because it needed to be retooled.

By late July 1996, the insurance payments were still trickling in and Feuerstein had received only $78 million, far short of the $302 million total in coverage that he was counting on. The insurance companies kept demanding more detailed documentation and were refusing comprehensive payments until a cause of the fire was determined. His bank loans were now more than $100 million and were rapidly climbing higher.

By September 1996, the Flock production was still not up and running, and Feuerstein was experiencing the consequences of the delays. They had simply run out of time and would miss the 1997 upholstery-buying season. He would have to wait a full year before the unit could begin earning income. He again had to announce that the delay would be several months. His Flock production manager had tried hard to get the line into production but had failed and felt he had to resign. Feuerstein took full responsibility for the failure. As he met with the 400 workers who had been waiting patiently to return to work, he remarked with bitter disappointment that he had "made a profound mistake" and that he was uncertain when, if ever, they would be able to return to the Flock production line. He urged them to get on with their lives and stated that he would provide an additional three months of medical insurance while they looked for new jobs.

Over the next several months, Feuerstein continued to make progress. He and his employees worked diligently, slowly rebuilding the company, literally brick by brick. By late fall 1996, as the leaves began to turn, Feuerstein allowed himself the luxury of reflecting back over the past ten months and was generally pleased with what he saw: His manufacturing lines were running on new computer-controlled machines, the model of technology and efficiency. Close to 700,000 yards of Polartec were rolling off the line each week. His Woven line was back in full swing and producing a new and higher-quality fabric than before the fire. Nearly 2,000 workers were back on the job, and more would be rehired in the months to come.

> **Strategy 8**
> *Find something to celebrate and something to laugh about!*

Months earlier, Feuerstein had planned a company-wide gala celebration to thank his employees and celebrate the success they'd had in rebuilding the company. In an uncharacteristic move, Feuerstein canceled the celebration at that time, because he was barely hanging on to key customers, and each minute of production was essential. Although he viewed celebration and recognition as critical, at that time he had neither the time nor money for an event that would have shut down operations for a half day.

A dedication eventually took place, however, in September 1997. It was a gala event with more than 15,000 guests in attendance, including all employees and family members, along with local and national political, religious, financial, business, and media leaders.

The Results

Just over one year after the fire, the insurance companies had paid about $180 million of the expected $302 million. In the months following, the fire investigation exonerated Malden Mills of any negligence, and slowly the insurance companies began to pay the remaining millions due the company. His company was beginning to reach pre-fire revenues, and when asked about the experience, Feuerstein beamed with deep pride as he recalled what had become known as the "Malden Miracle":

> You attempt in the business world to try to combine, even though they're two different things, the idea of business and everything that it stands for and the principle of faith and everything faith represents. Most people don't think of it as one. For them, business and faith are two separate worlds. In the world of business you eradicate the faith, and in the world of the faith you eradicate the business. . . . Each day and each year all of our efforts have to be focused on trying

to take the business world and the moral and ethical teach-
ings and bring them together and work out an intelligent
balance toward the ideal of making them one.

Feuerstein was recognized for his actions on behalf of his community and employees by President Clinton, who hailed him as a national
hero. The American Jewish Historical Society awarded him the Emma
Lazarus Award, for reflecting "the very best Jewish traditions."
Feuerstein was only the fifth person to receive the award in the society's 104 years of existence. Boston University and Merrimack College
awarded him honorary degrees in humanities and ethics, and the Jewish community recognized him with the Orthodox Union's Kesser
Shem Tov Award.

More important, Feuerstein delivered on his promise to his employees and the community. In his own words:

When all is moral chaos, this is the time for you to be a
mensch. In Yiddish, the word *mensch* means more than just
a man. It carries a sense of righteousness and obligation that
it is up to you to act and to be an example to all when there
is nothing to guide you in terms of morality and ethics. It's
not up to the whole community anymore, it's not up to your
club, it's not up to your school, it's not up to your family.
You're out there all alone in the world, and in the last analysis you've got to do something. In those situations, I stand
forward, and I do what needs to be done.

PART THREE

Continuing Your Expedition

16

Learning to Lead at
The Edge

It's never too late to be what you might have been.

George Eliot

The ten strategies outlined in Part One of this book provide a road-map for leaders who want to take their organizations to *The Edge*—to help them achieve their greatest potential. This chapter focuses on the personal dimension of the journey—the behaviors, attitudes, and ways of thinking about life that help individuals to realize their full potential as leaders. Specifically, it outlines a number of qualities and actions that—in my experience—contribute to living, learning, and thriving at *The Edge*.

Cultivate Poised Incompetence

When my son Jonathan turned sixteen, he got his own car, a Toyota Celica that was in good condition for a vehicle with about 90,000 miles on the odometer. Trying to be a good father, I spent a lot of time going over the importance of car maintenance, trying to remember everything *my* father told me to do.

Each parent stresses certain lessons or tasks as if they are the most important in the world. For my mother, it was choosing exactly the right word and pronouncing words exactly the way they were supposed to be pronounced. For my father, one of the central tasks in life was checking the engine oil and keeping an eye on the dipstick.

I was not as religious about watching the oil as my dad, but in an effort to be a good parent, I did my best to pass on the tradition to Jonathan. As a result, my son put all his teenage energy into getting the Celica into shape: washing, waxing, scraping off rust, dabbing on touch-up paint, and most important of all, watching the oil.

Jonathan watched the dipstick like a hawk, waiting for his big moment to add oil. When the time finally came, I was inside playing my guitar. Jonathan came in, brimming with excitement, and asked for a funnel. I went out to the garage, got him one, and then went back to playing.

A little while later, he came in and said, "Dad, this one's too big. I need a smaller funnel." So I went out to the garage a second time and got another funnel, saying, "This should do it. It's the smallest I have." It never occurred to me to ask why he needed such a small funnel.

After a while, I went outside to see how he was doing. He had an extremely frustrated expression on his face. "What's the problem?" I asked.

He pointed at the engine. I looked down and saw an extraordinary creation. It was a marvel of mechanical engineering. Jonathan had taken a roll of duct tape and attached a piece of glass tubing from his chemistry set to my small funnel. With this contraption, he was pouring oil . . . can you guess where? He wasn't pouring it into the normal hole on top of the engine, but into the hole for the dipstick, which is about the size of a pencil. He said, "Dad, this is taking forever!" And it probably would have.

When I showed him the two-inch hole over the manifold that most people use to add oil, it came as quite a revelation. The story did have a happy ending. We finished the job in about three minutes, and we still laugh about Jonathan and the dipstick.

What's the point of this story? Leaving aside my limitations as an auto mechanics coach, I can think of two. One is that—in the spirit of Strategy 10 ("Never give up")—with enough creativity and determination, you can accomplish the mission even if your strategy is not perfect. Jonathan was getting oil into the engine, even if it was taking him a while to do it.

A second point is that developing any skill is a journey that starts at the beginning with a certain level of ignorance and incompetence. When we look at people who are exceptional at their craft, we often think they were born with that knowledge. One of the interesting aspects about getting older is that you find that some of your friends actually make it to positions of real responsibility—and you knew them when.

Two of my Naval Academy classmates fit this description. John Dalton became the Secretary of the Navy, and Chuck Krulak became the Commandant of the Marine Corps. Both were talented individuals who showed early promise. But when I saw them at the Pentagon, thirty years after graduation, with everyone saluting, I did a double-take. I knew them both from plebe year at Annapolis, when we were first learning how to spit-shine our shoes, and before they had distinguished themselves as exceptional leaders.

In doing research on Shackleton's life, I discovered to my amazement that before his first trip to the South Pole he had never pitched a tent; he had never slept in a sleeping bag; he had never slept in a tent overnight; and he had never lit a Primus stove. He had never done any of these basic tasks and yet, eventually, he developed the skills to lead an expedition that would triumph over overwhelming obstacles in the most hostile environment on earth.

I do not recommend going to Antarctica without knowing how to set up a tent. I do know, however, that we all have to start somewhere. The first key to learning to lead at *The Edge* is this: Cultivate poised incompetence. You have to be willing to be incompetent in order to learn. Just because you don't know what you are doing doesn't mean you have to be embarrassed or upset or convinced something's wrong with you.

There are countless stories of people who moved from incompetence to great proficiency: The Red Baron crashed on his first solo landing; Michael Jordan was cut from his high school basketball team; and in the beginning of his administration, Abraham Lincoln was seen as an equivocating, mediocre president.

To achieve the ultimate level of skill in any profession—particularly the profession of leadership—means accepting a level of incompetence. It also means constantly raising the bar and learning the next task while maintaining a sense of poise, grace, and good humor.

Learn to Love the Plateau

I once had an opportunity to spend some time with a writer and martial arts expert named George Leonard, and I was impressed by many of his ideas. Leonard, who has studied the topic of mastery, argues that a basic ingredient in the process involves a willingness to live in that most dreaded of all places—the plateau, the level place in the learning process.[1]

Our culture places tremendous emphasis on instant gratification, quick fixes, and sound bites. We are busy people, and we do not have time for things that take time. In fact, there is no higher compliment than being called a "quick study." I actually saw an infomercial for a videotape called *Become a Zen Master in Thirty Minutes.* Presumably, for $29.95 and a half-hour of your time, you can compete with the Dalai Lama for enlightenment!

In this culture of ever-increasing clock speed, if events do not move quickly, we are easily convinced that something is seriously wrong. What's taking this plant so long to grow? Let's pull it up and see what the problem is.

The truth is that some things do not happen overnight. Yes, there can be spurts of learning, but they often occur after extended periods of practice in that flat place, the plateau. Whether you are learning a martial art or learning to be a leader, you need to develop the capacity to stay in that frustrating place when there are no immediate signs of progress.

Now, there are many ways of being on the plateau. You can kick back and coast. You can tune out and pretend it does not exist. Or you can embrace the plateau with the same focus, energy, and passion that you would if you were getting the instant reinforcement and affirmation that we all love.

I believe that the journey of learning to lead means accepting the reality that leadership skills are developed through long periods of striving with only moderate signs of progress. This means that learning to love the plateau is an essential part of learning to lead at *The Edge.*

Come to Terms with Fear

Although most people don't like to talk about it, fear seems to be an integral part of life. Every leader that I have been close to—close enough that they would really level with me—has described times that fear has loomed large in his or her life. Dealing with uncertainty, managing ambiguity, and not always knowing what to do come with the territory of being a leader.

In fact, nature has programmed us to be afraid of perceived threats, and this physiological mechanism has an important function: It helps us avoid danger. Biologists have identified a part of the brain called the amygdala whose function is just that—producing the reaction of being afraid.

Thanks to many years of biogenetic programming, we are quite skilled at being afraid. The problem is that to make a difference in the world, you often have to enter into territory where things can go wrong. Where there is risk, you can fail. You can be embarrassed. Sometimes there are more severe consequences: People can lose jobs, and sometimes, people can even die. There are many circumstances or events that trigger fear.

If fear is that much a part of life at *The Edge*—if it is that important a part of being human—we ought to know something about it. We ought to make a friend of it, as Joe Hyams suggests in his book *Zen in the Martial Arts*.[2] Making a friend of fear means understanding what is most personally intimidating to us and embracing it rather than pulling back.

The things that provoke fear are different for each of us. Some people are afraid to stand up in front of a group of people to deliver a speech. Others are afraid to take a personal financial risk or deal with the unknown. As Virginia Satir, the well-known family therapist, once remarked, "Most people prefer the certainty of misery to the misery of uncertainty."

Making a friend of fear means, first of all, understanding what it is that scares you. Second, it means understanding your personal reaction to fear. For example, when you are fearful:

> ➤ How does your body respond?
> ➤ What do you say to yourself?
> ➤ How do you feel?

You may be like Roberto Goizueta, the former CEO of Coca-Cola, who was asked whether he slept well at night, given all the competition in his industry. "Yes, I sleep like a baby, " he replied. "I wake up every two hours and cry."[3]

Finally, making a friend of fear means developing a way to detoxify the fear so that you can maximize your own effectiveness. For example:

> ➤ You can write about it.
> ➤ You can talk to other people about it.
> ➤ You can think about ways in which you have successfully dealt with fear in the past.
> ➤ You can ask friends for suggestions.
> ➤ You can do something else so terrifying that you forget about what you were afraid of in the first place.

A final observation on fear: Sometimes we think that fear is an obstacle that prevents us from accomplishing something. We say to ourselves, "I can't do that, I'm afraid." However, I learned in Vietnam just how much people are capable of achieving while being really scared.

Experiencing fear, therefore, does not mean that you cannot accomplish something. It doesn't even mean that something is wrong. In many circumstances you are supposed to be afraid. It just means that while you are doing it, you are going to be afraid—perhaps even terrified. The more you accept and engage your fears, the less they will stand in the way.

Find an Environment That Supports Learning

If you want to develop the ability to lead at *The Edge,* then find an organization that promotes good leadership. Robert Scott learned to be a leader at Dartmouth, where he received the best education the Royal Navy could provide. He later honed his skills by observing naval leaders firsthand, drawing his own conclusions about what it meant to be a leader.

As I have noted earlier, however, the Royal Navy of the time was a flawed institution, still basking in the glow of Horatio Nelson's past victories. Only such a navy would be content with muzzle-loading weapons while others had adopted the cutting-edge technology of breech-loaded guns. A complacent organization will produce complacent leaders.

The Royal Navy of the 1880s is ancient history, but what strikes closer to home are modern examples of complacency and inadequate leadership. David Nadler, in his provocative book, *Champions of Change,* recounts the eighteen months during 1992 and 1993 in which the CEOs of more than a dozen companies were forced to leave their jobs. Some of the most respected CEOs in the country were forced out of their jobs at IBM, General Motors, American Express, Eastman Kodak, Eli Lilly, AlliedSignal, Westinghouse, Digital Equipment Company, and Compaq. Nadler argues persuasively that the common denominator was that each was an industry leader with a sustained record of success. Each CEO was a victim of the "success syndrome."[4]

The characteristics of the Success Syndrome are eerily reminiscent of the old Royal Navy:

> ➢ *Codification.* Informal policies once successful become rigid policies.

> *Internal focus.* Threats from outside forces, such as competitors, are ignored.
> *Arrogance and complacency.* The belief that competitive problems are "only temporary."
> *Complexity.* Internal politics and the preservation of power become primary objectives.
> *Conservatism.* The culture becomes risk-averse.
> *Disabled learning.* New insights are not incorporated into the organizational memory.

As history demonstrates, the presence of these factors can have dire consequences for the organization. These characteristics also have direct implications for leadership. "Junior officers" model their successful seniors; and they behave in ways that are reinforced by the dominant culture of the organization.

The essential point is this: If you want to realize your full potential as a leader, look at the culture of the organization where you work. If it fits the characteristics of the Success Syndrome, find another. In the right environment, you are much more likely to become an Ernest Shackleton—not a Robert Scott.

Practice the Art of Thriving

Chapter 4 dealt with the vital importance of maintaining one's stamina as a leader at *The Edge*. There is, however, a more expansive way of thinking about taking care of yourself. I refer to this broader perspective as "the art of thriving."

The art of thriving focuses on sustaining career achievement and personal well-being throughout the life cycle. I believe that people who do this successfully are able to integrate the five components of the life structure shown in Figure 16-1.

Each individual has a unique set of needs. The ability to develop a sense of mastery in each of these five areas—work, relationships, renewal, physical health, and purpose—while also establishing a balance among them, is essential to personal vitality and thriving.

Work

It is interesting to look at work from the perspective of those who experience it with a sense of passion and excitement. In talking about

Figure 16-1. The "art of thriving" life structure.

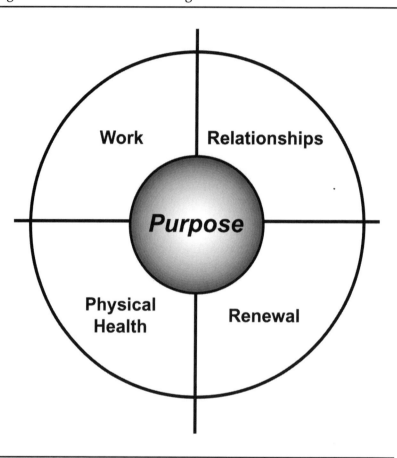

performing his music, Isaac Stern remarked that playing the violin is not just a "job" but a way of life. "It's a way of speaking, a way of expressing something . . . this ecstatic moment when you are at one with the phenomenon of man's creativity. That's very special. That's what is meant by being a musician."

You don't have to be a violinist to experience work as creative expression. On the contrary, I think it can happen in any profession, from computer technology to investment banking. The critical task is to make sure that your unique strengths are brought to bear on a task that provides satisfaction and meaning. In testing the extent to which work contributes to a sense of vitality in your life, here are some questions you may want to ask yourself:

> Are you using your unique strengths and distinctive abilities in your work?
> Are you enjoying what you are doing? Are you having any fun?
> Are you intrinsically interested in the work you are doing? Do you find the substance of the work engaging?
> Is your work a creative expression of who you are?

If the answers to these questions are generally yes, then you—like Isaac Stern—are fortunate. If the answers are generally no, however, it may be time to rethink this part of your life. The problem may lie with the work itself, or it may be a "systems problem" originating somewhere else in the life structure.

Relationships

The importance of supportive social relationships in managing stress and promoting individual well-being has been demonstrated repeatedly. Having others to whom you can turn provides a "psychic balm" that heals many wounds. For high achievers, however, establishing such relationships can be a problem. Life in the fast track leaves little time for developing the kind of mutual relationships that give the greatest support.

This is especially true during times of transition—such as when you are moving, joining a new organization, or starting a new job. During these periods of change, previous social support systems are often uprooted. To make matters worse, the challenges of a new environment and the attendant anxieties about "measuring up" may make it seem as if there is no time for socializing.

Taking the time to develop relationships is more important than ever in times of transition, but you will need to give the relationships in your life special attention. Some questions you may want to ask yourself periodically are:

> Where are your sources of support and nurturance?
> Who are the people in your life who care about you as a person, rather than simply as a representation of a job title?
> Do you have a sense of belonging in some group or community other than work?

> ➤ Are you making time to nurture the relationships that are important in your life?

Physical Health

The Spartans had an expression: "You cannot have a healthy mind without a healthy body." Physical health contributes to good decision making, and many successful leaders I have studied point to sheer energy as an important contributor to their achievement. Unfortunately, the importance of having a sound physical foundation is overlooked when things get hot. Basic needs such as sleep, food, and regular exercise are worth tracking. Some questions to ask:

> ➤ Are you getting enough sleep, and are you resting well when you fall asleep?
> ➤ Are you eating a balanced diet? Are you using caffeine as a substitute for sleep or exercise?
> ➤ Are you getting enough exercise? Regular exercise is a proven stamina builder. It doesn't mean you need to participate in a triathlon. Just walking briskly three times a week makes a major contribution, and walking can be done without equipment while you are on the road. The critical point, especially while traveling, is to plan your exercise in advance and to think of it as an important part of your job.
> ➤ Are you setting aside time—at least fifteen minutes a day—for concentrated relaxation and "decompression"?

Renewal

Some people attend to all the factors previously mentioned and still experience a sense of burnout and ennui. This problem often originates from a failure to create space for what I call "renewal"—the uniquely personal activities that bring a sense of revitalization into your life. Here are some questions about renewal to examine:

> ➤ Is there space in your life for you to engage in "regenerative" activities?
> ➤ Are there times when you can forget the needs of others and lose yourself in nonwork activities that are absorbing and renewing?

Sense of Purpose

The final element in the art of thriving involves the ability to find a deeper sense of meaning in life. This sense of purpose is ultimately grounded in an underlying set of values about what is important, right, or worthwhile. For some people, this purpose has a spiritual basis. For others it may be connected to beliefs about the importance of scientific progress, technological advances, or creating knowledge. For still others a sense of purpose is rooted in the need to contribute to humanity or to give to others. Once again, I return to Isaac Stern as an example. He has commented: "I've been playing concerts since I was fifteen. The world has been very nice to me, and I've taken a lot of things. I have to give something back."

Whatever the source, an ability to find meaning and purpose is an extremely important determinant of "stress hardiness" and longevity. Keeping track of the way you are feeling about these deeper issues is important. Lacking this underlying sense of direction, it is extremely difficult to maintain peak performance and personal effectiveness. Spend some time reflecting on the following questions:

➤ How do you feel about the direction your life is taking?
➤ What are the deeper values that guide your work?
➤ Are the other parts of your life—work, relationships, physical health, and renewal—consistent with this sense of purpose?

Balance

The final skill in the art of thriving is the ability to find balance among all five elements. Of course, no one can create and maintain perfect balance in life. Personal and professional growth involves change, experimentation, risk, and mistakes. The art of thriving is not based on an artificial attempt to establish rigid equanimity. On the contrary, its essence lies in the ability to know when life is out of balance and when you need to restore balance.

Developing this ability is a lifelong process. Morihei Uyeshiba, the famous martial arts teacher, was once asked by a student, "Master, how is it that you are never off balance when you are attacked?" His reply serves as a metaphor: "I am often off center—but I recover so quickly you never notice."

Mastering the art of thriving, then, means having the courage to explore the unknown, the willingness to risk losing your balance, and the tenacity to find that balance again. It is a demanding journey, but the rewards are great.

Relax . . . It Takes Time to Play Like Yourself

A final observation on leading at *The Edge* comes from my ongoing quest to play the tenor saxophone. On this journey I have spent a great deal of time on the plateau— perhaps even at "base camp"—but have yet to be discouraged. One reason for my perseverance is the encouragement of my teacher, Steve, a superb player who brings out the best in everyone.

I always tape my lessons so that I can hear what Steve does, and also so that I can listen to myself and learn what I need to do to perform better. I usually have to grit my teeth when I listen to my own playing, but one day I went to a section of the tape where I had been improvising over a song called "Blue Bossa." I was amazed. I was incredible. I was fluid. I was creative. I was almost flawless. Then the tape continued and I heard my own voice asking a question. Wow, I was so great I could talk and play the tenor saxophone at the same time.

Then it hit me: I had actually been listening to Steve. It was deflating, to be sure, but I recovered. At my next lesson, I said, "Steve, I'm very discouraged. Am I ever going to be able to improvise like that?" He took out his pencil and wrote out one word on my music: T-I-M-E.

Learning takes time. Once you understand that, you realize that the process of becoming a leader, or a musician, has to unfold. Yes, you need to practice. Yes, you need to work hard. Yes, there are tricks and techniques. But the uniqueness of your personal style has its own timetable. As the great trumpet player Miles Davis once said, "I can always tell when someone is trying to copy me or another musician. Sometimes you have to play for a long time before you can play like yourself."

17

Epilogue: A Perspective on Success and Failure

Was Shackleton a success or a failure as a leader? True, he led his crew to safety in what was arguably the greatest adventure in the history of polar exploration. The fact remains, however, that the Imperial Trans-Antarctic Expedition did not achieve its goal: It did not cross Antarctica.

Shackleton's critics have pointed out that, given the severe ice conditions, he should never have left South Georgia in the first place; that he should have had more or different equipment; and that he failed to plan for every possible contingency, as well as listing other flaws. On the other side of the ledger, there are those who lionize Shackleton as a leader. These supporters believe that he embodied everything that a leader should be.

I believe that any attempt to categorize Shackleton as a success or a failure misses the point. There is no debate about whether the expedition met its original goal. It did not. The question of whether Shackleton was successful as a leader does not have a simple or definitive answer. Any conclusion depends on the criteria by which Shackleton's leadership is judged.

There is little doubt that as an individual, Shackleton demonstrated an extraordinary level of determination and tenacity. But he did more than that. He also created a team with such strong bonds that, on the verge of starvation, they were willing to share their last rations. It was a team that worked together against enormous odds to overcome staggering obstacles. Although Shackleton failed to cross

Antarctica, he delivered on the promise contained in the original advertisement for the expedition: Those who sailed on *Endurance* did, indeed, receive "honor and recognition."

Depending on the yardstick used to measure success, Shackleton can be seen as a success or a failure, or a little of both. I believe that the more important question raised by Shackleton's adventure, and by the other accounts in this book, is a much more personal one: How do you measure your own success as a leader? What are the standards by which you assess your own performance?

One obvious benchmark of success is whether you accomplish what you set out to do—whether you achieve your stated goals. Even this straightforward measure, though, is more complex than it first appears. Whether you reach your objective depends not only on your own effort and ability, but also on external forces—the metaphorical equivalents of sea and ice conditions.

There are other variables in the equation that directly affect the probability that you will accomplish what you set out to do. What is the degree of difficulty of your goal? How far are you willing to reach? How high do you want to set the bar? You can greatly improve your odds of succeeding by setting low targets and easy goals. That strategy, while ensuring "success," is not at the core of leading at *The Edge*.

The spirit of reaching for *The Edge* is one of exploration—of breaking new ground and pressing the limits. This process of exploration carries with it the inherent risk that your original mission will fail, or that it may have to be changed as a result of new discoveries.

Of course, nobody likes failure, or even unpredictability—especially in today's business environment. I have tried to imagine the questions that would be directed toward Christopher Columbus if he were a CEO meeting with Wall Street analysts:

> Mr. Columbus, you promised sail to Japan, to establish a trading station with Asia, to build a relationship with the Emperor of China, and to bring back spices and gold. You accomplished none of this. Instead, you landed in the wrong place, and you brought back only corn, cotton, hammocks, and, well . . . some cigars. You may have discovered a New World, but you failed to deliver on your commitments. How do you explain your lackluster performance?

Unfortunately, the decision to explore new terrain—whether geographical, intellectual, or economic—carries with it inherent risk and uncertainty. There is simply no assurance that things will work out exactly as planned. Furthermore, there is no formula for determining the right level of difficulty at which goals should be set. What is certain, however, is that individuals who want to do extraordinary things—to reach for *The Edge*—must be willing to set lofty goals. And they must also be willing to risk the possibility that others will see the outcome of their efforts as a failure.

There are, then, many standards for judging success. Some of them include:

> ➤ Achieving your stated goals
> ➤ Achieving new goals, if the original goals must be changed
> ➤ Accepting bold challenges
> ➤ Avoiding failure
> ➤ Finding honor and recognition
> ➤ Achieving economic success
> ➤ Demonstrating loyalty to comrades

Each person must decide which of these (or other) standards are important and how each should be weighted. This weighting is, ultimately, a question of values. These values, in turn, determine how a leader will behave.

Vilhjalmur Stefansson, the leader of the *Karluk* expedition, displayed his values in an early dispatch from the Arctic that declared:

> . . . [T]he attainment of the purposes of the expedition is more important than the bringing back safe of the ship in which it sails. This means that while every reasonable precaution will be taken to safeguard the lives of the party, it is realized by both the backers of the expedition and the members of it, that even the lives of the party are secondary to the accomplishment of the work![1]

The values embedded in this message left Stefansson free to abandon the expedition. They also later enabled him to minimize the deaths of eleven men, arguing that "the loss of a dozen lives for scientific progress" was small when compared with the millions who perished in World War I. He neglected to add the roles that arrogance, dereliction of duty, and incompetent leadership had played in the tragedy. From Stefansson's perspective, however, the expedition was a great success. It furthered our understanding of "the friendly Arctic," and it enhanced his personal career ambitions.

Shackleton, in stark contrast, was as completely committed to bringing his crew safely home as Stefansson was nonchalant about the fate of *Karluk* and its crew. The night after the destruction of *Endurance*,

Shackleton lay awake in his tent, completely focused on his responsibility:

> The task was now to secure the safety of the party, and to that end I must bend my energies and mental power and apply every bit of knowledge that experience of the Antarctic had given me. The task was likely to be long and strenuous, and an ordered mind and a clear programme were essential if we were to come through without loss of life.[2]

It was this sense of responsibility that led him, time and again, to think of others before he thought of himself; to give his mittens and boots to those in greater need; and to volunteer for the first, and longest, watches.

On the boat journey to South Georgia, it was Shackleton's concern for the well-being of those left behind that moved him to confide in Frank Worsley, "Skipper, if anything happens to me while those fellows are waiting for me, I shall feel like a murderer."[3] This same sense of responsibility enabled him to work tirelessly to find a ship and rescue his comrades on Elephant Island.

This level of genuine concern was what inspired the unswerving loyalty that Shackleton generated to the end of his life. It was what moved Worsley to say:

> . . . [W]hen looking at Shackleton's grave and the cairn which we, his comrades, erected to his memory on the wind-swept hill of South Georgia . . . it seemed to me that among all his achievements and triumphs . . . his one failure was the most glorious. By self-sacrifice and throwing his own life into the balance he saved every one of his men. . . .[4]

However others may view his accomplishments, there is little doubt about how those closest to Shackleton felt about him as a leader—and as a comrade.

I believe that Shackleton and others who have faced the limits of human endurance have left an invaluable legacy. This legacy incorporates the leadership strategies outlined in this book, but it extends beyond that. The lessons drawn from the experiences of others can help individuals to clarify their personal values and to make decisions about the kind of people they want to be as leaders. By defining ourselves, we will be better able to reach *The Edge*—wherever and whenever we choose to pursue it.

PART FOUR

Resources for
Leading at The Edge

Resources

This section of the book contains several tools designed to help you continue the process of learning and developing your leadership skills. The Critical Leadership Skills Survey is an instrument to help you assess the extent to which you typically practice the ten strategies outlined in *Leading at the Edge*. The survey is intended to stimulate thinking about your leadership style; it is not meant to be a final, categorical assessment of your leadership ability.

The questionnaire will, however, allow you step back and reflect, and it can be an effective feedback instrument as well. I have found that having others complete the Critical Leadership Skills Survey and assess my leadership style is an enlightening, productive experience.

The second resource—Your Leadership Expedition: A Personal Development Plan—provides a way of bringing together, in a comprehensive plan for professional development, your insights from the Critical Skills Survey and your responses to the questions posed in the Expedition Log at the end of Chapters 1–10.

Finally, Further Readings from *The Edge* includes a list of books dealing with experiences at the *Survival Edge*. It includes additional readings both about the Shackleton saga and other survival accounts.

One of my goals is to continue to expand the list with stories that illustrate effective and ineffective leadership and teamwork at *The Edge*. I am interested in accounts that illustrate the use of the ten strategies in both business and survival situations. If you have a story to contribute, I would be pleased to hear from you. I can be contacted through my e-mail address, Dennis.Perkins@SyncreticsGroup.com, or you can write to me at:

The Syncretics Group, Inc.
250 West Main Street
Branford, CT 06405
Phone: 203-481-6118
www.SyncreticsGroup.com

Critical Leadership Skills Survey

Instructions

In answering these 30 questions, think about your behavior in a particular role or situation. For example, your frame of reference might be:

> › The way you demonstrate leadership as the formal head of a group or organization
> › Your peer leadership as a member of a work team
> › The way you lead and inspire yourself when dealing with personal or professional adversity

Please answer the questions about yourself using the following scoring categories:

> 1 = Never or almost never true
> 2 = Seldom true
> 3 = Sometimes true
> 4 = Often true
> 5 = Almost always true

If you have difficulty answering a question, choose the category that comes closest to describing the way you are.

Critical Leadership Skills Survey

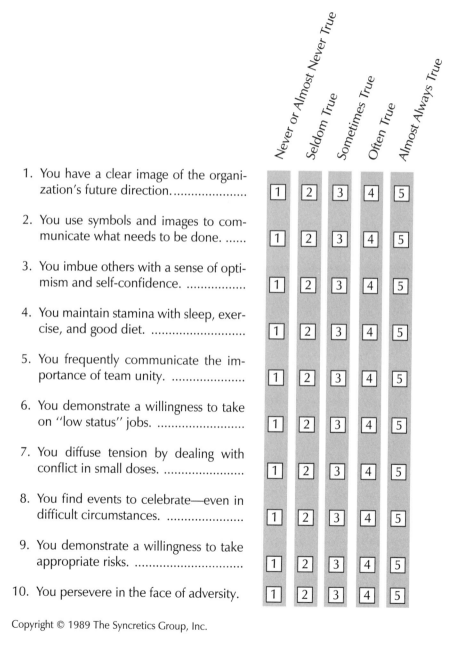

1. You have a clear image of the organization's future direction. .... `1` `2` `3` `4` `5`

2. You use symbols and images to communicate what needs to be done. ...... `1` `2` `3` `4` `5`

3. You imbue others with a sense of optimism and self-confidence. .... `1` `2` `3` `4` `5`

4. You maintain stamina with sleep, exercise, and good diet. .... `1` `2` `3` `4` `5`

5. You frequently communicate the importance of team unity. .... `1` `2` `3` `4` `5`

6. You demonstrate a willingness to take on "low status" jobs. .... `1` `2` `3` `4` `5`

7. You diffuse tension by dealing with conflict in small doses. .... `1` `2` `3` `4` `5`

8. You find events to celebrate—even in difficult circumstances. .... `1` `2` `3` `4` `5`

9. You demonstrate a willingness to take appropriate risks. .... `1` `2` `3` `4` `5`

10. You persevere in the face of adversity. `1` `2` `3` `4` `5`

Column headers: Never or Almost Never True / Seldom True / Sometimes True / Often True / Almost Always True

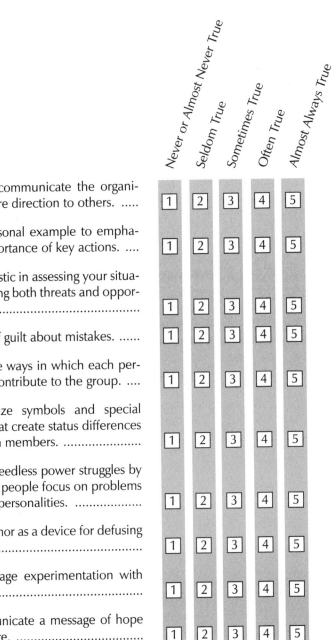

11. You clearly communicate the organization's future direction to others. ......

12. You use personal example to emphasize the importance of key actions. ....

13. You are realistic in assessing your situation (including both threats and opportunities). ....

14. You let go of guilt about mistakes. ......

15. You illustrate ways in which each person's skills contribute to the group. ....

16. You minimize symbols and special privileges that create status differences among team members. ....

17. You avoid needless power struggles by ensuring tht people focus on problems rather than personalities. ....

18. You use humor as a device for defusing tension. ....

19. You encourage experimentation with new ideas. ....

20. You communicate a message of hope for the future. ....

Never or Almost Never True
Seldom True
Sometimes True
Often True
Almost Always True

21. You direct others' energy toward realistic short-term goals. .... 　1　2　3　4　5

22. You use metaphor and stories to communicate ideas. .... 　1　2　3　4　5

23. You consider the merit of contradictory or "negative" views. .... 　1　2　3　4　5

24. You build renewal and relaxation into your daily life. .... 　1　2　3　4　5

25. You bring together the entire team for meetings and special events. .... 　1　2　3　4　5

26. You demonstrate genuine respect and concern for others. .... 　1　2　3　4　5

27. You maintain contact with "troublemakers" and dissidents. .... 　1　2　3　4　5

28. You provide opportunities for regular social activity. .... 　1　2　3　4　5

29. You emphasize learning from mistakes. .... 　1　2　3　4　5

30. You encourage people to step back and mobilize their creativity when faced with difficult problems. .... 　1　2　3　4　5

Scoring Instruction

STEP #1. Record your score for each question below. Each strategy is measured by three questions. Then total the scores for the three questions for each strategy.

Strategy 1:
Vision and Quick
Victories

Questions	Score
1	_____
11	_____
21	_____
TOTAL	_____

Strategy 2:
Symbolism and
Personal Examples

Questions	Score
2	_____
12	_____
22	_____
TOTAL	_____

Strategy 3:
Optimism and Reality

Questions	Score
3	_____
13	_____
23	_____
TOTAL	_____

Strategy 4:
Stamina

Questions	Score
4	_____
14	_____
24	_____
TOTAL	_____

Strategy 5:
The Team Message

Questions	Score
5	_____
15	_____
25	_____
TOTAL	_____

Strategy 6:
Core Team Values

Questions	Score
6	_____
16	_____
26	_____
TOTAL	_____

Strategy 7:
Conflict

Questions	Score
7	_____
17	_____
27	_____
TOTAL	_____

Strategy 8:
Lighten Up!

Questions	Score
8	_____
18	_____
28	_____
TOTAL	_____

Strategy 9:
Risk

Questions	Score
9	_____
19	_____
29	_____
TOTAL	_____

Strategy 10:
Tenacious Creativity

Questions	Score
10	_____
20	_____
30	_____
TOTAL	_____

Critical Leadership Skills Profile

STEP #2. Next, plot your profile below, using the "Totals" from Step 1, to create a graph.

	Vision and Quick Victories	Symbolism and Personal Example	Optimism and Reality	Stamina	The Team Message	Core Team Values	Conflict	Lighten Up!	Risk	Tenacious Creativity
15										
10										
5										
1										

Critical Leadership Skills Analysis Guide

1. Were there any suprises in your profile—low points or high points—that you didn't understand?

2. If so, examine the individual questions that made up each of the ten dimensions (corresponding to the ten strategies) you have plotted. Does that help explain your profile?

3. Of the ten strategies, which are your strongest or most developed?

4. Which of the strategies need to be strengthened or further developed?

Your Leadership Expedition: A Personal Development Plan

When embarking on an expedition, it is always useful to have a map. A conceptual map I have found helpful is shown in the Leadership Development Process. It depicts a systematic process consisting of five stages:

1. **Assessment.** Who are you now?
2. **Vision.** Who do you want to be?
3. **Overcoming barriers.** What are the obstacles that stand in your way, and how can they be overcome?
4. **Action.** What are the specific steps needed to move toward your vision?
5. **Sustaining.** How will you deal with setbacks and maintain momentum?

The stages are only guideposts, of course, and the development process does not always flow in one direction. In clarifying your vision, for example, you will probably gain insight into the person you are right now. The questions and exercises that follow will help clarify each of these stages, and they will refine your understanding of the leadership journey you have undertaken.

Assessment

1. What are your strengths as a leader—the skills, knowledge, and personal qualities that contribute to your ability to lead at the Edge?
2. What are your development needs—the areas which, if developed, would increase your effectiveness as a leader?

3. What are the activities that you find energizing—activities that stimulate you and that you find intrinsically enjoyable?
4. What are your core values about leadership—the deep beliefs that provide guidance and meaning?

Vision

1. Imagine that it is some time in the future. You have realized your full potential as a leader and are able to lead others to the limits of their performance.
2. Write a detailed, vivid description of who you are and what you will be doing. What is a typical day like for you? What will you be thinking and feeling? Try to capture that image in as much detail as possible.
3. Write a one-sentence, "high concept" statement that captures the essence of your vision.
4. Is there a concrete image that symbolizes your vision?

Overcoming Barriers

1. What are the barriers that stand between you and your vision? These obstacles may be external or internal, but they represent the "limiting beliefs" that prevent you from fully using your abilities.

List them below, casting each barrier in the form of an "I" statement (e.g., "I can't be a charismatic leader because I'm too introverted").

2. Select the barriers that represent the most problematic obstacles, and over which you have some degree of control.

3. Now generate as many ideas as possible for dealing with these obstacles. It is often helpful to get help from friends and colleagues who may see solutions that elude you. Some other strategies for generating ideas are:

> *Opportunity framing.* What hidden opportunities might be found in the problem?
> *Using a metaphor.* What concrete images can be used to represent the problem (e.g., a brick wall, a mountain, or an ice pack)? How you would deal with these symbolic barriers may suggest a solution.
> *"Chunking down."* Try to break the obstacles down into smaller pieces. Can you now get a toehold or a "lead in the ice"?

Action

1. Now that you have developed a vision and a set of strategies for overcoming obstacles, you can create a set of goals for moving toward your vision. To be most effective, these goals should be:

> *Specific.* For example, your goal may be to "take the conflict resolution seminar offered by X university," rather than more generally to "improve my conflict resolution skills."
> *Positive.* Goals should be stated in terms of "doing" rather than "avoiding" or "not doing."
> *Challenging yet attainable.* Stretch yourself, but don't set unreasonable expectations.

2. It is often helpful to create both a set of long-term (i.e., three to five years) goals and a set of short-term (i.e., six months to one year) goals.

Sustaining

List below the things that will enable you to sustain your leadership development process. Some questions to consider are:

1. What are your external sources of reinforcement? How will you get help and support from others?
2. What is your "backup plan" for dealing with adversity and setbacks?
3. When and how will you take time to reflect on your progress?
4. How will you reward yourself and celebrate success for interim accomplishments?
5. What are the tangible symbols that will help you stay focused on your vision?

Your Leadership Expedition Map

Using a large sheet of paper, construct a flowchart that shows the route of your expedition. The point of departure is your assessment, where you are right now. The destination is your vision. Trace the route that you will follow, showing key milestones with expected completion dates, along with major obstacles and how you will get past them. Feel free to be creative and to use vivid images with strong personal associations.

Further Readings from *The Edge*

Books on Ernest Shackleton

Alexander, Caroline. *The Endurance: Shackleton's Legendary Antarctic Expedition*. New York: Alfred A. Knopf, 1999.

Armstrong, Jennifer. *Shipwreck at the Bottom of the World: The Extraordinary True Story of Shackleton and the Endurance*. New York: Crown, 1998.

Fisher, Margery and James. *Shackleton and the Antarctic*. Boston: Houghton Mifflin, 1958.

Huntford, Roland. *Shackleton*. New York: New York: Carroll & Graf, 1999.

Lansing, Alfred. *Endurance: Shackleton's Incredible Voyage*. New York: Carroll & Graf, 1998.

McCurdy, Michael. *Trapped by the Ice! Shackleton's Amazing Antarctic Adventure*. New York: Walker, 1997.

Ralling, Christopher. *Shackleton, Greatest of All British Polar Explorers*. London: British Broadcasting Corporation, 1985.

Shackleton, Ernest. *South: A Memoir of the Endurance Voyage*. New York: Carroll & Graf, 1999.

Shackleton, Sir Ernest. *South: The Story of Shackleton's Last Expedition, 1914–1917*, ed. Peter King. North Pomfret: Trafalgar Square, 1992.

Worsley, F. A. *Endurance: An Epic of Polar Adventure*. New York: W. W. Norton, 1999.

Worsley, F. A. *Shackleton's Boat Journey*. New York: W. W. Norton, 1977.

Other Survival Accounts

Ambrose, Stephen E. *Undaunted Courage: Meriwether Lewis, Thomas Jefferson, and the Opening of the American West*. New York: Simon & Schuster, 1996.

Bailey, Maurice and Maralyn. *117 Days Adrift*. Dobbs Ferry, NY: Sheridan House, 1992.

Bickel, Lennard. *Mawson's Will*. New York: Avon, 1978.

Boukreev, Anatoli, and G. Weston DeWalt. *The Climb: Tragic Ambitions on Everest*. New York: St. Martin's Press, 1997.

Byrd, Admiral Richard E. *Alone: The Classic Polar Adventure*. New York: Kodansha International, 1995.

Callahan, Steven. *Adrift: Seventy-six Days Lost at Sea*. New York: Ballantine, 1987.

Caputo, Philip. *A Rumor of War*. London: Arrow Books Ltd., 1981

Cherry-Garrard, Apsley. *The Worst Journey in the World*. New York: Carroll & Graf, 1997.

Hayhurst, Jim, Sr. *The Right Mountain: Lessons from Everest on the Real Meaning of Success*. New York: Wiley, 1996.

Herzog, Maurice. *Annapurna*. North Salem, NY: The Adventure Library, 1995.

Heyerdahl, Thor. *Kon-Tiki*. New York: Washington Square Press, 1973.

Huntford, Roland. *The Last Place on Earth*. New York: Atheneum, 1985.

Junger, Sebastian. *The Perfect Storm: A True Story of Men Against the Sea*. New York: W. W. Norton, 1997.

Klaben, Helen, with Beth Day. *Hey, I'm Alive!* New York: McGraw-Hill, 1964.

Kocour, Ruth Anne, with Michael Hodgson. *Facing the Extreme: One Woman's Story of True Courage, Death-Defying Survival, and Her Quest for the Summit*. New York: St. Martin's Press, 1998.

Krakauer, Jon. *Into Thin Air: A Personal Account of the Mt. Everest Disaster*. New York: Villard, 1997.

Leslie, Edward E. *Desperate Journeys, Abandoned Souls: True Stories of Castaways and Other Survivors*. Boston: Houghton Mifflin, 1988.

Maclean, Norman. *Young Men and Fire: A True Story of the Mann Gulch Fire*. Chicago: The University of Chicago Press, 1992.

McKinlay, William Laird. *Karluk: The Great Untold Story of Arctic Exploration*. New York: St. Martin's Press, 1977.

Mitchell, Richard G., Jr. *Mountain Experience: The Psychology and Sociology of Adventure*. Chicago: The University of Chicago Press, 1985.

Nalepka, James, and Steven Callahan. *Capsized: The True Story of Four Men Adrift for 119 Days*. New York: Harper Collins, 1992.

Potterfield, Peter. *In the Zone: Epic Survival Stories from the Mountaineering World*. Seattle, WA: The Mountaineers, 1996.

Read, Piers Paul. *Alive: The Story of the Andes Survivors*. New York: Avon Books, 1975.

Simpson, Joe. *Touching the Void: The Harrowing First Person Account of One Man's Miraculous Survival*. New York: Harper and Row, 1990

Steger, Will, and Jon Bowermaster. *Crossing Antarctica*. New York: Alfred A. Knopf, 1992.

Stewart, George R. *Ordeal by Hunger: The Story of the Donner Party*. New York: Houghton Mifflin, 1988.

Trumbull, Robert. *The Raft: The Courageous Story of Three Naval Airmen against the Sea*. Annapolis, MD: Naval Institute Press, 1992.

Books on Leadership and Change

Carrison, Dan & Walsh, Rod. *Semper Fi: Business Leadership the Marine Corps Way*. New York: AMACOM, 1998.

De Pree, Max. *Leadership Is an Art*. New York: Dell, 1989.

Gardner, Howard. *Leading Minds: An Anatomy of Leadership*. Basic Books, 1995.

Nadler, David. *Champions of Change: How CEOs and Their Companies Are Mastering the Skills of Radical Change*. San Francisco: Jossey-Bass, 1997.

O'Toole, James. *Leading Change: Overcoming the Ideology of Comfort and the Tyranny of Custom*. San Francisco: Jossey-Bass, 1994.

Notes

The Shackleton Saga

1. Roland Huntford, *Shackleton* (New York: Carroll & Graf, 1999), p. 365.
2. Ernest Shackleton, *South: A Memoir of the Endurance Voyage* (New York: Carroll & Graf, 1999), p. 2.
3. Stephen J. Pyne, *The Ice: A Journey to Antarctica* (New York: Ballantine, 1988), pp. 4–5.
4. Alfred Lansing, *Endurance: Shackleton's Incredible Voyage* (New York: Carroll & Graf, 1998), p. 23.
5. Shackleton, op. cit. p. 4.
6. Ibid. p. 11.
7. Ibid. p. 34.
8. F. A. Worsley, *Endurance: An Epic of Polar Adventure* (New York: W. W. Norton & Co., 1999), p. 20.
9. Lansing, op. cit. p. 60.
10. Ibid. p. 95.
11. Ibid. p. 116.
12. Ibid. p. 280.
13. Sir Ernest Shackleton, *South: The Story of Shackleton's Last Expedition 1914–17* (North Pomfret: Trafalgar Square, 1992), p. 3, (Peter King, Ed.)

Chapter 1

1. Ernest Shackleton, *South: A Memoir of the Endurance Voyage* (New York: Carroll & Graf, 1999), p. 82.
2. Roland Huntford, *Shackleton* (New York: Carroll & Graf, 1999), p. 456.

3. Huntford, op. cit. p. 455.
4. Ibid. p. 456.
5. Adam Brandenburger and Barry Nalebuff, "Inside Intel," *Harvard Business Review* (November/December 1996), p. 168.
6. Huntford, op. cit. p. 224.
7. Norman R. Augustine, "Managing the Crisis You Tried to Prevent," *Harvard Business Review* (November/December 1995), p. 147, and Eileen Murray and Saundra Shohen, "Lessons from the Tylenol Tragedy on Surviving a Corporate Crisis," *Medical Marketing & Media*, Vol. 27, No. 2 (February 1992), p. 14.
8. Greg Brenneman, "Right Away and All at Once: How We Saved Continental," *Harvard Business Review* (September/October 1998), p. 162.
9. Ibid.
10. William Laird McKinlay, *Karluk: The Great Untold Story of Arctic Exploration* (New York: St. Martin's Press, 1977), p. 30.
11. Margery and James Fisher, *Shackleton and the Antarctic* (Boston: Houghton Mifflin, 1958), p. 352.
12. Huntford, op. cit. p. 390.
13. Ibid. p. 386.
14. Ibid.
15. Fisher, op. cit. p. 339.
16. Ibid. p. 342.
17. Ibid. p. 356.
18. Huntford, op. cit. p. 465.
19. J. P. Donlon, "The CEO's CEO," *Chief Executive* (July/August 1998), pp. 28–37.
20. Ibid.
21. Shackleton, op. cit. p. 162.

Chapter 2

1. Alfred Lansing, *Endurance: Shackleton's Incredible Voyage* (New York: Carroll & Graf, 1998), p. 64.
2. F. A. Worsley, *Endurance: An Epic of Polar Adventure* (New York: Jonathan Cape and Harrison Smith, 1931), p. 18.
3. Worsley, op. cit. p. 19.
4. Ibid.
5. Ernest Shackleton, *South: A Memoir of the Endurance Voyage* (New York: Carroll & Graf, 1999), p. 77.

6. Linda Hill and Suzy Wetlaufer, "Leadership When There Is No One to Ask: An Interview with Eni's Franco Bernabe," *Harvard Business Review* (July/August 1998), p. 93.
7. Shackleton, op. cit. p. 83.
8. Worsley, op. cit. p. 23.
9. Gordon Bethune, *Worst to First* (New York: John Wiley & Sons, Inc., 1998), p. 36.
10. Sir Ernest Shackleton, *South* (New York: The Macmillan Company, 1920), p. 135.
11. Quoted from Orde-Lees Diary, Roland Huntford, *Shackleton* (New York: Carroll & Graf, 1999), p. 511.
12. Philip Caputo, *A Rumor of War* (London: Arrow Books Ltd., 1981), pp. 91–92.
13. Robert F. Dennehy, "The Executive as Storyteller," *Management Review*, Vol. 88, No. 3 (March 1999), pp. 40–43.

Chapter 3

1. F. A. Worsley, *Endurance: An Epic of Polar Adventure* (New York: W. W. Norton & Co., 1999), p. 53.
2. Roland Huntford, *Shackleton* (New York: Carroll & Graf, 1999), p. 217.
3. Huntford, op. cit. p. 92.
4. Martin E. P. Seligman, *Learned Optimism: How to Change Your Mind and Your Life* (New York: Pocket Books, 1998), pp. 207–234.
5. Worsley, op. cit. p. 6.
6. Ibid. p. 4.
7. Sir Ernest Shackleton, *South* (New York: The Macmillan Company, 1920), p. 121.
8. Huntford, op. cit. p. 465.
9. Margery and James Fisher, *Shackleton and the Antarctic* (Boston: Houghton Mifflin, 1958), p. 359.
10. David Leonhardt, "The Saga of Lloyd Ward," *Business Week* (August 9, 1999), p. 58.
11. Worsley, op. cit. p. 4.
12. Ibid. pp. 4–5.
13. Alfred Lansing, *Endurance: Shackleton's Incredible Voyage* (New York: Carroll & Graf, 1998), p. 207.
14. Fisher, op. cit. p. 372.
15. Lansing, op. cit. p. 235.

16. Hal Lancaster, "Herb Kelleher Has One Main Strategy: Treat Employees Well," *The Wall Street Journal* (August 31, 1999), p. B1.
17. Piers Paul Read, *Alive* (New York: Avon Books, 1975), pp. 81–82.
18. The Chinese character is typically not interpreted in this way, with one symbol representing "danger" and the other "opportunity," but both individual elements are embedded in the compound character. I appreciate the assistance of John Montanaro and Diana Ho in helping me with the interpretation of this figure.
19. Martin Puris, *Comebacks: How Seven Straight-Shooting CEOs Turned Around Troubled Companies* (New York: Times Books, 1999), pp. 106–111.
20. Lansing, op. cit. p. 105.
21. Patricia Sellers, "CEOs in Denial," *Fortune*, Vol. 139, No. 12 (June 21, 1999), p. 80.
22. Albert Rothenberg, M.D., "Janusian Thinking and Nobel Prize Laureates," *American Journal of Psychiatry*, 139:1 (January 1982), pp. 122–124.
23. Nina Munk, "How Levi's Trashed a Great American Brand," *Fortune*, Vol. 139, No. 7 (April 12, 1999), p. 82.
24. Ibid.

Chapter 4

1. F. A. Worsley, *Shackleton's Boat Journey* (New York: W. W. Norton, 1977), pp. 58–59.
2. Roland Huntford, *Shackleton* (New York: Carroll & Graf, 1999), pp. 110–113, 115.
3. Huntford, op. cit. p. 145.
4. Sir Ernest Shackleton, *South* (New York: The Macmillan Company, 1920), p. 99.
5. Shackleton, op. cit. p. 91.
6. Worsley, op. cit. pp. 169–170.
7. Huntford, op. cit. p. 687.
8. Ibid. p. 690.
9. Alex Taylor III, "Neutron Jurgen Ignites a Revolution at Daimler-Benz," *Fortune*, Vol. 136, No. 9 (November 10, 1997), p. 144.
10. Anatoli Boukreev and G. Weston DeWalt, *The Climb: Tragic Ambitions on Everest* (New York: St. Martin's Press, 1997).
11. Jon Krakauer, *Into Thin Air: A Personal Account of the Mt. Everest Disaster* (New York: Villard, 1997), p. 202.

12. Shari Caudron, "Corporate Creativity Comes of Age," *Training & Development* (May 1998), p. 50.
13. Worsley, op. cit. p. 188.
14. Shackleton, op. cit. p. 75.
15. F. A. Worsley, *Endurance: An Epic of Polar Adventure* (New York: W. W. Norton & Co., 1999), p. 171.
16. Huntford, op. cit. p. 613.
17. Carol Hymowitz, "Damark's Unique Post: A Manager Who Helps Work on Relationships," *The Wall Street Journal* (September 7, 1999), p. B1.
18. Peter Frost and Sandra Robinson, "The Toxic Handler: Organizational Hero—and Casualty," *Harvard Business Review* (July/August 1999), p. 96.
19. Joe Simpson, *Touching the Void* (New York: Harper & Row, 1990), pp. 103–104.
20. Simpson, op. cit. p. 113.
21. Michael Dell, *Direct from Dell: Strategies That Revolutionized an Industry* (New York: Harper Business, 1999), p. 56.

Chapter 5

1. F. A. Worsley, *Endurance: An Epic of Polar Adventure* (New York: W. W. Norton & Co., 1999), p. 46.
2. Alfred Lansing, *Endurance: Shackleton's Incredible Voyage* (New York: Carroll & Graf, 1998), p. 17.
3. Margery and James Fisher, *Shackleton and the Antarctic* (Boston: Houghton Mifflin, 1958), pp. 343–344.
4. Jon Krakauer, *Into Thin Air: A Personal Account of the Mt. Everest Disaster* (New York: Villard, 1997), p. 163.
5. Krakauer, op. cit. p. 241.
6. Peter Burrows and Peter Elstrom, "The Boss," *Business Week* (August 2, 1999), pp. 76–84.
7. Personal interview with Joan Imhof, Branford, CT, May 7, 1999.
8. The use of the "Tap Code" was taken from the video *Return with Honor* (Santa Monica: American Film Foundation, 1998).
9. Gloria Gordon, "Wow! This Guy Can Communicate!" *Communication World*, Vol. 16, No. 7 (August/September 1999), pp. 17–20.
10. Roland Huntford, *Shackleton* (New York: Carroll & Graf, 1999), p. 461.
11. Huntford, op. cit. p. 467.

12. Fisher, op. cit. p. 343.
13. Suzy Wetlaufer, "Driving Change: An Interview with Ford Motor Company's Jacques Nasser," *Harvard Business Review,* Vol. 77, No. 2 (March/April 1999), pp. 76–88.
14. F. A. Worsley, *Shackleton's Boat Journey* (New York: W. W. Norton, 1977), p. 134.
15. Huntford, op. cit. p. 424.
16. Worsley, *Endurance,* p. 53.

Chapter 6

1. F. A. Worsley, *Shackleton's Boat Jour*ney (New York: W. W. Norton, 1977), pp. 20–21.
2. Roland Huntford, *The Last Place on Earth* (New York: Atheneum, 1985), p. 523.
3. Several months after this chapter was written, Margaret Holtman came upon a piece in the *New York Times* Book Review ("The Race to the Bottom," October 31, 1999, p. 43) in which Caroline Alexander makes a similar observation. My perspective on Scott was formed and written prior to the publication of the *New York Times* article.
4. Huntford, op. cit. pp. 562–563.
5. V. E. Fuchs, "Scott and Amundsen," *Geographical Journal* (July 1980) Volume 146 No. 2, pp. 272–274.
6. Huntford, op. cit., p. 151.
7. Ibid. p. 157.
8. Ibid. p. 151.
9. Ibid. p. 144.
10. Roland Huntford, *Shackleton* (New York: Carroll & Graf, 1999), p. 13.
11. Huntford, *Shackleton,* p. 57.
12. Ibid., p. 425.
13. Sir Ernest Shackleton, *South* (New York: The Macmillan Company, 1920), p. 92.
14. F. A. Worsley, *Endurance: An Epic in Polar Adventure* (New York: W. W. Norton & Company, 1999), p. 93.
15. Edward Lawler, *From the Ground Up: Six Principles for Building the New Logic Corporation* (San Francisco: Jossey-Bass, 1996), p. 85.
16. Personal interview with Scott Sklar, Novato, CA, June 14, 1999.
17. Huntford, *Shackleton,* p. 456.

18. F. A. Worsley, *Endurance,* p. 106.
19. Alfred Lansing, *Endurance: Shackleton's Incredible Voyage* (New York: Carroll & Graf, 1998), p. 127.

Chapter 7

1. Roland Huntford, *Shackleton* (New York: Carroll & Graf, 1999), p. 435.
2. Harold Horwood in *Sea Tales: The Deadly Arctic Expedition* (New York: New Video Group, 1997).
3. William Laird McKinlay, *Karluk: The Great Untold Story of Arctic Exploration* (New York: St. Martin's Press, 1977), p. 99.
4. George R. Stewart, *Ordeal by Hunger: The Story of the Donner Party* (New York: Houghton Mifflin, 1988), p. 63.
5. Stewart, op. cit. p. 66.
6. Huntford, op. cit. p. 26.
7. Ibid. p. 499.
8. Ibid. p. 424.
9. Ibid. p. 423.
10. Ibid. pp. 537–538.
11. Dennis N. T. Perkins, *Ghosts in the Executive Suite: Every Business Is a Family Business* (Branford, Conn.: The Syncretics Group, 1986), p. 11.
12. Huntford, op. cit. p. 435.
13. "AT&T Names Top Leaders for Two Communications Companies," *AT&T News Release,* October 12, 1995.
14. Alfred Lansing, *Endurance: Shackleton's Incredible Voyage* (New York: Carroll & Graf, 1998), p. 95.

Chapter 8

1. Ernest Shackleton, *South: A Memoir of the Endurance Voyage* (New York: Carroll & Graf, 1999), pp. 46–47.
2. Roland Huntford, *Shackleton* (New York: Carroll & Graf, 1999), p. 419.
3. Huntford, op. cit. p. 428.
4. Ibid. p. 437.
5. Ibid. p. 468.

6. Shackleton, op. cit. p. 111.
7. Alfred Lansing, *Endurance: Shackleton's Incredible Voyage* (New York: Carroll & Graf, 1998), p. 206.
8. Lansing, op. cit. pp. 208–209.
9. William Laird McKinlay, *Karluk: The Great Untold Story of Arctic Exploration* (New York: St. Martin's Press, 1977), pp. 67–68.
10. Lon Smith, "Letter to Hartford Life Employees," September 3, 1998.
11. Huntford, op. cit. p. 472.
12. F. A. Worsley, *Endurance: An Epic of Polar Adventure* (New York: W. W. Norton & Co., 1999), pp. 53–54.
13. Huntford, op. cit. p. 426.
14. Ibid. p. 448.
15. This story is reconstructed from material taken from the Manual of the Judge Advocate General final investigative report concerning the aircraft mishap involving Bureau Number 159892, which occurred on October 26, 1978; and the VP-9 Memorial Page (www.vpnavy.com/vp9586.html), which includes material from a *Reader's Digest* article, "We Are Ditching, Ditching, Ditching!" by Earl and Miriam Selby, September 1979, pp. 112–118.
16. Kevin and Jackie Freiberg, *Nuts! Southwest Airlines' Crazy Recipe for Business and Personal Success* (New York: Broadway Books, 1998).

Chapter 9

1. F. A. Worsley, *Endurance: An Epic of Polar Adventure* (New York: W. W. Norton & Co., 1999), p. 114.
2. Roland Huntford, *Shackleton* (New York: Carroll & Graf, 1999), p. 497.
3. Worsley, op. cit. p. 65.
4. Ibid., p. 89.
5. Ernest Shackleton, *South: A Memoir of the Endurance Voyage* (New York: Carroll & Graf, 1999), p. 159.
6. Shackleton, op. cit. p. 175.
7. Sir Ernest Shackleton, *South* (New York: The Macmillan Company, 1920), p. 180.
8. Adrian J. Slywotzky and David J. Morrison, *The Profit Zone: How Strategic Business Design Will Lead You to Tomorrow's Profits* (New York: Times Business, 1998), p. 6.

9. Personal interview with Randy MacDonald, Stamford, CT, April 30, 1999.

10. Jeremy Useem, "Internet Defense Strategy: Cannibalize Yourself," *Fortune* (September 6, 1999), p. 121.

Chapter 10

1. Roland Huntford, *Shackleton* (New York: Carroll & Graf, 1999), p. 561.

2. Steven Callahan, *Adrift: Seventy-six Days Lost at Sea* (New York: Ballantine Books, 1987), pp. 138–139.

3. Callahan, op. cit. pp. 222–223.

4. Ibid. p. 224.

5. Ibid. pp. 210–211.

6. Huntford, op. cit. p. 462.

7. Ibid. p. 460.

8. F. A. Worsley, *Endurance: An Epic of Polar Adventure* (New York: W. W. Norton & Co., 1999), p. 151.

9. Worsley, op. cit. p. 155.

10. Ibid. p. 156.

11. Ernest Shackleton, *South: A Memoir of the Endurance Voyage* (New York: Carroll & Graf, 1999), p. 208.

12. Robert D. Hof, Steve Hamm, and Ira Sager, "Sun Power," *Business Week* (January 18, 1999), p. 64.

Chapter 16

1. George Leonard, *Mastery: The Keys to Success and Long-Term Fulfillment* (New York: Plume, 1992), pp. 39–49.

2. Joe Hyams, *Zen in the Martial Arts* (New York: Bantam, 1982), p. 103.

3. "A Conversation with Roberto Goizueta and Jack Welch," *Fortune* (December 11, 1995), Vol. 132 No. 1, p. 96.

4. David A. Nadler, *Champions of Change* (San Francisco: Jossey-Bass, 1997), pp. 67–71.

Epilogue

1. William Laird McKinlay, *Karluk: The Great Untold Story of Arctic Exploration* (New York: St. Martin's Press, 1977), p. 6.

2. Ernest Shackleton, *South: A Memoir of the Endurance Voyage* (New York: Carroll & Graf, 1999), p. 77.
3. F. A. Worsley, *Endurance: An Epic of Polar Adventure* (New York: W. W. Norton & Co., 1999), p. 107.
4. F. A. Worsley, *Shackleton's Boat Journey* (New York: W. W. Norton, 1977), p. 220.

Index

Acknowledgments for Previously Published Materials (continued from copyright page)

Grateful acknowledgment is made to the following sources for permission to reprint from previously published material. The publisher has made diligent efforts to trace the ownership of all copyrighted material in this volume and believes that all necessary permissions have been secured. If any errors or omissions have inadvertently been made, proper corrections will gladly be made in future editions.

Excerpts from ADRIFT by Steven Callahan. Copyright © 1986 by Steven Callahan. Reprinted by permission of Houghton Mifflin Co. All rights reserved.

Excerpts from ENDURANCE by Alfred Lansing. Copyright © 1959 by Alfred Lansing. Reprinted by permission of Curtis Brown, Ltd.

Excerpts from TOUCHING THE VOID by Joe Simpson. Copyright © 1988 by Joe Simpson. Reprinted by permission from Jonathan Cape, Ltd./ The Random House Archive and Library.

Excerpts from SHACKLETON'S BOAT JOURNEY by F. W. Worsley. Copyright © 1977 by W. W. Norton & Company, Inc. Used by permission of W. W. Norton & Company, Inc.

Excerpts from ENDURANCE: AN EPIC OF POLAR ADVENTURE by F. A. Worsley. Copyright © 1931 by the Estate of F. A. Worsley. Used by permission of W. W. Norton & Company, Inc./ Sheil Land Associates.